The Fall of the GDR

The Fall of the GDR

Germany's Road to Unity

David Childs

An imprint of **Pearson Education**

Harlow, England · London · New York · Reading, Massachusetts · San Francisco · Toronto · Don Mills, Ontario · Sydney
Tokyo · Singapore · Hong Kong · Seoul · Taipei · Cape Town · Madrid · Mexico City · Amsterdam · Munich · Paris · Milan

Pearson Education Limited

Edinburgh Gate
Harlow
Essex CM20 2JE
England

and Associated Companies around the world

Visit us on the World Wide Web at
www.pearsoneduc.com

First published in Great Britain in 2001

ISBN 0 582 31569 7 PPR

British Library Cataloguing-in-Publication Data
A catalogue record for this book can be obtained from the British Library

Library of Congress Cataloging-in-Publication Data
Childs, David, 1933–
   The fall of the GDR : Germany's road to unity / David Childs.
     p. cm. — (Themes in modern German history series)
   Includes bibliographical references and index.
   ISBN 0–582–31568–9 (alk. paper) — ISBN 0–582–31569–7 (ppr : alk. paper)
      1. Germany (East)—Politics and government—1989–1990.   2. Socialism—Germany
(East)   3. Protest movements—Germany (East)   4. Opposition (Political science)
5. Germany—History—Unification, 1990.   I. Title.   II. Series.

DD289 .C45 2000
943'. 10878—dc21
                                                                          00–061359
10 9 8 7 6 5 4 3 2 1
06 05 04 03 02 01

Typeset by 35 in 10/13pt Sabon
Produced by Pearson Education Asia Pte Ltd
Printed in Malaysia, PJB

Contents

List of abbreviations

AVL   *Aktionsbündnis Vereinigte Linke* [Action Alliance United Left]

BFD   *Bund Freier Demokraten* [League of Free Democrats]

CDU   *Christlich-Demokratische Union* [Christian Democratic Union, the name for the Christian Democrats in both parts of Germany]

CPSU   Communist Party of the Soviet Union

CSU   Christlich Soziale Union [Christian Social Union]

DA   *Demokratischer Aufbruch* [Democratic Awakening]

DBD   *Demokratische Bauernpartei Deutschlands* [Democratic Farmers/Peasants Party of Germany]

DFD   *Demokratischer Frauenbund Deutschlands* [Democratic Women's Federation of Germany]

DFP   *Deutsche Forumpartei* [German Forum Party]

DGB   *Deutscher Gewerkschaftsbund* [German Trade Union Federation, the main West German trade union body]

DJ   *Demokratie Jetzt* [Democracy Now]

DSF   Gesellschaft für Deutsch-Sowjetische FreundSchaft [Society for German Soviet Friendship]

DSU   *Deutsche Soziale Union* [German Social Union]

DTSB   Deutscher Turn- und Sportsbund [the official sports; body of the GDR]

FDGB   *Freier Deutscher Gewerkschaftsbund* [Free German Trade Union Federation, the GDR trade unions]

FDJ   *Freie Deutsche Jugend* [Free German Youth]

FDP   *Freie Demokratische Partei* [German Democratic Party]

FRG   Federal Republic of Germany

GDR   German Democratic Republic

GST   *Gesellschaft für Sport und Technik* [Society for Sports and Technology]

HVA   Hauptverwaltung Aufklärung [Main Administralian Intelligence, the foreign intelligence branch of the MfS]

IFM   *Initiative Frieden und Menschenrechte* [Initiative for Peace and Human Rights]

IM   *Inoffizieller Mitarbeiter* [unofficial collaborator, informer working for the MfS]

KGB	*Komitet gosudarstvennoi bezopasnosti* [Committee for State Security of Soviet Union]
KPD	*Kommunistische Partei Deutschlands* [Communist Party of Germany]
LDPD	*Liberal-Demokratische Partei Deutschlands* [Liberal Democratic Party of Germany]
MfS	*Ministerium für Staatssicherheit* [Ministry for State Security]
NATO	North Atlantic Treaty Organisation
NDPD	*Nationaldemokratische Partei Deutschlands* [National Democratic Party of Germany]
NF	*Neues Forum* [New Forum]
NVA	*Nationale Volksarmee* [National People's Army, the GDR's armed forces]
PDS	Partei des Demokratischen Sozialismus [Party of Democratic Socialism, successor to the SED]
SDP	*Sozialdemokratische Partei* [Social Democratic Party, initial name of this party in the GDR in 1989]
SED	*Sozialistische Einheitspartei Deutschlands* [Socialist Unity Party of Germany]
SPD	*Sozialdemokratische Partei Deutschlands* [Social Democratic Party of Germany]
Stasi	*Short for Staatssicherheitsdienst* [State Security Service, Operated by the MfS]
UFV	*Unabhängiger Frauenverband* [Independent Women's Association]
ZK	*Zentralkomitee* [Central Committee of the SED]

Preface

Just before starting my degree course at the London School of Economic and Political Science, and just after the crushing of the East German revolt of June 1953, I made one of my first trips to Berlin. It was for entirely personal reasons. On a previous occasion I met, at the World Youth Festival, the son of the Blumenthal-Barby family, who lived in Treptow, East Berlin. The kind and intelligent Blumenthal-Barbys invited me back. The head of the family, a medical practitioner and member of the SED, had turned to Communism as a result of his experiences in the German Army medical corps in the 1914–18 war. He had suffered at the hands of the Nazis and lost his older son to them. He hoped the new Germany would be different from the old. During my 1953 visit he gave me a book to read. It was Orwell's *Nineteen Eighty-Four*! Over a few weeks hearing the eyewitness accounts of his family members and of other Berliners, I came to the conclusion that the German Democratic Republic was not very German and was certainly not democratic. Disillusioned though he was with Ulbricht's Reich, the doctor stayed in East Berlin and remained a Marxist idealist to the end of his life in the 1960s. I retained my interest in Berlin and Germany and was urged to keep up my contacts with the East by the SPD Member of the Bundestag and later Federal Ambassador to Yugoslavia, Peter Blachstein, with whom I became friends, after meeting him when I was a student in Hamburg. Blachstein introduced me to Luxemburg's critique of Lenin, and I remain grateful to him for that and much else.[1] Equally important for me was Wolfgang Leonhard's fascinating *Die Revolution Entlässt Ihre Kinder* (1955). Later, from the British Labour Party, the MPs Konni Zilliacus, Anthony Greenwood and Richard Crossman also urged me to study developments in 'the other Germany'.

With a few breaks and under a variety of different auspices, I visited the GDR on many occasions until its final demise in 1990. Despite the Wall, trips in the 1960s produced a somewhat more optimistic picture than in the 1950s. The SED appeared at last to be introducing economic reforms, and cultural policy was slightly more relaxed. This was of course in keeping with trends in the Soviet Union. When one visited the GDR on official visits the hosts were often victims of the Third Reich, like the woman who had been a child prisoner in Auschwitz, or the former *Kriegsmarine* NCO who deserted to the French resistance movement.[2] There was Professor Franz

Loeser, son of a Rabbi, who had served as a sergeant in the British Royal
Army Medical Corps.[3] There was also Kurt Goldstein, who had survived
the International Brigades, Auschwitz and Buchenwald, who became head
of the radio station Voice of the GDR.[4] Individuals like these were very
often the public face of the GDR to the Western journalist, academic, politician or 'peace friend'. Among many others, I also encountered Walter
Ulbricht and the British journalist John Peet,[5] who was one of the few
'defectors' from West to East, and Margarete Wittkowski, President of the
State Bank, who had spent years of exile in Finchley. My first book on the
GDR, called by the publisher simply *East Germany*,[6] was the product of
this period. Its positive reception in West Germany, the USA, Britain and
elsewhere encouraged me to remain wedded to GDR studies.

In 1978 I spent five weeks in Rostock, East Berlin, Jena and Weimar on
a visit arranged by the British Council. It was both interesting and depress-
ing. On arrival at Schönefeld airport a veteran Communist from the Foreign Ministry took me through customs and we were driven at speed to the
Hauptbahnhof. My host gave me repeated warnings at the station to watch
my baggage as it could easily be stolen. In the first-class compartment from
Berlin to Rostock no one spoke. I was shocked by the very poor conditions
I found at GDR universities. The student accommodation, the scarcity of
writing materials, the overcrowding and the poor food were worse than
expected. I, like many others, had believed that, to an extent, the Communists had sacrificed private consumption for public services. That trip convinced me that everything was equally bad: trains, schools, universities and
hospitals. Far worse, however, was the atmosphere of fear. Support for the
regime appeared to be minimal. Even official hosts, when entirely alone
with you, and some appeared afraid of being alone with this strange person
from Britain, expressed their disillusionment with the regime. On the other
hand, one or two SED professors went out of their way to attack Britain.
This period led to the publication of my highly successful *GDR: Moscow's
German Ally* (1983, 1988) and my edited *Honecker's Germany* (1985). In
the GDR I was put in the category of 'imperialist ideologue'.[7] Meanwhile
Professor Loeser had sought political asylum in the USA.

During the 1980s I travelled to the GDR any number of times and
found the situation changed little. I also attended conferences of the Aspen
Institute (West Berlin, 1987, 1989), attended by top SED members, the
Gesellschaft für Deutschland Forschung (West Berlin) and other bodies in
the GDR, West Germany, Britain and the USA. I became convinced the end
was not far off. The East Germans simply needed the green light from
Moscow. In Bonn, on the other hand, the great majority, irrespective of
political persuasion, accepted the division of Germany certainly for as far
as they could see. It was regarded as almost obscene, or certainly out of

touch or off-message, to mention German re-unification. My work of that period, *East Germany to the 1990s: Can It Resist Glasnost?* (1987), for the Economist Intelligence Unit, reflected these experiences. I did, however, manage to infiltrate the following message into that slim volume:

> An event in Moscow, another severe winter, a sudden breakdown of supplies, an over reaction by the security police, an East German Chernobyl, a historical anniversary, any of these could provide the spark for strikes and/or demonstrations. They would be suppressed immediately but that might not prevent long-term consequences.[8]

During *Die Wende* I made many journeys to the GDR as I was writing the pamphlet *Germany on the Road to Unity* (1990) for the Economist Intelligence Unit. I attended the special conference of the SED–PDS in December 1989 and the CDU special conference. I was present at the last demonstration of 1989 in Leipzig. As the end of the GDR came in sight I attended a conference organised by the *Institut für Internationale Politik und Wirtschaft der DDR* (February 1990), at which I met Professor Christa Luft, and shook hands with West German Foreign Minister Hans-Dietrich Genscher and Egon Bahr. Subsequently I observed the elections of March and December 1990. It was an exhilarating period and I was delighted with the results, that is, the restoration of German unity by peaceful and democratic means. I did feel sorry for those idealists who believed in what they were doing, however, including a few Gorbachev supporters who wanted the GDR to develop 'socialism with a human face'.

It was Richard Popplewell, then my colleague at Nottingham University, who suggested we do a book on the GDR's Ministry for State Security (MfS or Stasi). In the course of the research for that book, *The Stasi: The East German Intelligence and Security Service* (1997), the idea for the present volume formed, and I interviewed many individuals with both volumes in mind. They are acknowledged below. The German Academic Exchange Service gave me some financial help on that occasion, for which I remain grateful. Although I had expected some Stasi interest in me, I was still shocked when I saw the documents which survived, including those indicating that the Stasi had its agents watching my activities in Britain. Of course, in the GDR itself you expected to be watched. Hotels where foreigners were quartered were usually bugged. In the modern hotels you were on video as well even when going to the bathroom! All letters were read routinely. Some East Germans who corresponded with Westerners always put in each letter at least one sentence praising the SED. One point often forgotten by those not involved in such research was the consideration one had to have for contacts and friends behind the Iron Curtain. You could leave and need not return. They could not. Occasionally, your phone call was received with 'You've got the wrong number.' The person you had called feared someone else could be listening! Occasionally, your friend, colleague or acquaintance did not turn up for a meeting. It was just not worth the risk! Occasionally, you rang someone you had spent a very pleasant evening with in East Berlin, just to say you had reached West Berlin safely. Your call was unexpected and you were dismayed to hear a Stasi man on the other end. All this did have some influence on what was written. For instance, especially in my early days I attempted to criticise the SED-regime by reference to its own Marxist-Leninist aims and its own publications. Some of us, including Blachstein, hoped the GDR would develop a 'third way'. Such naïve hopes were dashed by the time Honecker took over in 1971. I think my *Marx and the Marxists: An Outline of Practice and Theory* (1973) reflects this.

Another consideration was that many people found it difficult to believe that the Soviet bloc was as bad as it was in both material and political terms. You could easily be accused of presenting horror stories or Cold War propaganda! As one reviewer of my *East Germany to the 1990s* put it in the respected journal *International Affairs* (Chatham House), Childs 'sometimes allows his evident dislike of the Honecker regime to cloud his evaluation of the factors shaping contemporary East German politics'.[9] I wonder what he thought a year later! I did not discover what Madeleine Albright and the CIA operative thought about my message 'GDR kaputt' when I spoke in Washington, DC, in September 1986. When I put the same case in California in April 1989 I was met with a hostile response from a considerable minority of my largely academic audience.

In this volume, as in the past, I use the terms 'socialist', 'socialism', 'Communist', and so on, for convenience, simply as they were used by the SED and in the Western media. I do not, however, believe that the SED or Soviet regimes had much to do with pre-1914 German, or other West European, socialist movements, or even with the ideals and ideas of Marx and Engels, Bebel, Luxemburg or Mehring.

David Childs
Nottingham, July 2000

Notes

1. Rosa Luxemburg, *Die Russische Revolution: Eine kritische Würdigung*, ed. Peter Blachstein, Hamburg, 1948.
2. Kurt Hälker, 'Ein Spaziergang an der Seine führte zur Wende in meinem Leben', in Dora Schaul (ed.), *Résistance: Erinnerungen deutscher Antifaschisten*, Berlin, 1973.
3. Franz Loeser, *Die unglaubwürdige Gesellschaft: Quo vadis DDR?* Cologne, 1984.

4. Friedrich-Martin Balzer, *Wir sind die letzten – fragt uns, Kurt Goldstein Spanienkämpfer, Auschwitz- und Buchenwaldhäftling, Reden und Schriften 1974– 1999*, Marburg, 1999. I only interviewed Goldstein after the fall of the GDR.

5. John Peet, *The Long Engagement: Memoirs of a Cold War Legend*, London, 1989.

6. *East Germany*, London/New York, 1969. Among over 30 reviews were: *Die Zeit* (Hamburg), 3 October 1969; *Problems of Communism* (USIA, Washington, DC), September/October 1970; *Times Literary Supplement* (London), 27 November 1969. Peet gave his view in *Democratic German Report*, 5 November 1969.

7. Dieter Müller in *Beiträge zum marxistisch-leninistischen Grundlagenstudium*, XXIV. Jg., 1985, Heft 3, p. 52.

8. David Childs, *East Germany to the 1990s: Can It Resist Glasnost?*, London, 1987, p. 95.

9. *International Affairs*, 64, 1988.

Acknowledgements

André Andrich, *Neues Forum*, Dresden; Dr Sabine Bergmann-Pohl, MdB, formerly President of the Volkskammer; Dr Sc. med. Kay Blumenthal-Barby, Berlin/Göttingen; Dr Heinrich Bortfeldt, formerly *Akademie für Gesellschaftswissenschaften beim ZK der SED*; Dr Manfred Braune, CDU, Leipzig; Dr Eberhard Brecht, MdB; Elfriede Brüning, writer, Berlin; Wolfgang Dehnel, MdB; Colonel Prof. Dr Helmut Eck, formerly of the *Hochschule des MfS*, Potsdam-Eiche; Colonel Klaus Eichner, formerly head of *Bereich 'C'* of Department IX of the HV A; Dr Helmut Ettinger, formerly diplomatic service of the GDR, PDS, Berlin; Joachim Fiegel, PDS, Bonn/Chemnitz; Bernt Förster, Leipzig University; Monika Friedrich, *Gauck-Behörde*, Berlin; Dipl.-Psych. Svetla Friedrich, Leipzig; Prof. Dr Walter Friedrich, former Director of the *Institut für Jugendforschung*, Leipzig; Horst Gibtner, MdB, formerly Minister of Transport of the GDR; Dr Wolfgang Gudenschwager, CDU, Berlin; Dr Karlheinz Guttmacher, MdB; Adolf Haidegger, CDU, *Bürgermeister*, Colditz; Hildegard Hannan, *Stadtmuseum*, Oranienburg; Dieter Herberg, FDP, Leipzig; Prof. Dr Uwe-Jens Heuer, MdB; Matthias Hinkel, Leipzig; Prof. Dr Hartmut Jäckel, Free University, Berlin; Dr Dietmar Keller, MdB, former Minister of Culture of the GDR; Egon Krenz, formerly General Secretary of the SED and Chairman of the Council of State of the GDR; Vera (Wollenberger) Lengsfeld, MdB; Dr Ekkehard Lieberran, PDS, Bonn; Roger Loewig, painter, Berlin; Heidemarie Lüth, MdB; Dr Michael Luther, MdB; Friedrich Magirius, *Stadtpräsident* Leipzig and *Superintendant der Nikolaikirche*, Leipzig; Lothar de Maizière, formerly Minister-President of the GDR; Captain Wilfried Mannewitz, formerly of the MfS; Roland May, SPD, Leipzig; Rudolf Meinl, MdB; Dr Hans Modrow, MdB, formerly Minister-President of the DDR; Uwe Müller, formerly SPD, Leipzig; Dr Hermann Pohler, MdB; Gerd Poppe, MdB; George Pumfrey, PDS, Bonn; Klaus Reichenbach, MdB, formerly Minister in the Office of the Minister-President of the GDR; Hans Jürgen Richter, MdL, SPD, Chemnitz; Colonel Dr Klaus Rösler, formerly head of Department XII of HV A; Christina Schenk, MdB; Dr Gerald Schmidt, CDU, Berlin; Richard Schröder, formerly Chairman of the SPD group in the Volkskammer; Dr Sigrid Semper,

MdB; Werner H. Skowron, MdB; Dr Gerald Thalheim, MdB; Rolf Thieme, CDU, Dresden; Cenzi Troike-Loewig, Berlin; Dr Wolfgang Ullmann, MdB; Joachim Walther, writer, formerly *Gauck-Behörde*, Berlin; Konrad Weiss, MdB; Wolfgang Wiemer, SPD, Bonn; and many others who did not wish to be identified.

Chapter 1

The GDR in 1988 – a stable state?

Geriatrics lead the SED

As the military band goose-stepped its way past the East Berlin reviewing stand followed by other military units, and delegations of the Free German Youth and mass organisations, the East German leaders smiled confidently at their followers below. The date was 7 October 1988 and the occasion was the 39th anniversary of the founding of their state, the German Democratic Republic (GDR), in 1949. Most of them remembered that first celebration. Certainly Erich Honecker, General-Secretary of the ruling Socialist Unity Party (SED) and head of state, Willi Stoph, head of government, Kurt Hager, SED secretary responsible for ideology, and Erich Mielke, Minister for State Security, had been there in 1949 celebrating the new state amid the ruins of the old. They had grown old in the service of the GDR. Honecker was 76, Stoph 74, Hager 76 and Mielke already 81. The other 22 members and candidate members of the Politburo of the SED were nearly all as old. The man widely tipped to succeed Honecker, Egon Krenz, was regarded as a youngster at 51. The age factor did mar the image of the GDR. The leaders of the two countries most important for the GDR, the Soviet Union and the Federal Republic of Germany (West Germany), Mikhail Gorbachev and Helmut Kohl, were 56 and 58 respectively. In practical terms, age mattered in that the SED leaders found it difficult to adapt to the changing situation. It mattered too in that they appeared determined to cling to power at all costs. Many citizens of the GDR could not see why their leaders should go on and on when they were classified as pensioners at 65 and forced to retire.

The SED leaders lived since 1960 in a forest settlement on the outskirts of Berlin known as Wandlitz. On 31 May 1960 they had decided that in future all full and candidate members of the Politburo who worked in Berlin should live there.[1] Started in the 1950s, it was justified on the grounds of security. The settlement was surrounded by a high wall and patrolled by members of the guards regiment Felix Dzershinski of the Ministry for State Security (MfS). In it was a restaurant, a medical complex, a fitness centre and, naturally, a supermarket. Krenz later wrote that the conditions in the

1

settlement were not as luxurious as many outsiders thought. Nevertheless, he conceded that many East Germans would have found the housing luxurious given the very bad conditions which still existed in the GDR.[2] As a result of the SED leaders living in Wandlitz, they were even more cut off from the people they claimed to represent than they would otherwise have been. Krenz later freely admitted this. Not only that, they were cut off from each other. If they were known to be socialising with each other, this could lead to suspicions that they were 'forming a faction', one of the greatest crimes in the Communist political world. For that reason they rarely visited each other socially.[3] Only Honecker was allowed to have friends among his Politburo colleagues.

Who were the 'prisoners' of Wandlitz?

Erich Honecker was born in the Saar, the son of a coal miner, in 1912. He took up an apprenticeship as a roofer, but his interest was politics from childhood. He joined the German Communist Party (KPD) youth organisation in 1926 and the KPD in 1929. In 1930–31 he studied at the Lenin School in Moscow. After the Nazi seizure of power in 1933 he worked in the KPD underground. Arrested in 1935, he was sentenced to ten years' imprisonment in 1937. In 1945 he was charged with building up a youth movement which became the Free German Youth (FDJ) in 1946. He served as its Chairman until 1955. Honecker was rewarded for his suffering and loyalty by being elected to the Executive Committee of the SED in 1946. In 1950 he was elected candidate member of the Politburo, becoming a full member in 1958. Walter Ulbricht, SED chieftain, 1950–71, treated him almost as a son, but this did not stop Honecker seizing his chance to overthrow Ulbricht in 1971. He then attempted to secure his position by promoting his own men to the ruling Politburo. His wife, Margot, was his eyes and ears in the government as Minister for People's Education and the only woman minister. She also served as a member of the Central Committee (ZK), first as a candidate, 1950–63, and then as a full-member from 1963 to 1989. The couple met in the FDJ.

Honecker's colleagues in the Politburo, ranked according to the year they became full members of that body, were, in 1988, as follows.

Willi Stoph served as a Deputy Chairman of the Council of Ministers (deputy head of government), 1954–62, First Deputy Chairman, 1962–64, Chairman, 1964–73, Chairman of the Council of State, 1973–76, and then Chairman of the Council of Ministers again until 1989. He was born in Berlin in 1914 and completed his apprenticeship in the building trade. He joined the Communist youth moment in 1928 and the KPD itself in 1931. He served in the artillery in the war as an NCO. He turned again to the building industry and Communism after 1945 and was soon on his way up the ladder! In **1953** he was already a member of the Politburo. He proved flexible enough to be moved from building to military matters. He held office as the GDR's first Defence Minister, 1956–60, after helping to create disguised military units when he was Minister of Interior, 1952–55. He was given the GDR's highest military rank, *Armeegeneral* in 1959. In 1973 Honecker moved him to be Chairman of the Council of State, titular head of state. This was a setback. He recovered his position as Chairman of the Council of Ministers in 1976 after Honecker's nominee, Horst Sindermann, stepped down.

Born in the industrial town of Chemnitz in 1910, **Erich Mückenberger** grew up in a Social Democratic Party (SPD) milieu. He completed his apprenticeship as a machine-fitter and enrolled in the SPD youth movement in 1924. Three years later he joined the SPD itself and worked as a functionary of the Reichbanner, the party's para-military wing. His anti-Nazi activities after 1933 brought him several months in Sachsenburg concentration camp in 1935 and a ten-month jail sentence in 1938. After service in the wartime Wehrmacht, he re-joined the SPD in 1945, supporting merger with the Communists the following year. He rose speedily through the ranks of the new SED, joining the ZK in 1950. In the same year he joined the Politburo as a candidate, becoming a full member in **1958**. As ZK Secretary for Agriculture, 1953–60, he played a decisive part in the forced collectivisation of farming in the GDR. Various other positions followed, including chairmanship of the SED group in the Volkskammer, 1980–89.

Born 1909 in Berlin, **Alfred Neumann** had been active in the workers' sports movement. He had fled to Moscow and took part in the Spanish Civil War. Interned by the French and handed over to the Gestapo, he was sentenced to a term of imprisonment in the same jail as Honecker at Brandenburg. He served briefly in a penal battalion before the war's end in 1945. He built his career in Berlin, holding office as deputy mayor in the crucial years 1951–53. Between 1953 and 1957 he was First Secretary of the SED Berlin organisation. He was a member of the ZK from 1954, joining the Politburo at the same time as a candidate member. He was elected to full membership in **1958**. From the 1960s his main responsibilities were in the government, and for many years he was a First Deputy Chairman of the Council of Ministers.

Born in 1921, **Kurt Hager** was regarded as one of the most influential members of the Politburo. An old KPD member, he had spent the war years in the sanctuary of England. From 1952 he headed the department responsible for science and universities, having been appointed Professor of Philosophy at the Humboldt University, East Berlin, in 1949. His rise under Walter Ulbricht, SED leader until 1971, was swift. He was 'elected' to full membership of the ZK of the SED in 1954 after serving as a candidate from 1950. In 1955 he was appointed a Secretary of the ZK responsible for science, education and culture. After being promoted to candidate member-ship of the Politburo in 1959, he was 'elected' to full membership in **1963**. He also headed the Politburo's ideological commission. Thus Hager wielded enormous power over every aspect of the GDR's cultural life. He could prevent writers being published, could arrange for good or hostile reviews to appear praising or denouncing works by particular writers, artists or directors. He could prevent artists or academics going abroad. He had final say over university appointments and much more. His main rival for power in these areas was General Erich Mielke, head of State Security.

Günter Mittag was Honecker's only friend in Wandlitz. Born in Stettin in 1926, he worked on the Reich railways before taking up full-time political work. He served as SED Secretary with responsibility for the economy, 1962–73 and 1976–89. He had been an economic reformer under Ulbricht in the 1960s, but threw out his reforming zeal when he joined Honecker's inner circle in the 1970s. A candidate member of the Politburo from 1963, he became a full member in **1966**. He was a sick man for many years and died in 1994.

Like Honecker, Hermann Axen (see below) and Neumann, **Horst Sindermann** had seen the inside of Nazi jails and, unlike Honecker, concen-tration camps. He spent six years in Waldheim prison and Sachsenhausen and Mauthausen concentration camps. Born in Dresden in 1915, he at-tended grammar school and was soon involved in Communist activities. He started his post-war career as editor of various Communist newspapers. He was a candidate member of the ZK in 1958, a full member after 1963, and a member of the Politburo from **1967**. From 1976 he was President of the Volkskammer.

Born in Leipzig in 1916, **Hermann Axen** was another grammar school boy who joined the Communist youth movement and served a prison sen-tence for his political activities, 1934–37. He fled to France, and after being interned there in 1940 was handed over to the Gestapo. He was deported to Auschwitz and, as a Jew, was very lucky to survive. He knew Honecker as a co-founder of the FDJ and worked with him in this movement. How-ever, he was elevated to the Politburo under Ulbricht, first as a candidate in 1963, and then as a full member from **1970**. A Secretary of the ZK from 1966, he was responsible for the relations between the SED and other Communist parties.

Werner Krolikowski was born in Silesia in 1928. Although his father was a worker, he was trained as a white-collar administrator. He joined the SED in 1946. His big chance came in 1960 when he was appointed First Secretary of the SED Dresden district organisation. Elected to the ZK in

1963, his elevation to the Politburo followed in **1971**. Honecker gave him Mittag's job as ZK Secretary for the Economy in 1973, but in 1976 he was moved to the Council of Ministers as First Deputy Chairman.

Erich Mielke was born in Berlin into a working-class family in 1907. After education with a scholarship at the *Kollnisches Gymnasium*, Berlin, he took up an apprenticeship with a road haulage firm. He soon followed his parents into the KPD and was active in the para-military and sports organisations of the party. He was known as a strict vegetarian, non-smoker and total abstainer from alcohol. He fled to the Soviet Union in 1931 to avoid arrest for his part in the shooting of two policemen. He received training at the Comintern's military school and was sent to Spain, where he served as an officer in the Communist secret police during the Civil War, 1936–39. For a time he was interned in France, but he was back in Berlin soon after the end of the war in 1945. He immediately took up security work and played a key role in building up the state security system of the Soviet Zone/GDR. After a variety of top security jobs, he was finally appointed Minister for State Security in November 1957. He reached the Politburo in **1971**. He was given the GDR's highest military rank, *Armeegeneral* in 1980.

Born in 1927, **Harry Tisch**, like Stoph, served in the Wehrmacht. He joined the Communist Party in 1945 and made his way first in the trade union movement and then in the SED apparatus. Between 1961 and 1975 he headed the SED organisation in Rostock. He joined the Politburo in **1975** after being a candidate member, 1971–75. From 1975 he was Chairman of the GDR trade union federation, the FDGB.

Seen for some time as the white hope of SED reformers, **Werner Felfe** was born near Dresden in 1928, the son of a worker. He completed his apprenticeship in commerce. At the war's end he joined the KPD and FDJ. By 1946 he was working full-time for the SED. He switched to FDJ work, and, owing to his association with Honecker, climbed the ladder of that organisation. He was deputy head of the FDJ, 1954–57, serving as Honecker's deputy, 1954–55. His career then suffered a setback during the limited and abortive de-Stalinisation drive after the XX Congress of the Soviet Communist Party (CPSU). The FDJ was accused of 'sectarianism' and he was moved to a lesser post outside the youth movement. Felfe proved himself flexible and orthodox enough to work his passage to position of second secretary of the SED's Halle district organisation in 1968. Ulbricht was on the look-out for comrades not suspected of being in sympathy with the Prague Spring of that year. Honecker promoted him to first secretary in 1971. In 1973 he was elected candidate member of the Politburo and in **1976** a full member. He was given responsibility for agriculture in 1981. Under Felfe there was a certain relaxation of the tight collectivism in agriculture. Peasant farmers were allowed a little more scope to sell the produce of their private plots. Allotment holders, hobby cultivators, were also encouraged in this direction. Felfe died in 1988, thus enhancing Krenz's claim as heir apparent.

Berlin-born (1928) **Joachim Herrmann** was a close associate of Honecker in his capacity as ZK Secretary, since 1978, for Agitation and Propaganda. This meant he had responsibility, subject to Honecker's veto, for the media. He served as editor-in-chief for the lifeless *Neues Deutschland* between 1971 and 1978, and before that, *Junge Welt*, the organ of the Free German Youth. A candidate member of the Politburo from 1973, Herrmann became a full member in **1976**.

Horst Dohlus, born in Plauen in 1925, completed his apprenticeship as a hairdresser in Plauen before being called up in the Wehrmacht. In 1946 he joined the SED and worked in the Wismut uranium mines, but by 1949 he had been appointed a full-time SED functionary in the mines. After a course at the CPSU university in Moscow, he was moved to the brown coal industry. Elected to the ZK as a candidate in 1950, he was promoted to full membership in 1963 and to the Politburo in **1980**.

Egon Krenz was born in Kolberg (now in Poland) in 1937. He mother was a working woman and he did not know his father, a tailor. It would be true to say that the SED became his father. He was a loyal child of the GDR and was rewarded for it. He made his career in the youth movement. Between 1964 and 1967 he studied at the university of the CPSU in Moscow. He was put in charge of the Young Pioneers in 1971, serving until 1974, and as Chairman of the FDJ until 1983. From **1983** he was a member of the Politburo with responsibility for security and youth. He also a member of the Council of State, 1981–84, and a Deputy Chairman, 1984–89. For years Krenz was regarded as heir apparent to Honecker.

Werner Jarowinsky had a remarkable childhood in that he was born in Leningrad (1927). His father, a worker, repatriated the family to Germany in the 1930s. After training as a sales representative, Jarowinsky served in the Wehrmacht, 1943–45. He joined the KPD/SED in 1945 and went on to study economics at the Humboldt University in Berlin. After working as a university lecturer and gaining his doctorate, he went on to work at the Ministry of Trade and Supplies. Elected to the ZK in 1963, he joined the Politburo in **1984**.

Günther Kleiber was one of the post-war FDJ generation. He was born in 1931 in Eula, the son of a worker. He worked as an electrician in the brown coal industry before taking a mature student access course in Dresden. From there he went on to study electrotechnology in Rostock and Dresden. After working as secretary of the SED organisation at the Technical University in Dresden, 1962–63, he joined the state apparatus. Elected to the ZK and candidate membership of the Politburo in 1967, he became a full member in **1984**. He served as a Deputy Chairman of the council of Ministers, 1971–89.

Günter Schabowski, born in Anklam in 1929, had risen at speed through the SED's ranks, which caused some to have their doubts about him. He had trained as a journalist working for *Tribüne*, the trade union paper, in the 1950s. He joined the SED in 1952 and worked on *Neues Deutschland*, serving as its editor-in-chief, 1975–84. In that capacity he promoted the personality cult around Honecker. Honecker promoted him to candidate membership of the Politburo in 1981 and then full membership in **1984**. He was a ZK Secretary from 1986 and head of the Berlin SED organisation from 1985. He was regarded as a Honecker loyalist.

Werner Eberlein was born in West Berlin in 1919, the son of a KPD functionary. In 1934 his family emigrated to the Soviet Union, where his father was subsequently imprisoned under Stalin. In Siberia he trained as an electrician. On his return to Germany in 1948 he was immediately given work by the SED. After completion of studies at the CPSU university in 1954, he worked as a journalist for *Neues Deutschland*. Various SED posts followed, including that of First Secretary in Magdeburg, 1983–89. In 1981 he reached the ZK and in **1986** the Politburo.

Heinz Keßler took over in 1985 as Minister for Defence on the death of Heinz Hoffmann. Born into a Communist working-class family in Lauban, Silesia, in 1920, he served his apprenticeship as a metal turner before being called up in the Wehrmacht in 1940. He defected to the Soviets in 1941 and was a co-founder of the National Committee for a Free Germany. After the war he rose rapidly in the military wing of the People's Police. In 1950 he was put in charge of building up an airforce, with the rank of major general. After training at the Soviet Air Force academy, 1955–56, he was appointed Deputy Minister for Defence in 1956. Other senior military posts followed. Although he was elected to the SED executive in 1946, which became the Central Committee, he did not reach the Politburo until **1986**.

Only a member of the Politburo from **1986** to 1989, **Hans-Joachim Böhme** was born in Bernburg (Saale) in 1929. After a working-class childhood, he joined the SPD in 1945 and went into the SED a year later. He made his way via the FDJ and the SED, becoming the First Secretary of the SED Halle in 1981. In that year he was elected to the Central Committee.

Siegfried Lorenz was born in Annaberg in 1930 and took a similar path to Kleiber, taking his access course at Leipzig University. He climbed the FDJ ladder, serving on Central Council, 1961–76. He was head of the Youth Department of the ZK, 1967–76. A candidate member of the ZK from 1967, full membership was achieved in 1971. Full membership of the Politburo came in **1986** after only one year as a candidate. Lorenz was First Secretary of the SED Karl-Marx-Stadt district, 1976–89.

Lenin: 'not deceived by...slogans like freedom'

It is difficult to be certain to what extent the Politburo members believed their own propaganda. They were not great intellects and made no contribution to furthering the theory of socialism. It is doubtful that many of them had ever read much of the literature of Marxism. Of the Soviet Union, most of them knew little. Even those of the pre-war generation, like Honecker and Hager, probably only read Lenin and Stalin as interpreted by the CPSU. Lenin was presented not only as the great revolutionary leader but also as a great theorist of Marxist science. Lenin, as well as Stalin, offered them the ammunition to justify their dictatorship and even the dictatorship of one person.

> The Soviet Socialist Democracy is in no way inconsistent with the rule and dictatorship of one person: that the will of a class is at times best realised by a dictator who sometimes will accomplish more by himself and is frequently more needed...

And,

> we are not going to let ourselves be deceived by such high-sounding slogans like freedom, equality, and the will of the majority, and those who call themselves democrats...[4]

Lenin had proved he could win against the odds in 1917 and in the civil war, and Stalin proved he could do the same by smashing the Nazi Wehrmacht between 1941 and 1945. This must have made an enormous impression on the veterans of the inter-war period and on the generation which followed. Many of the difficulties and much of the unpleasantness in the Soviet Zone could be explained away by the historical backwardness of Russia, the losses of the Second World War, and the corruption and confusion wrought by Nazism. In private older communists could admit that 'mistakes had been made', but such mistakes had to be seen against the broader historical picture. They followed Lenin in believing

> If we are not anarchists, we must admit that the state, i.e., *coercion*, is necessary for the transition from capitalism to socialism. The form of coercion is determined by the degree of development of the given revolutionary class, and also by special circumstances, such as, for example, the heritage of a long and reactionary war and the forms of resistance put up by the bourgeoisie or the petty bourgeoisie.[5]

Their own individual survival and success was enough proof for them that Lenin was right and that they had history on their side! The victory of Mao in China, decolonisation, Soviet space successes in the 1950s and 1960s and the victory of Ho Chi Minh's forces in the Vietnam War all pointed in the same direction. The international recognition of the GDR in the 1970s had been forced on the Imperialist Camp and was further proof of the correctness of the policies of the CPSU and the SED. The early mastery of nuclear weaponry by the Soviet Union had prevented a third world war and saved Castro's Cuba. Waverers and doubters wanted to leave the GDR and the security of the Socialist Camp to go to West Germany for bananas, Volkswagens and holidays in Spain. These opportunists and defeatists were just the same sort of people who had been bribed by Hitler's 'good times' in the 1930s, and look where that led – Warsaw, Coventry and Auschwitz, followed by Stalingrad, Hamburg, Dresden and the fall of Berlin! By holding firm, victory would go ultimately to the peace forces led by the Soviet Union.

The Politburo

Of the 22 full members of the Politburo in 1988, only 9 were born in what was or was to become the GDR, another 4 were Berliners, 4 were from the lost territories beyond the Oder–Neisse line, 2 were from West Germany, and 1 was born in Russia. Only two appeared to be from middle-class backgrounds. Of the 14 who were old enough, 6 had been imprisoned by the Nazis and 6 had served in the Wehrmacht, while 3 had served in the Spanish Civil War. Neumann was in all three groups. They were men of limited experience and limited intellectual horizons. By 1988, 14 of the 22 had reached the Politburo under Honecker. Honecker looked impregnable. Like his predecessors, the real threat to him came from Moscow.

The Politburo met once a week, but, its deliberations were often of a purely formal kind. Various members would give reports on their particular areas and would not expect colleagues to interfere. Honecker often did his main wheeling and dealing either before or after the meetings with Mittag and Mielke and Herrmann. The General Secretary drew up the agenda and usually no one sought to change it. Reports were circulated during the week, like those of Mielke on the security situation, but this did not mean they were discussed. Honecker was very powerful, but he could not escape the fact that several of his colleagues had direct links with their counter-parts in Moscow. This was true of Mielke with the KGB, Axen with the CPSU's foreign relations department, Stoph with the Soviet state apparatus (and defence contacts), and Kessler with the Soviet defence establishment.

The Central Committee (ZK) officially elected the Politburo, but the ZK was much like the Volkskammer (to which most Politburo members be-longed) in that it had formal power but not real power. Its members rarely met outside its official deliberations unless it was in the official meetings of a ministry or of other bodies of which they were members. The real power was exercised by Honecker and before him by Walter Ulbricht, through the

General Secretary of the SED Chairman of the Council of State Chairman of the National Defence Council Erich Honecker	Secretaries of the ZK of the SED Hermann Axen Horst Dohlus Kurt Hager Joachim Herrmann Werner Jarowinsky Egon Krenz Werner Krolikowski Günter Mittag Inge Lange

President of the Volkskammer Horst Sindermann	Minister for National Defence Heinz Keßler	Minister for State Security Erich Mielke

Chairman of the Council of Ministers Willi Stoph	First Deputy of the Chairman Günter Kleiber	First Deputy of the Chairman Alfred Neumann	Chairman of the State Planning Commission Gerhard Schürer

First Secretaries of Districts (*Bezirke*) Hans-Joachim Böhme Werner Eberlein Siegfried Lorenz Gerhard Müller Günter Schabowski Werner Walde	Chairman of the FDGB Harry Tisch

Chairman of the Central Party Control Commission Erich Mückenberger

Chairman of an Agro-Industrial Organisation Margarete Müller

Commissions and Working Parties of the Politburo	
Foreign Policy Commission	Hermann Axen
Agitation	Joachim Herrmann
Culture	Kurt Hager
Women	Kurt Hager
Economics	Günter Mittag
Youth	Egon Krenz
Commission of Heads of Institutes of the SED	Kurt Hager
Working Party on the Balance of Payments	Günter Mittag

Commission for the Co-ordination of
   Economic, Cultural & Scientific Technical
   Relations of the GDR with the States of Asia,
   Africa and the Arab Areas
	Günter Mittag

Figure 1.1 Responsibilities of Members and Candidate Members of the Politburo (Summer 1989)

party *Apparat*, the SED's band of full-time officials who acted according to a strict hierarchy (see Figure 1.1). At the head was the Secretariat (*Sekretariat*). In 1988, this was made up of ten secretaries, with Honecker, General Secretary, acting as its chairman. They included Hermann Axen, international relations; Horst Dohlus, SED publications; Werner Felfe, agriculture; Kurt Hager, culture and science; Joachim Herrmann, agitation and propaganda; Werner Jarowinsky, trade, supplies and the churches; Egon Krenz, security, youth and sport; Günter Mittag, the economy; and Inge Lange, women. Günter Schabowski, First Secretary of the Berlin SED organisation, was also a member of the Secretariat. The secretaries were expected to report directly to Honecker. All, except for Lange, were full members of the Politburo. She was a candidate member for many years. The Secretariat met once a week and controlled the promotion or demotion, assignment or re-assignment of cadre, which gave it a powerful hold on the reins of power. It clearly had tremendous powers of patronage. It was responsible for formulating and transmitting directives to SED groups in the state organs, armed forces, economy and mass organisations. Altogether, there were about 2,000 full-time officials who worked in the 'Big House', as the ZK building was known.[6]

Democratic Centralism

Article 47, paragraph 2 of the constitution laid down, 'The sovereignty of the working people, which is implemented on the basis of democratic centralism, is the fundamental principle of the state structure.' Democratic Centralism meant control by the SED of all aspects of the state. It also meant that the SED itself was subject to this principle. The Politburo would put forward its proposals to the ZK, which would normally meet four times a year. That body usually agreed without any dissenting voices. It was the official governing body of the SED between the congresses, held every five years, and its resolutions had the force of law. They were passed down to the 15 district First Secretaries, many of whom were themselves members. Within the district organisations the same Democratic Centralism principle applied. In normal times there was only formal discussion, not controversy. If SED members discussed party matters outside the monthly members' meetings they were in danger of being accused of 'factionalism', especially if three or more were present. The party leaders appeared to have all the best cards in their hands! As Hans Modrow was later to admit, it was impossible for any party member who had expressed an opinion different from those of the Politburo to be elected as a delegate to a party congress, to the ZK or other bodies.[7] He also admitted that the SED's democratic constitution was only on paper.[8]

The ZK was formally elected by the SED congress on the proposal of the outgoing ZK. Most members, once elected, remained on the Central Committee indefinitely. It had grown in numbers over the years from a mere 51 full members and 30 candidate members in 1950 to 111 full and 44 candidates in 1958. When Honecker took over in 1971, it consisted of 135 full and 54 candidate members. The XI congress elected 165 full and 53 candidate members to the ZK. They included most of the SED's elite. Ten SED ministers out of 33 were either full or candidate members. Among those not on the ZK were the Minister for Light Industry, the Minister of Finance, the President of the State Bank, the Minister for Electro-technology and the Head of the Office for Youth Questions. This gave some idea of the Politburo's priorities. The leaders of the 'mass organisations' such as FDJ, DFD, FDGB, and so on, were all members. All 15 District First Secretaries were members of the ZK and three of the five were rectors of the party's own universities. The most significant of them was Professor Dr Otto Reinhold. One noticeable trend in the Honecker period was the growing numbers of military, police and state security members of the ZK.

The SED's leading role

The SED dominated every aspect of life and society in the GDR. Article 1 of the constitution of 1968, as modified by the law amending the constitution of 7 October 1974, stated, 'The German Democratic Republic is a socialist state of workers and farmers. It is the political organisation of the working people in town and countryside led by the working class and its Marxist-Leninist party.' The 'Marxist-Leninist party' was of course the SED. The use of this term left open the possible change of the party name to Communist at a later date. The four other parties – the Christian Democratic Union (CDU), the Liberal Democratic Party of Germany (LDPD), the National Democratic Party of Germany (NDPD) and the Democratic Farmers' Party of Germany (DBD) – accepted in their constitutions the leading role of the SED. The government, officially called the Council of Ministers, was totally dominated by the party. The Chairman of the Council of Ministers and his two first deputies were all SED members. There were nine other deputy chairmen, of whom five were SED with one each from the CDU, LDPD, NDPD and DBD. Of the other 33 ministers, all were SED members. The CDU held the Ministry for Posts and Communications, the DBD the Ministry for Protection of the Environment and Water, the NDPD member was Chairman of the State Contracts Court. Finally, the LDPD member, Hans-Joachim Heusinger, was Minister of Justice, a post he had held since 1972. The Council of Ministers and all its ministers were subject to accepting the 'proposals' (*Vorschläge*) of the SED. The way the government operated is revealed below in relation to the GDR Minister for Posts and Communications. This was equally true of the collective head of state, the Council of State. Honecker was its Chairman and under him were eight deputies. In addition there were 20 ordinary members, a secretary and a head of chancellery. Stoph, Sindermann, Krenz and Mittag were deputy chairmen and there were another four who were the leaders of the four allied parties: Manfred Gerlach (LDPD), Gerald Götting (CDU), Heinrich Homann (NDPD) and Günther Maleuda (DBD). Interestingly, in a state that claimed to have achieved sexual equality, there was only one woman minister, Margot Honecker. In the Council of State seven women served as ordinary members. Honecker was also Chairman of the National Defence Council, a body whose exact membership was a secret but which included the important Politburo members.

According to Article 48 of the GDR constitution, the Volkskammer (People Chamber) 'is the supreme organ of state power' in the GDR. 'It decides in its plenary sessions the basic questions of state policy.' The Volkskammer is 'the sole constituent and legislative organ' of the GDR. 'No one can limit its rights.' Given that, it was essential for the SED that it always dominated the Volkskammer. This was achieved through the other parties bound in the National Front, agreeing to the SED getting the lion's share of candidates in the single-list elections held every five years. To some extent this was disguised by SED members standing as FDJ, DFD or trade union nominees. In any case, the Volkskammer met only for a few days each year, to receive progress reports or formally pass legislation. There was never any controversy, and voting was almost always unanimous. In fact, the only exception was when the Volkskammer legalised abortion in March 1972. Then 14 CDU members voted against and 8 abstained. This had been undoubtedly agreed with the SED beforehand. The 15 district councils operated in the same way, as did the town councils. Elections to the Volkskammer and the 15 district councils were last held on 8 June 1986. According to the official results 99.94 per cent was given to the National Front candidates. There were no other candidates. Virtually every voter went to vote. There was strong pressure to do so. As most people lived in blocks of flats, it was relatively easy for the National Front co-ordinators in each block to pressurise their fellow tenants to vote. It was easy for the sick, hospitalised and travellers to vote. Once at the polling station, all the voter had to do was to identify themselves, take their ballot paper, and, if supporting the official list, simply fold it and put it in the box. Only if the voter rejected one or more of the candidates did they need to go to one of the booths provided, thus drawing attention to themselves. They had to reckon that the election official would note their name. Most people feared there would be consequences if they did not vote or if they used the booths.

In 1988 the chairmen of all 15 GDR administrative districts (*Bezirke*) were members of the SED and 14 of them were men. Irma Uschkamp was the exception in Cottbus. Of the mayors, of the 28 most important towns, 27 were SED members. The exception was Professor Dr Gerhard Baumgärtel of Weimar, who belonged to the CDU. This was not an accident. Weimar was regarded as playing an important propaganda role abroad. There were only two women among the 28 mayors.

It goes without saying that the SED dominated all military, police, security, state and economic bodies in the GDR. Heinz Adameck chaired the State Committee for Television, and he and his five committee members were all SED and all were men. A committee of four SED members, all male, governed the radio. Günter Pötschke headed the only news agency, ADN. Pötschke and his six deputies were all SED comrades, all were male. In 1988, the rectors of all the GDR's nine universities were SED members and all were men. Of the nine academies, all were run by men, of whom seven were SED and two were non-party. One of them was Professor Dr Konstantin Spies of the medical academy, the *Akademie für Ärztliche Fortbildung* in Berlin. The SED rightly believed it needed to treat the medical profession with kid gloves, and it therefore had to avoid the appearance of subjecting non-SED medical practitioners to disadvantage. All the professional organisations of the GDR were headed by male comrades, the best-known being Hermann Kant, President of the Writers' Union, and Professor Dr Hans-Peter Minetti, President of the Creative Theatre Workers. All the main 'mass organisations', such as the FDJ, KB, DSF, GST, DTSB and the DFD were headed by members of the SED. Obviously, the DFD had women at its head! Ilse Thiele was its long-serving Chairperson. The allied parties each had one deputy chairperson in the leadership of the DFD and there was also a second SED member. Almost all other public bodies, such as the German Red Cross and the Federation of Co-operatives, were headed by male members of the SED. The only exceptions were the Peace Council of the GDR, whose President was Professor Dr Günther Drefahl, a 66-year-old chemist. The Peace Council's mandate was to pursue world peace according to the SED's interpretation of the Soviet line. The League for Friendship Among the Peoples had as its President Gerald Götting, head of the CDU. Full-time SED members staffed both bodies.

The 1986 XI Congress of the SED

In January 1986, in preparation for the XI congress, the Secretariat gave details of SED membership. The SED, it claimed, had 2.3 million full and candidate members out of an adult population of about 12.5 million. It was claimed that 58.2 per cent of them were workers. As Honecker and his fellow Politburo members and all full-time functionaries were classified as workers, this figure must be treated with great caution.[9] The figures were manipulated to suit the SED's needs. Women were said to make up 35 per cent of the membership. In 1946 21.5 per cent were women, and in 1967 26 per cent. The SED was proud of the fact that 371,000 members were university graduates and 503,000 had graduated from technical colleges (*Fachschulen*). Members were expected to attend monthly meetings, pay subscriptions according to their incomes, and take part in various SED activities, including courses on party policy. According to the Secretariat, 1.9 million of them had attended a course lasting over three months. Most of those in the SED were members by choice. They were individuals who wanted advancement in society and knew SED membership was a prerequisite for the highest positions in almost any sphere. It was virtually impossible to occupy *any* position in the state administration, police, armed forces, education or the media without SED membership. Most foremen and women in industry were members. There were still some idealists in the SED, but equally there were ordinary members with little interest in politics. Party members who were fit were expected, where appropriate, to take part in a unit of the *Kampfgruppen der Arbeiterklasse* (fighting groups of the working class). These were in effect party militias organised at factories and offices throughout the GDR. They were designed to quell any attempt at 'counter-revolution'. Approaching the office of the economic journal *Die Wirtschaft*, one Monday morning, the author was alarmed as a truck screeched to a halt beside him and out jumped a dozen or so men in combat gear and steel helmets carrying Kalashnikov rifles. They were journalists who had spent the weekend 'in the field'.

At the XI congress of the SED in April 1986, Honecker appeared impregnable. He had pushed through changes in the composition of the Politburo which meant that half its members had joined since he had taken over in 1971. With an average age of over 64, they were individuals of limited experience. They greeted Gorbachev but did not even pay lip service to self-criticism. Instead the SED announced its utopian plans to make the GDR a world leader in the 'key technologies', including computer-aided design and manufacturing, robotics, nuclear energy, laser technology and biotechnology. In its attempts to achieve these aims it readily sacrificed more traditional industries, including the consumer sector. The fact was that the GDR, like its 'socialist' neighbours, was in decline. It had relied on exporting a range of industrial, oil and agricultural products at bargain-basement prices to the West to import essential supplies. But increased competition from Asia had cut demand for these exports. The fall in oil prices had been another blow. The GDR's defence and security expenditure was another crippling burden. In the 1980s it was forced more than ever to seek loans from the

15

West and encourage remittances from the millions of East Germans who lived in the West to their relatives in the GDR. Western television and radio and Western visitors, without consciously doing so, brought with them ideas which gained currency in the GDR. The relative success of the Greens in West Germany captured the imagination of many young East Germans. The Greens appealed because they were not part of the Western Establishment, were better educated, were often conscientious objectors to military service, and did not flaunt BMWs or other expensive consumer goods. Such young people in East and West were concerned about the environment and opposed nuclear energy.

Allies of the SED

Those who had ambitions but could not bring themselves to apply for SED membership often chose one of the four other parties in the GDR. They could only join with the approval of the SED. Their activities were controlled through the department for allied parties of the ZK of the SED and through the MfS. The 'allied parties' could not, for example, recruit industrial workers or members of the armed organs of the GDR. Their members came mainly from the small traders, artisans, medical practitioners, farmers and the remnants of the old middle classes. They were regarded as part of the past rather than of the future. Nevertheless, in the 1980s the SED gave them a slightly larger role.[10] Since the 1950s these parties had recognised the 'leading role' of the SED and were proud to pursue the tasks mapped out for them by the leaders of 'the party of the working class'. They held their congresses in 1987. Like the SED congresses, these were rituals with no real discussion. Their leaders once again emphasised their loyalty to the SED. They were all expanding at this time. Membership of the CDU stood at 140,000. The DBD claimed 115,000 members. The NDPD claimed a membership of 110,000, and the LDPD 104,000. Citizens of the GDR with no ambitions at all still needed to be in an official body in order to work. Membership of one of the FDGB's affiliated unions was a necessity for any employee. Membership stood at about 9.5 million in the mid-1980s. The union's role was to ensure discipline in the workplace, to ensure that its members were working effectively to realise the aims of the five-year plan. Union officials controlled a wide range of welfare facilities and holiday hostels. Membership of the Free German Youth was also all but compulsory. This body claimed a membership of 2.3 million, that is, about three-quarters of those aged between 14 and 25. To outsiders it was difficult to understand the almost blanket membership of the DSF. Most working adults were members. The point was that this was a way of showing one's loyalty without having too many obligations. Apart from paying the modest subscriptions, little more was required. Ironically, interest, as opposed to membership, increased to a degree during the Gorbachev years. There was also the GST. This was a military sports organisation modelled on a similar body in the Soviet Union. Most young male adults were involved in the GST's activities at one time or another, and those wishing to gain entrance to higher education were strongly advised to join it. All male university students were required to do a four weeks' military camp. Women students were expected to take part in civil defence.

To a very large extent, jobs and professions were controlled by the SED, FDJ and the MfS. School leavers were directed to particular trade or professions or to work in particular enterprises. In theory this was voluntary. In practice it took a strong-minded individual to go his or her separate way. Would-be university students were directed into particular disciplines. It was virtually impossible to get into English studies, medical or music studies. At the end of a degree course, very many students went where they were directed in terms of location, enterprise and particular job within that enterprise. Their previous political and military activities were taken into consideration by the graduation commissions responsible for finding them work. Only if they had good connections, or there were special personal circumstances, could a mediocre posting be changed. Whatever their views in private, it was difficult for the citizens of the GDR to escape the embrace of the SED either directly or indirectly.

Reagan (1987): 'Mr Gorbachev, tear down this wall!'

Honecker went on about 'imperialist plots' against the GDR, but he was glad to be seen with such 'enemies' as Helmut Schmidt (1981), Franz Josef Strauß (1983, 1987), and even Chancellor Kohl. Indeed, he was most anxious to be seen on the world stage, especially visiting Western capitals or receiving Western leaders. He knew that most East European leaders, before Gorbachev that is, cut no ice with ordinary East Germans. He hoped pictures of himself with such Western politicians would legitimise him in the eyes of his own people. In 1985 Honecker received the French Prime Minister Laurent Fabius, the Finnish President Kalevi Sorsa, SPD Chairman Willy Brandt and, at the beginning of the year, Johannes Rau (SPD), the Prime Minister of Northrhine-Westphalia, the biggest state of the Federal Republic. In 1986 he received a group of US senators, the Belgian Prime Minister, Wilfried Martens, and made state visits to Sweden and China. In June 1987 he was in the Netherlands, and in September he made his long-awaited visit to Bonn. There was a price to be paid for such a visit. The East German people were looking for greater freedom as a result of the visit. One world statesman who avoided him was President Ronald Reagan.

He visited Germany in 1987, including Berlin. But the President did not make the few short steps through Checkpoint Charlie to see Honecker.[11] Instead, Reagan, probably seen by very many East Germans watching Western television, called rhetorically, looking towards the Berlin Wall, to the absent Soviet leader Gorbachev, 'Come to this gate! Mr Gorbachev, open this gate! Mr Gorbachev, tear down this wall!'[12] Apparently, before Reagan had made this public call he had told Hans-Jürgen Heß, Director of the then semi-redundant Reichstag building, 'This wall will fall' and, 'be sure, this will be very soon'.[13] No one thought that within less than two years the Wall would be open and redundant. The aged leaders of the SED had no intentions of following Gorbachev. One line of argument they used was that they were *ahead* of Gorbachev in many areas. They had a private service sector of the kind Gorbachev had just legalised. Their economy was functioning and they had always retained more than one party.

Sputnik banned

As the leaders of the GDR watched developments in the Soviet Union, they became afraid of where Gorbachev was heading. They started to distance themselves from the idea, which they had fully accepted in the past, that policies introduced in one socialist state had any relevance to the situation in another. The interview which Hans-Dieter Schütt, editor in chief of the youth paper *Junge Welt*, gave to the West German weekly *Die Zeit* (27 June 1986) caused dismay in reform-friendly circles in the GDR. Schütt, while careful to praise the Soviet Union for defeating Nazi Germany, went on to say that he did not consider the Soviet Union a model in terms of technology and progress. Not many years earlier he would have lost his job and been expelled from the party for such a comment. When the Soviet feature film *Repentance* was broadcast on West German television in autumn 1987, it was strongly criticised in *Neues Deutschland* and *Junge Welt*. An allegory about small town small-mindedness and political repression which was critical of the Stalin era. A beloved City Father dies and his body is continuously – and mysteriously – exhumed.[14] For many thinking East Germans, unlike Schütt, the Soviet Union was at last becoming interesting. Soviet publications, so often despised, became worth looking at. This was particularly true of the monthly publication *Sputnik*, which was a kind of Soviet equivalent of *American Express*. It had first appeared in 1967 and of its one million copies about 180,000 were printed in German. *Sputnik* was in no sense a journal just of politics. It tried to serve the interests of a wide audience and was generously illustrated. Subscribers in the GDR were shocked, if they noticed it, by a short statement published in

Neues Deutschland (19 November 1988). This was from the Ministry of Post and Communications. The Ministry had crossed the magazine off its list of publications it would carry because it did not serve Soviet–German friendship but instead published distorted history contributions. This was not the first time that a Soviet publication had been banned. The Soviet journal *Neue Zeit*, also a publication aimed at foreign readers, had been banned previously. After the fall of the SED, the Post Minister, in whose name *Sputnik* had been banned, Rudolph Schulze, of the SED-satellite CDU, said he only learned of the ban when he read about it in *Neues Deutschland*.[15] Schulze was a Deputy Chairman of the GDR Council of Ministers, 1969–89. His *démenti* revealed just how little power ministers had relative to the Politburo of the SED and the security organs. The ban brought anger and resignation in some SED and intellectual circles in the GDR. In a celebrated reply, Kurt Hager, Politburo member responsible for ideology, asked his interviewer from the West German weekly *Stern* (10 April 1987), 'If your neighbour changed his wallpaper in his flat, would you feel obliged to do the same?' Hager and his colleagues deceived no one with such rhetoric. But reformed-minded members of their own party were downcast by such utterances. A few months later, the candle of reform flickered dimly at the X Writers' Congress (24–6 November 1987). Hermann Kant, its President, mumbled noises in the direction of *glasnost* and there was some criticism of the GDR press from other speakers.

Frau Margot Honecker, wife of Erich, member of the Central Committee of the SED and Minister of People's Education since 1963, had her say on 13 June 1989. At the ninth GDR Pedagogic Congress, an important political as well as educational event, she attacked reforms in neighbouring states. In a hard-line speech, she said it was not clear what those who talked about the free market economy and pluralism had in mind. She had no doubt that they sought 'not the strengthening of socialism, but the return to capitalism'. What was needed, she continued, were young people who could fight, who helped to strengthen socialism, who stood up for socialism, defended it by word and deed and, 'if necessary, with weapons in their hands'. She came out strongly in favour of education based on Marxist-Leninist ideology.[16] Her words were rather ominous: 'with weapons in their hands' was certainly meant as a veiled threat. A few days earlier, Erich Honecker, her husband, had been a little more diplomatic. Asked by American journalists about reforms in 'the socialist camp', he responded:

> We are anxious to find in each case such solutions as suit our national conditions best. This does not of course mean that we would underrate the experience gathered by the other socialist countries. On the contrary; we are actively involved in the exchange of experience with them. In the process, we would be well advised not to copy from the other socialist countries.[17]

That seemed to be that. There seemed to be little hope of reform from within the leadership of the SED itself. The death of Politburo member and Secretary of the ZK for Agriculture, Werner Felfe, in summer of 1988 had removed the last hope for rapid change from within. A member of the Council of State, the 60-year-old Felfe had been seen by some as a likely successor to Honecker and, rightly or wrongly, was associated in some people's minds, including Egon Krenz, with a more Gorbachev-style approach.[18] The younger Krenz himself was written off as Honecker's protégé. Only outside the SED could anything be attempted.

On 17 January 1988, in Berlin, dissidents attempted to plead their case by joining the annual march commemorating the murder of Karl Liebknecht and Rosa Luxemburg in 1919. They unfurled banners reminding their fellow-citizens that Luxemburg had supported free speech and the right to differ. Some carried pictures of Gorbachev, which were torn down by the General Mielke's Stasi operatives. At least 100 of the would-be demonstrators were arrested. Later that month others were arrested and imprisoned. Some, like Stephan Krawczyk and Freya Klier, were expelled to West Germany, and others, like Bärbel Bohley, to Britain. Protests were held all over the GDR. They were held in churches because churches were the only places in which the SED permitted a modicum of free speech. In Bonn all the parties in the Bundestag protested.

Despite the fall in church attendance and membership of the decades of SED rule, the churches remained influential. In fact, the influence of the Evangelical Church, the most important of the Christian denominations in the GDR, had grown over the 1980s. The Evangelical Church had accepted the political and economic structures of the GDR but reserved the right to speak out on particular issues which it regarded as fundamental to human rights. It had opposed military instruction in schools and the denial of social service as an alternative to compulsory military service. These were burning issues for a considerable minority of parents and young people. In March 1988, Honecker discussed developments with Bishop Werner Leich, Chairman of the GDR Conference of Evangelical Church Leaders. In the summer of 1988 reform in the GDR topped the agendas of four regional Evangelical Church congresses (Halle, Görlitz, Rostock and Erfurt). In Halle, Manfred Stolpe, Vice-Chairman of the Federation of Evangelical Churches of the GDR, called for *perestroika*. Earlier, according to *Neues Deutschland* (10 June 1988), Kurt Hager, speaking to the ZK of the SED, warned: 'there can be no room in the Church for anti-state activities'. With over forty years of experience behind him, ensuring the security of the SED and its state, Mielke was still confident he could nip in the bud any opposition 'conspiracy', inside or outside the churches, with his informers, like 'Maximilian' and 'Torsten', already placed in the opposition groups.

Notes

1. Egon Krenz, *Wenn Mauern fallen*, Vienna, 1990, p. 75.
2. *Ibid.*, p. 77.
3. *Ibid.*, p. 78.
4. Lenin quoted in David Shub, *Lenin*, Harmondsworth, 1966, p. 443.
5. Shub, *op. cit.*, p. 443.
6. Arnold/Modrow, in Hans Modrow (ed.), *Das Große Haus*, Berlin, 1994, p. 11.
7. *Ibid.*, p. 17.
8. *Ibid.*, p. 20.
9. *Ibid.*, p. 12. Among many others, by 1988 the middle levels of the medical profession were classed as 'workers', as were army officers and cadet officers.
10. Peter Joachim Lapp, *Ausverkauf: Das Ende der Blockparteien*, Berlin, 1998, p. 20.
11. John O. Koehler, *Stasi: The Untold Story of the East German Secret Police*, Boulder, CO, 1999, p. 145. Apparently Ronald and Nancy Reagan paid a private trip to East Berlin in 1978.
12. Dennis L. Bark and David R. Gress, *A History of West Germany 2 volumes*, Oxford, 1993, II, p. 524.
13. Daniel Friedrich Sturm, 'Ronald Reagan sagte den Mauerfall voraus', *Das Parlament*, 27 August/3 September 1999.
14. *Leonard Maltin's 1998 Movie and Video Guide.*
15. Stefan Wolle, *Die heile Welt der Diktatur*, Berlin, 1998, pp. 294–5.
16. *Informationen*, No. 12, 30 June 1989, pp. 6–7.
17. *Foreign Affairs Bulletin* (GDR), 21 June 1989.
18. Krenz, pp. 24–5.

Chapter 2

The GDR's flawed development

A modern economy – in 1945

The GDR leaders were proud of their state. They regarded it as one of Europe's leading states and the world's most modern socialist state. In economic terms it was ahead of the other Soviet bloc countries on the basis of the range of the products it produced and their sophistication. Yet many believed they had squandered their inheritance. In 1945 the part of Germany which became the Soviet Zone and then the GDR was possibly the most modern area of Europe. In 1944 about 25 per cent of the population of the German Reich lived in the area which became the GDR, yet 29 per cent of the Reich's industrial production originated there. The area was noted for its production of optical equipment, office machines (the forerunners of computers), motor vehicles, aircraft, chemicals, scientific instruments, electrical engineering products, machines and machine tools, pottery and glass, textiles and clothing, toys, musical instruments, wood products and book publishing. And even though cities like Berlin, Leipzig, Dresden and Halle had been devastated by allied bombing and by ground fighting, much remained. Many towns fell without a fight. Subsequently the Soviet Zone was taken apart for reparations by the Soviets and it is almost a miracle that it survived. Many of the top designers, technologists, scientists and managers were forced to work in the Soviet Union for up to ten years. The Americans who briefly occupied much of the southern industrial hub in the summer of 1945 had evacuated others. Of those who remained, many joined the exodus to the West at later stages. The census of June 1961 in West Germany revealed that 3,099,000 Germans in the Federal Republic were originally from the Soviet Zone/GDR. The population had been about 18 million in 1946. In addition, a further 2,766,000 Germans, who had originally sought refugee status there from the territories behind the Oder–Neisse Line, had subsequently left for West Germany.[1] Moreover, this was no orderly movement. The numbers rose and fell according to the political and economic situation. Disproportionately more of the young, educated and skilled left. If someone did not turn up for work on Monday morning, their boss did not know whether they were just ill or whether they had joined the exodus to the West.

Lack of raw materials

One other problem was that the Soviet Zone lacked the hard coal and steel needed to feed the sinews of industry. In 1938, only 7 per cent of Germany's iron and steel products originated in what became the Soviet Zone, although the population there constituted 32 per cent of the Reich's population.[2] The industry suffered heavily from Soviet dismantling policies. Only about 2 per cent of Germany's hard coal was produced in the area of the Soviet Zone/GDR before the war and the area was actually running out of reserves.[3] The well-developed chemical industry suffered from the fact that 80 per cent of the sulphuric acid came from West Germany. Although before 1945 33 per cent of German motor vehicle production originated in what became the Soviet Zone/GDR, its factories delivered only 14 per cent of such essentials as tyres, spark plugs, pistons and glass. Many of the dyes for the textile industry also came from the West. One natural resource it did possess was uranium, now needed for the new nuclear industry. But the Soviets took charge of this and the East German economy benefited little from it. When the Soviets did give the green light for the GDR to develop a nuclear energy capacity, they saw to it that their client was dependent on their technology. It has been concluded that 'The situation in the energy sector and the historical dependence on Soviet nuclear technology played a significant role in the economic downfall of the GDR.'[4]

The Soviet Zone also suffered from the loss of pre-war trading partners like the UK, France, Denmark, Sweden and the Netherlands. Instead it was linked to the more backward economies of Eastern Europe. By the time the GDR was established in 1949, the Soviet Zone was still in a very poor condition and was already falling behind the new West German state. It was also handicapped by the Stalinist command economy.

Ulbricht's unrealistic targets

Central state planning was in force and, under the first five-year plan of 1951–55, the task was to produce massive reparations deliveries to the Soviet Union, build up heavy industry, and pay for the new armed forces. All of this meant austerity for the mass of the population. Stalin died in March 1953, and some of his more extreme policies were reversed. A more consumer-orientated economic policy was introduced. But this came too late to prevent the revolt of June 1953, which started in East Berlin and engulfed many of the key towns of the GDR. This was crushed by the intervention of the Soviet armed forces. Following the line of Soviet leader Nikita Khrushchev at the XX congress of the CPSU in 1956, the second five-year plan, 1956–60, continued this relatively consumer-friendly policy.

Food rationing was finally abolished in the GDR in May 1958. Again, following the CPSU, the SED embarked on entirely unrealistic economic policies in 1958. It set the GDR the goal of overtaking West Germany in the per capita consumption of all-important food and consumer products by 1961.[5] Khrushchev had declared that the Soviet Union would overtake the USA by that date. The SED now pushed for collectivisation of agriculture and handicrafts. At the end of 1954, 75.5 per cent of the agricultural land belonged to private farmers, in 1958 it was still 62.2 per cent, but by the end of 1960 only 7.6 per cent remained in private hands.[6] These measures were forced through against the opposition of many of those affected. The result was a rapid escalation of the numbers going West. In addition to farmers, these included electricians, plumbers, carpenters, barbers and tailors. Khrushchev's threats against West Berlin also caused fear and uncertainty in the GDR and helped to convince more East Germans that it was time to abandon the GDR. In desperation, SED leader Walter Ulbricht got the Soviet Union to agree to the sealing off of East Berlin, the last escape route for refugees, by means of the Berlin Wall.

The Wall helped the GDR economy to the extent that it at least stabilised the labour force. It also led to many East Germans coming to the conclusion that they should try to make the best of a bad job. In Moscow Khrushchev continued with de-Stalinisation at the XXII congress of the CPSU in 1961. Ulbricht felt obliged to follow. The New Economic System was announced at the VI congress of the SED in 1963. Its aim was to put the economy on a more rational basis. The GDR was to concentrate on what it was good at. The remaining private sector was to be encouraged. More emphasis was to be put on quality rather than just quantity, and consumer products were to be given priority. The more 'liberal' cultural policy also gave the hope of better times to come.

Such hopes were dashed in a quite dramatic way by the palace coup against Khrushchev in 1964 and his replacement by Brezhnev. Even more dramatic was the invasion of Czechoslovakia in 1968 by the Soviet Union and its Warsaw Pact allies to crush the 'Prague Spring'. This was the attempt by the Czechoslovak Communist Party to introduce 'socialism with a human face' after the dark days of Stalinism. Ulbricht himself was forced to resign as SED leader in 1971, although he remained titular head of state until his death in 1973.

Erich Honecker replaced Ulbricht first as SED leader and then as head of state. He too promised a better life for the GDR population. He offered the cultural élite a policy of 'no taboos'. This meant that, providing artists and writers supported the socialist system, they would be free to pursue the themes which interested them and adopt the forms which did justice to these themes. No longer would rigid 'Socialist Realism' be enforced.

Honecker faced several pressures when he made these promises. Firstly, there had again been near-revolution in neighbouring Poland. Secondly, improved relations with West Germany after the setting up of the coalition led by Willy Brandt in 1969 presented a new challenge to the SED. One of these challenges was the increased number of tourists from West Germany, many of whom were there to see their relatives. One indicator of the development of human contacts between West and East Germans were the increasing number of telephone calls from West Germany to the GDR. In 1972 there were 5.1 million calls from the Federal Republic or West Berlin to the GDR. By 1985 there were over 25 million such calls.[7] Thirdly, by the early 1970s most East Germans were able to receive West German television programmes, which gave them a better window on the world, including the Soviet bloc, than did the GDR media. The importance of the West German electronic media cannot be emphasised enough, even though they did not attempt to stir up discontent in the GDR.

Oil imports and defence burdens

Honecker soon faced another challenge. This was the sudden oil price rise in 1973 following the Arab–Israeli War. Most of the GDR's oil came from the Soviet Union, which put up its prices in 1975. This was a savage blow to the GDR economy, which was so heavily dependent on imported fuel. In March 1977 Gerhard Schürer, Chairman of the State Planning Commission, and Günter Mittag, SED Economy Secretary, both Politburo members, sent a letter to Honecker warning him of growing financial difficulties in paying for imports.[8] According to their estimate, the GDR needed, in 1978, 11 billion marks to make interest payments and pay back foreign credits, yet it was only expected to earn 9.3 billion from its exports. The GDR had to borrow from Western banks to help repay earlier loans. Moreover, as the Soviet Union was unable to maintain its deliveries of oil and other vital raw materials to the GDR, the GDR had to look to states outside the Soviet bloc for substitutes. In the early 1980s the situation continued to deteriorate as Western states instituted a boycott of all Soviet bloc states in retaliation against the declaration of martial law in Poland.[9] Owing to strikes, Poland was itself unable to deliver coal to the GDR. Worse was to follow in 1979 with the second international oil crisis. Other raw material imports also cost more. Far fewer resources could be used to raise living standards, far more had to be used to meet export commitments. A self-inflicted injury was the nationalisation of most of the remaining partly privately owned businesses in 1972. These mixed state–private undertakings accounted for 10 per cent of industrial production in 1971 and were particularly important in textiles and light industry. The continuing large

25

expenditure on the armed forces and the security apparatus represented a heavy drain on the GDR's slender resources. According to the International Institute for Strategic Studies in its report on the military balance, 1986–87, GDR defence expenditure rose from the equivalent of $6.7 billion in 1981 to $7.7 billion in 1984. This represented $457 per capita in 1984 and compared with $328 per capita in the wealthier West Germany. This was higher than all its Warsaw Pact allies except for the Soviet Union. According to the Institute, the GDR's defence spending was 7.7 per cent of national income compared with 4 per cent for Czechoslovakia, the next highest spender of the Warsaw Pact (excluding the Soviet Union). The armed forces swallowed up badly needed manpower and defence industries distorted the economy, especially the hi-tech branches. Inevitably, the GDR turned to arms exports to help its foreign exchange bill. During the Iran–Iraq war of the 1980s it was content to export to both sides.

In their competition with the West the SED leadership decided to concentrate building activity in Berlin in preparation for the celebrations surrounding the 750th anniversary of the founding of the city. This not only caused discontent in the provinces but also damaged the economy because essential work in other towns and cities had to be put back.

Honecker and his colleagues found that they had little leeway to manoeuvre if they wanted to maintain living standards, let alone improve them. They could attempt to modernise the economy by increasing exports. This project was decided upon and action was taken following the XI SED party congress in April 1986. The GDR was to become the Japan of the Soviet bloc. It was to develop its hi-tech industries and become a world leader in the industries of the future. This was to be achieved partly with the help of the Stasi's industrial espionage activities in the West and partly with the help of secret deals with Japanese manufacturers. Resources were concentrated on this project to the detriment of other branches of the economy. But it was totally unrealistic and made matters worse. Apparently Schürer, sometimes supported by Willi Stoph, advocated this disastrous policy to Honecker. He was prepared to cut subsidies to help find capital to support this development. Mittag and Werner Jarowinsky, Minister of Trade, who argued it entailed a hopeless misallocation of resources, opposed him. Jarowinsky agreed with his colleague on the need to cut subsidies, the cost of which had climbed from 8 billion marks in 1970 to 58 billion in 1989, outpacing by almost two to one the growth in national product.[10] Honecker backed microelectronics possibly without fully understanding the cost involved. As late as the summer of 1989 Honecker still believed his own propaganda. According to *Neues Deutschland* (15 August 1989) he believed that 'all in all the development of microelectronics in the GDR underlines the correctness of the path we have chosen'. In 1988 Schürer estimated that by the end of 1989 the GDR's indebtedness abroad would amount to 38.9 billion marks. He attempted to make it clear to Honecker that the GDR was on the verge of bankruptcy and presented reform proposals, including the cutting back of the costly, highly subsidised hi-tech enterprises. Honecker would not listen and even suspected a conspiracy against him.[11] In May 1989 Schürer warned once again that the GDR was on the verge of bankruptcy.

West German help to the GDR

On the whole the West German political establishment, irrespective of party, favoured helping the GDR. Naturally the feelings of kinship played an important part in this. If helping their kith and kin meant helping the SED regime, so be it. They would, however, attempt to gain humanitarian concessions from the GDR. The other important reason for helping was the fear of what would happen if widespread dissatisfaction led to an open revolt, as in Poland. In 1983 West German banks granted the GDR a loan of DM 1 billion. In return the GDR abolished the regulation under which West German children visiting the GDR were required to exchange a minimum sum of hard currency for each day spent in the SED state. A loan of DM 950 million in 1984 led to a reduction in the amount West German pensioners had to pay when visiting the GDR. These loans increased the GDR's credibility with non-German banks. West Germany was pumping money into the GDR by different routes over the decades, something which was not given too much publicity, for political reasons. West Germany, for instance, paid for the improvement of road, rail and canal links between the West and West Berlin, all of which were used by East Germans as well as West Germans. This also helped to increase the numbers of foreigners visiting Berlin who had to pay for GDR transit visas. West Germany also helped to finance the improvement of postal services between the two states. Moreover, it paid a high price for political prisoners it 'bought free' from the GDR. Between 1964 and 1989 the cost to West Germany was 3.5 billion marks for 33,755 prisoners. Rainer Barzel, then Minister for All-German Affairs, negotiated the arrangement with the GDR. The cost per prisoner depended on his or her education and the length of his or her sentence. For many years this was done under the cloak of secrecy. In additional, the Federal Republic enabled 2,000 children to join their parents in the West and re-united 250,000 individuals with family members in West Germany.[12] Apart from assistance from the West German state, the GDR benefited from gifts from West Germans to their relatives in the East, and from gifts from the West German churches to their co-religionists in the GDR.

Intershop resentment

Within the GDR a chain of Intershops was established where the best of Soviet bloc consumer goods were available as well as imports from the West. Like much else, this followed the Soviet pattern. The first was set up in 1955 in Rostock for foreign seamen. By the late 1960s Intershops had spread across the GDR and the range of goods was expanding. The really big expansion came, however, in the 1970s and 1980s with a very wide range of consumer goods on offer. For example, there were jeans from the USA, cameras from Japan, televisions, Salamander shoes, coffee and washing powder from West Germany, cigars from Cuba, wines from France and Italy, toys, whisky and DIY tools from Britain. Some goods, like cigarettes, were in fact manufactured under licence in the GDR and sold in the Intershops. The catch was that you needed convertible Western currency like the German mark, the US dollar or the Belgian franc to be able to shop there. Most East Germans had no way of earning such convertible currencies. It was only from 1974 that East Germans were allowed to hold foreign currency. The lucky ones were those with relatives in the West and a small number of GDR citizens who could earn Western currency, like writers, artists or transport workers whose work took them to the West. Most East Germans could look round these stores but could only take away with them food for thought. If the GDR was doing so well as its media always claimed, why were such quality goods not produced in the GDR? Why were they not available in the ordinary shops? The Intershops also proved divisive between those who somehow got the German mark and those who had only GDR marks. From 1956 the few East Germans who earned foreign currency could legally import goods through the *Geschenkdienst* (present service) in Berlin. This was used increasingly in later years by West Germans to send presents to their relatives in the GDR. Everything from electrical goods to furniture and cars could be bought.

Even in shops where the GDR mark could be used, there were the ordinary stores and the Exquisit and Delikat chain where better quality goods were available at much higher prices. Some of these goods were imported. The ordinary shops made a dismal impression indeed. The staff often took up a 'take it or leave it' attitude. There were constant shortages of everything. There were coffee and cocoa crises. People wasted much time queuing. A university lecturer explained with pride to the author that he was friendly with the local butcher and had been able to get the fillet steak being served from 'under the counter'. Grapefruit, oranges, lemons and bananas were hardly ever available. 'Are there grapes where you come from?' the small son of a medical specialist asked the writer in 1986. His father explained that he had investigated a queue on the way home from the night shift at

East Berlin's renowned Charité hospital and found grapes were being sold. The doctor drove a battered Trabant. His wife, also a medical practitioner, did not own a car. Old age pensioners boosted their incomes by queuing for others for automotive parts. All of this caused stress, disappointment and discontent. East Germans believed they worked as hard as West Germans yet they knew from television and from talks with relatives from the West that they were so much poorer. Something was wrong somewhere. The whole system was unfair. One other aspect of the shortages was that East Germans could not understand why it was that, if the GDR had such friendly relations with many Third World states, their products were not available in the GDR.

Another aspect of the SED's failure to provide enough facilities for its people was the lack of restaurants and other eating-out opportunities. Even when a restaurant was half empty, would-be customers still had to take up a suitably humble and obsequious pose at the door in the hope that the kind waiter would direct them to a table. Service was slow and often any number of items on the menu would not be available. Hard-currency restaurants in the Interhotels, on the other hand, were often virtually empty and the guest got immediate attention. East Germans felt like second-class citizens in their own country.[13]

The severe restrictions on travel were keenly resented. As a rule, only retired people could visit the West. Even then some were prevented for security or political reasons from travelling West. There could be a humiliating search of baggage in the customs hall in Friedrich Straße, Berlin, or elsewhere, as the jack-booted customs officer with the cynical smile rummaged through an old woman's underwear to ensure she was not trying to illegally export the crown jewels from the socialist state. It could be a lengthy procedure before the lucky traveller was allowed through to the West-bound train. The pensioners went without means and had to rely on the few marks given them by the West German state, so-called 'welcome money', and the generosity of the relatives who had invited them. It was somewhat humiliating. Travel to the West was about the only privilege pensioners had. Pensions for most people remained very low and contrasted unfavourably with those in West Germany. The few citizens allowed to go to the West on 'urgent family business', such as births, marriages and deaths of close family members, had to go through an even more tortuous process than the pensioners. Whether they were permitted to travel or not usually depended on the arbitrary decisions of local officials. Even then their spouses were forced to stay behind. In any case, up to the early 1980s the annual number travelling was only about 40,000. Under pressure from below and from West Germany, the granting of this right to travel was given more readily in the second half of the 1980s and 139,000 travelled West in 1985, 573,000 in 1986 and nearly 1.3 million in 1987.[14] Even then there was no clear right in law, and local officials made decisions in an arbitrary fashion. Those wanting to travel were often interrogated like criminal suspects. Holidays had to be spent at home or in GDR holiday resorts, often in trade union hostels or under canvas. Frequently husbands and wives were forced to take a break separately. The fortunate few who had money to spend could visit Soviet bloc states, where, in most cases, they were forced to pay high prices for second-rate accommodation. They visited Bulgaria, Czechoslovakia, Hungary, Poland, Romania and the Soviet Union, only to find that West Germans received better service in better hotels because they paid in hard currency. Many who visited the Soviet Union were shocked by the low standards prevailing, having been fed by the GDR media on the image of the USSR as the most modern and progressive state in the world.

Poor housing

Poor housing conditions were also a cause of discontent. The GDR media projected the image of a country where a massive housing programme was underway. Yet the few statistics available and even visits to prestige sites tended to reveal the opposite. The flats which most people lived in were small by West European standards. In his report to the XI SED congress, Honecker admitted that only 68 per cent of GDR homes had toilets and only 74 per cent had baths or showers. Much of the housing stock dated from before 1914. Little renovation was being done. Most of the housing built since 1945 was poor in construction and lacked modern amenities. Newer housing was mainly monotonous blocs of flats on large estates, which often lacked shopping and other facilities. DIY materials were also in short supply and plumbers and electricians, in the 1980s, usually demanded hard currency for their work. By comparison, whereas in 1986 38 per cent of the GDR's homes were built after 1945, in West Germany the percentage was 72,[15] and West Germany had been forced to cope with a far greater housing problem due to the large number of outsiders seeking to live there. The GDR's situation was the reverse. Deteriorating housing conditions included deteriorating water quality and refuse disposal. Modern waste disposal facilities hardly existed in the GDR.

The media were forever hammering the message that the GDR was a land of great 'social achievements' – low rents, low tariffs on public transport, free health care, subsidised basic foodstuffs and an excellent education system. All of this was only partly true.

Lack of GDR identity?

During the existence of the GDR and since there has been much discussion about the extent to which its citizens regarded themselves as part of separate and distinct nation from the West Germans. Germany was politic-ally united in 1871, after which it had three distinct political regimes until 1945. It also had several frontier changes in 1919, 1935, 1938 and 1945. All these changes forced a certain flexibility on Germans in terms of their political identities and loyalties. There were also big shifts of population. However, whatever the regime, there was only one German state demanding their loyalty and they had the consciousness of being part of a community recognised for its great achievements in science, technology and industry and, above all, culture. What Shakespeare was to the British or even Pushkin to the Russians or Racine to the French, Beethoven was to the Germans. Whatever the political regime, the feeling of being German persisted. 'Hitlers come and go but the German People go on,' said Stalin. Officially, the GDR did not attempt to change this in the 1950s and 1960s. The SED claimed it sought to overcome the division of the German people. Like the rival Federal Republic, it too kept up the rhetoric of German re-unification. Until the building of the Berlin Wall in August 1961 the contacts between family members living in East and West were often strong. Even after that date, letters were still exchanged.

From the early 1970s on, the contacts grew again, with increasing num-bers of West Germans visiting their relatives in the GDR or even meeting them in third countries such as Bulgaria, Czechoslovakia or Hungary. It was only at this time that the SED proclaimed the doctrine that the GDR had developed a separate identity and had little or nothing in common with West Germany. The doctrine of a separate GDR identity was taught as official doctrine from 1974 to the end of SED rule in March 1990. In that sense it did not have so long to take root. Of course, by that time, the great majority of East Germans had only experienced life separated from the West. In the author's many years of GDR watching, GDR citizens usually consciously regarded themselves as 'German' rather than identifying with either German state directly. There must, however, have been various de-grees of identification and alienation. For some there was a kind of negative identification with the GDR based on dislike of West Germans. Some were envious of the affluence of West Germans. They saw them in their designer jeans spending freely in Budapest, Moscow, Prague or even East Berlin or Leipzig, and thought they saw the ugly face of the Federal Republic. Some were glad to see the Federal Republic's squad defeated at international football or other sporting fixtures. Many were appalled by the crime and drugs problems which they saw aired on West German television. They thought their own republic was relatively crime-free partly because little publicity was given to crime in the GDR. However, from the television pictures they were able to see nightly, many found the Federal Republic a modern and exciting place, a place much more in touch with the world than their own republic. West German politicians such as Brandt, Schmidt and Strauß were lively and were seen on chat shows as well as in formal settings. Their private lives were discussed. Against them, Honecker, Stoph and their colleagues appeared to have no existence outside the grim formal proceedings of party and state occasions. Even their ability to deliver a public address compared badly with their West German rivals. East German viewers saw West German politicians facing sharp questioning by inter-viewers or voters. The same was true of the foreign politicians allied to the GDR and those allied to West Germany. Despite the criticism of American Presidents back home, on German television they came across as far more likeable and human than the Soviet or East European Communist leaders. Such images weakened any identification with the GDR.

Worse still, virtually every aspect of the GDR and its allies seemed drab, dreary and provincial compared with the Federal Republic. Internationally, West Germany was allied to other interesting and exciting places such as the United States, New York, Paris, London and Rome. By comparison the Soviet Union, Moscow, Warsaw, Sofia – and even Prague – seemed dull. The Soviet bloc was associated with little that was modern, stylish or chic, whether it was cars, clothes or consumer goods, or films, literature, archi-tecture, music or theories about modern society. Even the GDR's currency, with its light-weight coins, looked and felt shabby in comparison with Western currencies such as the pound, the dollar and, above all, the German mark. Many East Germans felt condemned to a life of boredom. Others felt angry. They knew either directly, from their parents, from the West German media, or even from museums, of German achievements and felt that only the SED system was holding them back from reaching those heights once again. Many felt demeaned at having to publicly acknow-ledge the system, having to vote at pseudo-elections, having to join SED-controlled organisations, and having to be very careful if they complained about anything. No wonder the Soviet German expert, diplomat Valentin Falin told Markus Wolf that East German support for the GDR was never higher than 30 per cent and normally much lower.[16]

The views of youth

Unlike Western countries, the Soviet bloc states never presented the results of objective opinion polls. These were introduced relatively late into the armoury of the ruling Marxist-Leninist parties and their dependencies and they were normally regarded as state secrets. Only occasionally were lim-ited results published. The GDR was no exception to this rule. However, research on youth was conducted there from the 1960s onwards. Given the situation in the GDR, any survey results must be treated with caution for it is likely that many of those questioned did not really believe in the anonymity of the poll. They would have been reluctant, therefore, to give unorthodox, dissenting views. For what they are worth, the poll findings of the *Zentralinstitut für Jugendforschung* (Central Institute for Research on Youth) in Leipzig, headed by Professor Walter Friedrich, revealed a loss of identification among GDR youth with 'their' state between 1975 and 1989. The question put to apprentices by Friedrich's assistants was 'Do you agree with the statement, "I am proud to be a citizen of our socialist state"?' The bulk of those asked would have been clear what answer was expected of them. In any case youngsters are unlikely to be able to differentiate between the state and the community in which they live. To say they reject the state would be almost like saying they reject their country, town and friends. In 1975, 57 per cent identified completely and 38 per cent did so with reservations. Only 5 per cent identified hardly or not at all. Ten years later the figures were 51, 43 and 6 respectively. In the following year, 1986, they were 48, 46 and 6. But in 1988, according to Friedrich, there was a dramatic fall in the percentage of those who identified completely. In May of that year only 28 per cent said they did so, while 61 per cent did so with reservations. Eleven per cent identified hardly or not at all. In October of the same year the figures were 18, 54 and 28. Finally, in September 1989 a survey of male-only apprentices showed only 16 per cent identified completely, 58 per cent partly and 26 per cent hardly or not at all.[17] These were all young people who had been indoctrinated in kindergarten, schools and places of work as well as in the official youth bodies to which they were virtually forced to belong. Their parents had to be careful what they said to them. Only Western television, which many of them saw, gave a different picture of the world. Friedrich's surveys were useful in showing the trend but probably greatly underestimated the doubts and disaffection which existed among GDR young people.

Was no one in favour of the SED regime? Certainly. There were the old Communists and there were a few old Nazis who had thrown in their lot with the Soviets and the SED. There were their offspring. There were others who had grown up in the Soviet Zone/GDR who had got satisfying jobs. Take someone who was 12 in 1945 and by his nature was inclined to back those in power. By loyalty and diligence he could have risen in many spheres of life in the GDR. The massive outpouring of potential job competitors before 1961 made this more certain. Many such individuals occupied the teaching profession at all levels, the armed forces, police and administration both nationally and locally, full-time jobs in the mass organisations, the top jobs in industry. In most cases they were, by nature, the opposite of individuals who joined Communist parties, Green parties or even Social Democratic parties in Western Europe in the same period. These GDR loyalists in responsible jobs gained a variety of minor privileges, including awards, in return for their conformity. As a very rough guide to their combined numbers, one can consider SED membership, which, as we saw, in 1988, stood at around 2.3 million out of an adult population, including pensioners, of about 13.3 million, that is, about 17.3 per cent. To these must be added some members of the 'allied' parties – LDPD, CDU, DBD and NPDP, and FDJ members not yet in the SED. The figure of 17.3 per cent comes remarkably close to the SED successor party (Party of the Democratic Socialism or PDS) vote in the March 1990 election.

A public opinion poll conducted in the GDR in June 1990 found that 78 per cent of those questioned believed that some of the things built up in the GDR over forty years were good and should be retained in the future united Germany. Only 16 per cent rejected this view, wanting things to change as quickly as possible to become like the Federal Republic.[18] This result is hardly surprising. The natural inclination is to say, 'Surely there must be some good here? Surely we must have done something right?' Many of those who experienced it were likely to say the same about the Third Reich, especially between 1933 and 1939.

Apart from most of the SED members and the others mentioned above, there were others, not supporters of the SED, who had a kind of GDR identity. They felt a kind of solidarity with their fellow citizens in the GDR, having been bound together in a *Schicksalsgemeinschaft* (community of fate) by the accident, in most cases, of having been caught on the wrong side of the post-war demarcation line. This kind of individual could be found among the church activists, in ecological groups, and so on. There were also some who harboured a certain pride in the GDR's achievements despite the odds, despite the lack of capital, despite the system. If it were admitted that everything in the GDR was third-rate, inefficient, outclassed, unjust and in part perhaps 'evil', then what did that say for its people who had put up with it for over 40 years? In such circumstances most people would want to salvage something to justify their own existence. As SED, and later PDS, member Professor Christa Luft put it, 'Inevitably one asks oneself: Was that a wasted life? I personally energetically deny that!'[19]

Notes

1. Bundesministerium für gesamtdeutsche Fragen (1969), p. 211.
2. *Ibid.*, p. 167.
3. *Ibid.*, p. 333.
4. Burghard Weiss, 'Nuclear Research and Technology in Comparative Perspective', in Krishe Macrakis and Dieter Hoffmann (eds), *Science under Socialism: East Germany in Comparative Perspective*, Cambridge, MA, 1999, p. 228.
5. Stefan Doernberg, *Kurze Geschichte der DDR*, Berlin, 1964, p. 320.

6. *Ibid.*, p. 17.
7. Bundesminister für Innerdeutsche Beziehungen, *Jahresbericht 1985*, Bonn, 1986, p. 25.
8. Hans-Hermann Hertle, *Der Fall der Mauer*, Opladen, 1996, p. 37.
9. *Ibid.*, p. 42.
10. Charles S. Maier, *Dissolution: The Crisis of Communism and the End of East Germany*, Princeton, NJ, 1997, p. 70.
11. Hertle, *Der Fall der Mauer*, pp. 68–71.
12. *Ibid.*, p. 77; Rainer Barzel, *Es ist noch nicht zu spät*, Munich, 1976, pp. 31–41.
13. Stefan Wolle, *Die heile Welt der Diktatur: Alltag und Herrschaft in der DDR 1971–1989*, Berlin, 1998, pp. 213–15.
14. Hertle, *Der Fall der Mauer*, p. 79.
15. Gernot Schneider, *Wirtschaftswunder DDR: Anspruch und Realität*, Cologne, 1990, p. 54.
16. Markus Wolf, *Spionagechef im geheimen Krieg*, Munich, 1997, p. 132.
17. The figures are taken from Elisabeth Noelle-Neumann, 'The German Revolution: The Historic Experiment of the Division and Unification of a Nation as Reflected in Survey Research Findings', *International Journal of Public Opinion Research*, Vol. 3, No. 3, 1991. The author interviewed Professor Friedrich having first met him in December 1989.
18. Rolf Reißig and Gert-Joachim Glaeßner (eds), *Das Ende eines Experiments: Umbruch in der DDR und deutsche Einheit*, Berlin, 1991, pp. 298–9.
19. Christa Luft, *Zwischen Wende und Ende Eindrücke: Erlebnisse, Erfahrungen eines Mitglieds der Modrow-Regierung*, Berlin, 1992 and 1999, p. 15.

Chapter 3

The Stasi and the internal security of the GDR

From K-5 to MfS

SED functionaries used to joke cynically that 'Vertrauen ist gut, Kontrolle ist besser.' (Roughly, 'Trust is good, but surveillance is better.') This revealed that ultimately they did not trust the people in whose name they ruled. Following the Soviet example, they justified the building up of an organ responsible for such surveillance, the Ministry for State Security (MfS), Erich Mielke's personal empire. In addition, the DVP carried responsibilities in this direction. Thirdly, the SED regarded itself as having the ultimate responsibility for the security of the GDR.

In his *Spionagechef im geheimen Krieg,*[1] General Markus Wolf, head of the foreign intelligence-gathering department (HV A) of the Ministry for State Security, 1950–87, claims his boss, Minister for State Security Erich Mielke, openly called himself a Stalinist.[2] He does not emphasise that the MfS never ceased to regard the Soviet Cheka as its model. This was the body set up in Soviet Russia in 1917; its acronym stood for Extraordinary Commission to Combat Counterrevolution and Sabotage. Headed by Feliks Dzerzhinski, a Polish intellectual, it was established with Lenin's blessing. As Alexander Solzhenitsyn has reminded us,[3] it waged a campaign of terror throughout the land. In the Soviet Zone of Occupation after 1945 the Soviet MGB/KGB built up a German satellite body known as *Kommisariat-5* or K-5. It had powers in Germany similar to its overlord in the Soviet Union. The only real restriction on its activities was the close oversight of the Soviet occupation authorities themselves. K-5 had its own internment camps where thousands of political opponents were held. These were from all parties and none, but many were Social Democrats who had opposed the merging of their party with the Communists in 1946 to form the SED. After the GDR was established in 1949 the Soviets granted it the right to have its own Ministry for State Security (MfS), which was established in 1950. The first minister was Wilhelm Zaisser, a loyal Stalinist who was, however, purged by Ulbricht in 1954 for 'defeatism' after the workers' revolt of June 1953. Ernst Wollweber, another veteran Communist and Soviet loyalist, who fell out with Ulbricht in 1957, followed Zaisser. Erich

Mielke had been a key figure in the setting up of the East German security and intelligence agencies from the very start, and in December 1957 was appointment Minister, a position he was to hold until 1989.

Although the GDR's security apparatus was outwardly modified in the years of Khrushchev's anti-Stalin campaign, being reduced from a full ministry to a state secretariat between 1953 and 1955, it never really changed its nature. Once Mielke took over it was set for a continuous expansion year by year. Over the Honecker period the full-time staff of the MfS expanded from 52,700 in 1973 to 81,500 in 1981.[4] Moreover, it employed a growing army of informers. Although no final figure can be given, it has been estimated that between one and two million citizens worked at one time or another as informers for the MfS.[5] The MfS employed more people than Hitler's Gestapo,[6] which is a shocking commentary on the GDR. The reason for this is clear: the maximum of only 30 per cent support for the regime, as reported by Falin was usually lower (see previous chapter). The Politburo hoped that by constantly expanding the numbers working for the MfS, either as full-time employees or as informers, it would be ready to quell any opposition before it became serious. It also believed that it compromised ever greater numbers of GDR citizens. If they were beholden to the MfS, they would be hardly likely to turn against it. Regarding the security side of the MfS's activities, Wolf himself uses the excuse, used so often by others in relation to Nazi crimes, that he did not know what was going on.[7] If in any way true, Wolf's account reveals how badly out of touch with the mood of the people the top echelons of the GDR's élite were. Falin's plausible estimate reveals why the MfS was a necessity for the SED dictatorship.

The Stasi and the police

Mielke's ambition was to cover the GDR from end to end with his informers and to infiltrate every institution – indeed everywhere where two or three of its citizens were gathered together. He sought information about everyone, from students in Jena to his colleagues in the Politburo. He intended to know everything that was going on, not only in opposition circles, or those so classified, but also among the police. The People's Police (DVP) was organised nationally on semi-military lines by the Ministry of the Interior, headed by a responsible minister. He was also in charge of the (armed) fire service, (armed) customs and excise service, civil defence and the prison service. At his disposal the minister had 18,000 heavily armed ever-ready detachments. He was also in charge of the 8,500 transport police who were trained and equipped with a variety of infantry weapons. In addition, there were 15,000 well-armed factory protection police. Finally, the minister commanded the 73,000 men and women of the *Schutzpolizei*. These were the ordinary police on the beat. The minister, Friedrich Dickel, aged 76 in 1989, had been in office since 1963. Before that he had been a deputy minister of defence. Dickel shared control of the 202,000-strong *Kampfgruppen* (factory militias) with the SED. He trained them with their assault rifles, mortars, machine guns and armoured cars, but could only deploy them on orders from the SED. Mielke was not without his own armoury. Those in charge of dismantling the MfS in 1990 found 124,593 revolvers, 76,592 sub-machineguns, 3,611 sniper rifles, 449 light machine guns, 766 heavy machine guns, 3,537 anti-tank weapons, 342 anti-aircraft machine guns, and various other guns, including 3,303 flare pistols. Even women cooks and nurses who were members of the Stasi were armed.[8]

Officially, the DVP was completely independent of the MfS. The practice was very different. Dickel held the same military rank as Mielke, that of *Armeegeneral*, but he was only a member of the ZK, whereas Mielke was also a member of the Politburo. Under the GDR's emergency decrees he could be required to put his forces under the control of the military or the MfS or any other body designated by the Defence Council. As a member of the ZK he took his orders from that body rather than the Chairman of the Council of Ministers, Willi Stoph. Mielke wanted indirectly to control the activities of the police through informers within it. This was done through the system of 'officers on special assignments', or OibE. They wore police uniforms but were undercover officers of the Stasi. The criminal police, a division of the DVP, was a particular target of the MfS. Its subdepartments covered serious crimes, economic crimes, youth, the frontiers of the GDR and certain religious groups. Many of the police's own informers were used by the Stasi to keep track of matters of interest.

Informers would listen in on conversations in bars, hotels and restaurants, trams, trains and buses. Normally, hotel receptionists would be recruited. Informers would prowl around the rail stations of big towns like Berlin, Leipzig, Karl-Marx-Stadt, Magdeburg, and so on. The telephone service in the GDR was out-of-date. Private subscribers could wait twenty years without getting a telephone. If an applicant waited an unusually short time it was likely that the Stasi had taken an interest. In Leipzig, in the 1980s, 1,000 phones were tapped daily.[9] The post in the GDR was surprisingly slow for a compact modern country. This was not just because the SED gave it low priority. It was also because the Stasi gave it a high priority. In Leipzig the Stasi employed 120 operatives to open between 1,500 and 2,000 letters daily in its headquarters. Letters from beyond the frontiers of the GDR were particularly suspect, as were letters destined for abroad. However, so were letters addressed to Honecker and other members of the Politburo.[10] Some individuals who had foreign contacts or 'pen pals' often found it a good idea to include at least a line or two supporting the peace policy of the GDR government or describing the latest economic successes of the GDR. Mielke's experts also hoped to monitor all the major thoroughfares in towns and cities. They had achieved their target in East Berlin and Leipzig, where TV cameras recorded shoppers as well as pickpockets, lovers as well as dissidents. SED protagonists argued that all these weapons are employed by Western states. That is true, but in the GDR the SED leadership and Mielke's Stasi aimed at total control. They never intended to face questions about their policies, let alone democratic, contested elections.

The Stasi, the SED and education

In addition to the armed forces and the police, all industrial units, every state office nationally and locally, all the 'mass organisations', schools and universities were under both SED and Stasi influence. In all these bodies the key individuals at all levels were party members. They were subject to party discipline, and the SED secretary within these bodies saw to it that party policy was enforced. The party secretary took it for granted that he or she would assist the Stasi if called upon to do so. Stasi officers would arrive and expect and get answers to their questions and have the right to search through any files on staff or students. The Stasi often had its own informers in these bodies who were unknown to their colleagues. In the case of Berlin's Humboldt University, it has been estimated that 25 per cent of the academic staff worked for the Stasi.[11] In the medical profession, research completed since the end of the GDR revealed that the Stasi had recruited informers in most of the hospitals in East Germany.[12] Heads of offices, schools, university departments and institutes were automatically regarded by the Stasi as GMS or *Gesellschaftlicher Mitarbeiter für Sicherheit*. Unlike the ordinary informers (IM), they would not necessarily have been required to sign any declaration obligating them to work for the Stasi. Teachers and professors were often expected to 'talent spot' for likely recruits. They were required to write reports on colleagues, on all visitors, especially from the West, and about any visits they had made outside the GDR. If a Finnish professor visited a colleague in the Institute for the Further Education of Medical Practitioners in Berlin, a report had to be written for the MfS. If a British academic visited Jena University, the Stasi expected a detailed report. Commissions interviewed those seeking admission to higher education on which sat SED officials, military officers as well as academics. In many cases IMs would also be present. It was taken for granted that would-be students had shown their enthusiasm for the Free German Youth. Young men greatly increased their chance of admission if they had completed three years' military service as volunteers and not just the normal compulsory service.

Literary informers

Another important area for the Stasi, which illustrates how Mielke, and his predecessors, attempted to control thought, was the literary life of East Germany. The Stasi infiltrated the GDR's literary world and mobilised writers, editors and publishers for its work within the republic and beyond. Joachim Walther[13] reveals that the Stasi recruited writers, literary editors, publishers and others in the literary world to act as informers. Those who wanted to write were faced with supervision by the ruling SED, by the writers' union, and by the legal framework, which could be used to make criticism illegal. What they did not know was that they were being screened by the Stasi through its informers. One example Walther mentioned was Armin Zeißler, deputy chief editor of the prestigious literary journal *Sinn und Form* from 1963 to 1988. He worked for department HAII of the MfS from 1984 to 1988. Among Zeißler's tasks was that of reporting on the literary/publishing scene in West Berlin and West Germany.[14] Likewise, the Stasi infiltrated *neue deutsche literatur*, the monthly journal of the writers' union. Informers manned key positions in publishing houses like Aufbau-Verlag. Klaus Gysi, a prominent figure in the GDR, served as informer 'Kurt' from 1957, having been recruited by a 22-year-old Stasi NCO, Peter Heinz Gütling. Gysi worked as head of the Aufbau-Verlag between 1956 and 1966. Gütling wrote of Gysi in 1957 that he had conscientiously fulfilled all the tasks set him and shown himself open, sincere and reliable.[15] Gysi had collected material which helped to convict the dissident SED intellectual Wolfgang Harich in 1957. Although Gysi was an atheist of Jewish background, at Christmas 1956 the Stasi gave him as presents a leather briefcase for himself and an electric train for his children.[16] Gysi gave up his informer activities in 1964. As the Stasi pointed out, they would meet him officially through his position as Minister of Culture, 1966–73.[17] He went on to serve as Ambassador to Italy and Malta, 1973–78 and State Secretary for Church Affairs, 1979–88. Gütling crept up the ladder in the Stasi, reaching the rank of major in 1980. He continued in his attempts to keep GDR literature clean and pure until the Stasi was abolished in 1989. Walther was himself a victim of the Stasi. After negative comments about his GDR loyalty by a British academic, he was prevented from taking up an invitation to Britain in the 1980s, and was banned from travelling abroad.

The cases of Fuchs, Havemann and Biermann

The prominent East German civil rights activist and writer Jürgen Fuchs, who died aged 48 in 1999, was a typical case which illustrates how intellectuals who were products of the GDR could become disillusioned and how they were persecuted when they voiced their doubts. Fuchs was born in the small East German town of Reichenbach. The son of an electrician, Fuchs had a classic GDR early life. He gained his *Abitur* (university matriculation) in 1969 and, following the polytechnic education system, completed an apprenticeship with the state railways, strangely still officially called the *Reichsbahn*. From there he did his compulsory military service in the National People's Army (NVA), 1969–71. He had proved himself worthy to be allowed to study and he took up a scholarship at the University of Jena. He chose social psychology and sociology, areas of study which had been rediscovered in the Soviet empire after the nightmare years of Stalin. During his student days Fuchs applied for membership of the SED and was admitted in 1973.

Fuchs, like many others, took SED leader Erich Honecker seriously when he proclaimed in 1971 that there were to be 'no taboos'. As long as East German writers and artists did not attack the fundamentals of socialism they were free to write or paint as they liked in terms of both style and content. Although influenced by the crushing of the Prague Spring in 1968, Fuchs was a GDR loyalist who wanted to improve the system, not abolish it. He believed in the regime's proclaimed objectives of social solidarity, power emanating from the people for the good of the people, anti-racism, anti-colonialism and, above all, the fight for peace. However, it was not long before he was in trouble with the SED for criticising the militarisation of the GDR in his first literary works. A confidential report about an evening of music and songs held in Bad Köstritz on 17 February 1975 was sent direct to Honecker by the Gera area secretary of the SED, Herbert Ziegenhahn. Ziegenhahn claimed that the majority of items on the programme criticised and slandered the principles and achievements of the GDR. He was disgusted that none of the guests protested about this.[18] Fuchs was expelled from the SED in April 1975 for 'enemy attacks against the basis of socialist society'; he also had his undergraduate dissertation rejected. Expulsion from the university and a ban of his works followed. Fuchs then worked as a transport worker and as a carer in a church-run children's home. He developed a friendship with the best-known GDR dissident, Professor Robert Havemann. Havemann took in Fuchs, his wife and child.

Havemann, a convinced Marxist, member of the KPD and a physical chemist, was sentenced to death by the Nazis for his resistance activity. He survived in the shadow of the gallows by doing research considered important for the war effort. After liberation by the Red Army, he became a strong supporter of Stalin and joined the SED. He was dismissed from a post in West Berlin for criticising American nuclear policy. He was then appointed professor of physical chemistry at the Humboldt University. He was awarded a GDR National Prize in 1959. Fired by the revelations of the XX congress of the CPSU, he became increasingly critical of Ulbricht's way of 'building socialism'. In 1964 he was expelled from the SED and sacked by the Humboldt University. Later he was placed under house arrest and subjected to harassment by the Stasi. His celebrity status in the West deeply embarrassed the SED and it was relieved when he died of cancer in 1982. However, his ideas continued to exercise an influence through Fuchs, Wolf Biermann and others, helping to stimulate many of those involved in the battles of 1989.[19]

In 1976, Fuchs joined over 150 other writers and artists in protesting against the withdrawal of GDR citizenship from the singer and writer Wolf Biermann, who was on a concert tour in West Germany. Among the most prominent were writers Christa Wolf, Volker Braun, Stephan Hermlin and Stefan Heym and sculptor Fritz Cremer. Cremer was persuaded to withdraw his signature. Biermann, the son of a Jewish Communist murdered in Auschwitz, left West Germany for the GDR in 1953. He studied at the Humboldt University, got involved with Brecht's Berliner Ensemble and started to compose his own songs. He was soon in trouble with the SED and was banned from public appearances most of the time. In 1963 he became friendly with Havemann. It was during a West German tour that the SED/Stasi struck. For supporting Biermann, Fuchs was arrested and charged with agitation against the state. He was held on remand for nine months and then expelled to West Germany. During his imprisonment his *Gedächtnisprotokolle* was published in the West.

Fuchs was the object of secret police attention from 1968, when he was still at school, until the secret police was abolished at the end of 1989. The Stasi attempted to discredit dissidents whether they still lived in the GDR or whether they had sought refuge in, or been expelled to, the West. Rumours were spread about them, their characters, associations and life-styles. Using undercover agents, attempts were made to turn them into heavy drinkers, sexual deviants, and so on. A secret police document dated 29 September 1982 reported on attempts to make Fuchs, already living in the West, feel insecure. Anonymous callers continuously telephoned him at night. Newspapers and magazines, including some which would compromise him, were ordered in his name. Taxis and emergency services were called to his flat. Without his knowledge or consent any number of home improvement firms dealing in fitted kitchens, bathrooms, oriental rugs, antiques, television repairs, and so on, were called in his name, and meetings in his flat were arranged at various times of the day or night or at weekends.[20] Sascha Anderson, the notorious Stasi agent who posed as a dissident writer, infiltrated Fuchs' circle in the 1980s.

After the fall of the GDR, Fuchs worked for the public body in charge of the Stasi archives, the *Gauck-Behörde* in Berlin. He, like others, was shocked by what the archives revealed. Both the large numbers of informers and the fact that they included writers like Anderson was a severe blow to idealists like Fuchs and Biermann.

'Swords into ploughshares'

In 1980 the Federation of Evangelical Churches in the GDR and other non-Catholic churches started the movement 'Frieden schaffen ohne Waffen' ('create peace without weapons'). This was at least in part in opposition to the introduction, in 1978, of compulsory pre-military training in schools for all 15- and 16-year-olds. This peace movement's badge was the figure of a man with a hammer destroying a sword. It carried the biblical quotation, 'Swords into ploughshares'. The badge was non-confrontational in that the figure on it had been created by an orthodox Soviet artist as a gift from the Soviet Union to the UN. Rather than approaching the movement as a potential ally, however, the SED banned the badge as far as possible. Policemen tore them from the coats of young people and school directors banned them in school. In May 1981 members of the Evangelical Church called for a 'social service for peace' as an alternative to compulsory military service. This was something which was taken for granted in West Germany. Those given this option in the West worked in old people's homes, hospitals, children's homes or did agricultural work. The State Secretary for Church Affairs, Klaus Gysi, the former Stasi informer, rejected the proposal, claiming that the GDR already had an alternative. This was service in the construction units of the NVA. Those recruited were not required to bear arms but were in every other respect subject to military discipline. After service they suffered disadvantage. On 25 January 1982 Pastor Rainer Eppelmann and Professor Robert Havemann issued their Berlin Appeal, which called for the whole of Europe to become a nuclear-free zone, peace treaties between the four victor powers and the governments of the two German states, followed by the withdrawal of all occupation forces from Germany. They wanted to ban war toys in the GDR, introduce peace studies in GDR schools, introduce social service for peace, stop all public displays of military might and end civil defence preparations.[21] At various times in the past the SED had itself advocated some or all of these proposals. It could have treated the signatories with generosity, offered to discuss with them, and attempted to integrate them in the official peace movement. Instead, they were criminalised and harassed by the Stasi. Over the 1980s the movement grew.

'Let us leave!'

Most East Germans were not like Havemann, Fuchs, Biermann, Pastor Eppelmann or the other dissidents. Like most people everywhere, they simply

Table 3.1 GDR Emigration Figures 1980–8

Year	Applications to leave the GDR	Applications withdrawn	Applications granted
1980	21,500	4,700	4,400
1981	23,000	5,000	9,200
1982	24,900	6,500	7,800
1983	30,400	5,600	6,700
1984	50,600	17,300	29,800
1985	53,000	11,300	17,400
1986	78,000	10,800	16,000
1987	105,100	12,800	7,600
1988	113,500	11,700	25,300

Source: Adapted from Frankfurter Allgemeine Zeitung, 18 May 1996.

wanted a quiet life. A minority of the more active were prepared to kick up a fuss to be allowed to go to West Germany. They were often not the most politically conscious elements. They were not interested in changing the GDR, just escaping from it to build a new life in the West. They were more likely to have relatives there already and often had training which meant they were likely to find work in the Federal Republic without too much difficulty. In the late 1970s and throughout the 1980s more and more GDR citizens attempted to emigrate legally (see Table 3.1). This method was adopted because illegal means had become ever more dangerous, and because the GDR had signed the Helsinki Final Act, in 1975, of the Conference on Security and Co-operation in Europe. This was attended by 35 heads of state, including Honecker and West German Chancellor Helmut Schmidt. Honecker basked in the glow of media attention as he was photographed sitting next to Schmidt and US President Gerald Ford. The Act guaranteed existing frontiers in Europe, which pleased the SED leadership. However, the Act also obligated all signatory states to observe human rights, including the right to free movement. GDR citizens got this information mainly from the Western news media. The GDR media said little about it. The GDR authorities did not give any information about procedures for those wishing to leave East Germany permanently and often denied that such procedures existed. It was a case of boldly going to the local town hall and applying to be released from citizenship of the GDR and being allowed to leave for West Germany. SED officials attempted to talk the applicants out of taking the action further. Threats and abuse would often be used. If the applicants were parents, they could face the threat that their children would be taken away from them, as they were obviously not fit to bring up children. If the applicant persisted, they would usually lose their jobs and their 'politically correct' friends and acquaintances would boycott them. A language teacher would end up scraping a living together by cleaning; an engineer would be reduced to casual work on a building site. The individuals concerned were sometimes subject to harassment and usually to Stasi attention. They could be arrested on trumped-up charges and jailed before being deported to the West. The problem for Honecker and Mielke was that the more they allowed people to leave, the more likely it was that others would want to follow them. This certainly seemed to happen in the 1980s. More and more citizens of the GDR were demanding, 'Let us leave!'

Mielke's Potemkin village

Historically, Field Marshal Grigori Potemkin, the eighteenth-century Russian soldier and statesman, is associated with the invention of 'Potemkin villages' to fool gullible outsiders. He used the technique to hoodwink his liege, Catherine the Great, whose carriage route was lined with apparently clean and prosperous villages. Stalin built on this Russian tradition to sucker many a foreign delegation with more elaborate deceptions. Himmler cynically did the same at Theresienstadt and elsewhere to hide the fate of the Jews. Mielke kept up the tradition in the GDR. It started with the route from the airport to the centre of Berlin getting special attention. The streets were cleaned, the façades were painted and the shop windows were filled. Security personnel were posted at short intervals along the route. If Ulbricht or Honecker visited a town, it got detailed attention before their arrival. The same treatment was given to any kindergarten, schools, hospitals, factories or NVA barracks before the distinguished guests appeared. The food in the canteens improved remarkably. Thus far, it could be objected, Mielke's practice was in line with that of most states in the UN. After all, when members of the British royal family go on visits time and money is spent on improvements before their arrival, and, depending on the situation, appropriate security precautions are set in train. But such measures cannot prevent determined protesters appearing to make their point. The visitors themselves can inform themselves about the problems of the area before they arrive. The writer is unaware whether Potemkin's well-intended deception was ever challenged by the monarch deciding to take a side tour. Nevertheless there is no record of Honecker, Stoph or their colleagues deviating from the path mapped out for them by their aides with Mielke's help.

Mielke's measures went well beyond those practised in democratic states. In the summer of 1973 Honecker took the risk of hosting the Communist-run X World Festival of Youth and Students in East Berlin. Most of those attending were either from the Soviet bloc and subject to the discipline imposed on them by their organisations, or from Western Communist bodies.

In addition, there would be much smaller groups of Westerners from non-Communist peace movements, Christian groups, Trotskyite bodies, and even one or two liberal or right-of-centre youth organisations. Mielke code-named his ministry's activities in relation to this event 'Operation Banner'.

Pleased though Honecker, Mielke and their colleagues were at the propaganda opportunity the festival presented, they were worried that it could all go badly wrong. Firstly, the many Western groups attending could decisively influence the GDR population, especially the youth. They also feared attempts by the guests to protest about civil rights issues, Warsaw Pact nuclear strategies or the Wall. Was it possible that there could be an attempt to storm the Wall? A third worry was that Westerners would be sought out by GDR oppositionists or 'asocial elements' and would go home with negative impressions.

Apparently no expense was spared to counter these dangers. Naturally, there was the usual beautification of all the buildings where the guests would be quartered or would visit. Secondly, thousands of FDJ members who had the privilege of taking part in the festival were specially schooled in every aspect of their behaviour. They were indoctrinated to answer bourgeois liberal, left radical and other lines of argument critical of the 'Socialist Camp'. Meanwhile, the security forces were ordered to ignore conduct which would not normally be tolerated. Westerners distributing leaflets, holding impromptu concerts or generally 'walking on the grass' were to be overlooked. On the other hand, every effort was made to ensure that Westerners met the right sort of people. Not only were the specially selected FDJ members there, there were members of the élite guards regiments ready to be bussed in civilian clothes to various events. Stasi informers were on permanent duty for the duration of the festival. All those and other trusted individuals were dispatched to strategic points where Westerners were likely to congregate. In case things should get out of hand, the guards regiment Feliks Dzershinski was on stand-by, as were units of the NVA, thousands of extra ordinary police and alert police units. All those on duty were ordered to use firearms only in the most extreme cases of emergency.

From Mielke's point of view, equally important was the removal of undesirables from Berlin and the prevention of undesirables from the provinces reaching the capital. His colleagues held interviews with 19,779 individuals advising them that they would not be welcome in Berlin. Thousands of others suffered from other forms of Stasi attention. Women who were designated HWG, 'frequently changing sexual intercourse', were taken out of circulation. Those regarded as mentally sick were sent to institutions. Problem children were taken into care. In the first half of 1973, 917 'criminal groups' with 5,258 members were 'dissolved' and 1,824 persons were taken into custody.

As it turned out, there was very little trouble and the festival was deemed a great success. Mielke was determined to build on this success and to apply the experience gained. Visits by Western football teams, athletics meetings, parliamentary delegations to the Volkskammer and tourist groups were all subject to similar controls. In the case of small tourist, peace or other groups one favourite tactic was to ensure that the visitors were fully occupied from dawn to dusk and beyond! When they visited a nursery, a school or a housing project, had a discussion with officials of the Friendship League, Peace Council, a trade union or other body, the ground had been carefully prepared well in advance. Their guides were obviously picked for their political, linguistic, diplomatic and interpersonal skills. They were allowed to make minor criticisms of GDR conditions, and were not to take offence at negative remarks. Occasionally, they even repeated political jokes.

One more example will suffice to illustrate the Stasi's hand in presenting the GDR to outsiders. On 13 December 1981 Chancellor Helmut Schmidt visited the small GDR town of Güstow. Under the codename 'Dialog' the Stasi got to work. In and around the town of 37,000 the Stasi identified 664 persons they deemed to be possible troublemakers. Their homes were watched, their telephones were put out of commission and the police were told to warn them not to be on the streets in the centre of Güstow on 13 December. At 06.00 the town was sealed off. Later the Stasi was given the order to 'spread a festive atmosphere' with lights, Christmas music and visitors. Appropriate cadres were posted on the left side of the road, the side on which Honecker would be sitting, to greet him as he drove by with Schmidt. When the two politicians arrived at the Christmas market in the main square, specially chosen comrades were there looking at the stalls and eating and drinking the traditional fare. They stopped to greet the two leaders. Later Schmidt was taken to an organ recital in the cathedral. Even the church had to play its part in the charade. Klaus Bölling, head of West Germany's diplomatic representation in the GDR, who went with Schmidt to Güstow, later described the atmosphere as worthy of Kafka. The Westerners were not completely fooled. Western journalists noticed that so many of the 'natives' spoke not with the local, Mecklenburg, accent but with Saxony accents.[22]

Mielke and Krenz

How did Mielke operate within the SED leadership? Egon Krenz recalled that as ZK Secretary responsible for the Security Department, Mielke had promised him full co-operation. However, in practice, Mielke spoke with Honecker after the Politburo meetings and he was left in the dark about their discussions.[23] Krenz described the Ministry for State Security as 'a state within the state'. He only got to know the true figure for the number of its operatives after the Ministry had been abolished. If he is to be believed, he was neither familiar with the organisational structure of the Ministry for State Security nor with the functions of the different departments.[24] Krenz's great disadvantage was that when he joined the Politburo in 1983 he was confronted by the leaders he had been taught to admire. Even as Security Secretary it would have been difficult for him to challenge Mielke and Honecker. And to whom could he have appealed when they ignored him? Mielke, for his part, appears to have been a born manipulator who always sided with those who appeared to be in the ascendancy. He was the longest serving security minister in the Soviet bloc, seeing 11 of his Soviet counterparts come and go. The only loyalty he showed, apart from to himself, was to the KGB, for he was aware that the future of the GDR was ultimately dependent on the Soviet Union.

Isolation of 'enemy negative persons'

The increasing flood of reports flowing to the regional centres of the MfS and then on to Berlin gradually overwhelmed Mielke's organisation. In 1989 there were some 500 situation reports, each sixty pages in length, about the internal situation in the GDR. Few of those they were intended for had the time or the inclination to read them all. Yet the reports revealed the growing dissatisfaction of the population. What to do? Mielke had drawn up plans for an emergency. This involved large-scale internment of suspected subversives, or 'enemy negative persons', as the Stasi labelled them. In many cases these were individuals who had simply applied to leave the GDR. Plans to arrest subversives were first mooted in the 1950s following the revolt in the GDR in June 1953 and the Hungarian revolution in 1956. In 1967 Mielke issued a directive which put these plans on a firmer footing. By the end of the 1970s he ordered his district commanders to draw up plans for a system of isolation camps. These would often be existing building such as old castles or educational buildings. As a general rule there would be one central camp in each district (*Bezirk*) of the GDR. Those with higher population densities, like Karl-Marx-Stadt, Halle and Gera, would have two. Over the years the planning became more precise, right down to how those interned were supposed to address their captors.[25] Mielke ordered his planners to ensure that there were enough informers among the detainees to make control and intelligence gathering easier.[26] Suspects were targeted. By December 1988, 85,939 individuals were listed as candidates for the isolation camps.[27] Those isolated could not receive or send post. In addition to keeping their quarters clean, they were expected to work.

The ultimate authority over security in the GDR was not, however, Mielke but the Chairman of the National Defence Council set up in 1960. This was Honecker. According to Manfred Gerlach,[28] a Deputy Chairman of the Council of State and member of the Defence Committee of the Volkskammer, at the end of 1988, a defence exercise was carried through by the Department of Security of the ZK and the Ministry of Defence of the GDR. This involved using all the armed units of the GDR, including the *Kampfgruppen*, against the population. Gerlach believed that, given the security doctrine of the SED, a bloodbath could have taken place under Honecker. Honecker issued an order on 26 September 1989, in which he claimed 'certain circles' in the Federal Republic and West Berlin, together with those in the GDR influenced by them, would use the preparations for the fortieth anniversary of the GDR to unleash an exceptionally tough campaign of agitation against the socialist system. He ordered reports, 'until further notice', to be sent to him directly every day at 08.00 about the situation in Berlin. In addition, he wanted immediate reports on any happenings of a politically provocative nature.[29] No advice was given about the use of force. Given the regime's massive investment in every department of repression and military power and its belief in its historical role, force had to be expected.

Notes

1. Markus Wolf, *Spionagechef im geheimen Krieg,* Munich, 1997; Markus Wolf with Anne McElvoy, *Man Without a Face,* New York, 1997. These two books vary in their contents.
2. Wolf, *Spionagechef,* p. 107.
3. Alexander Solzhenitsyn, *The Gulag Archipelago,* London, 1974, pp. 29–36.
4. Joachim Gauck, Die Stasi Akten Reinbek bei Hamburg, 1991, p. 61.
5. David Childs and Richard Popplewell, *The Stasi: The East German Intelligence and Security System,* London, 1996, p. 86.
6. Gauck, p. 61.
7. *Ibid.,* p. 49.
8. *Der Spiegel,* 11/1995, p. 96; *Der Spiegel,* 11 October 1999, pp. 108–9.
9. Bürgerkomitee Leipzig, p. 113.
10. *Ibid.,* p. 121.
11. *Welt am Sonntag,* 10 April 1994.
12. Childs and Popplewell, *The Stasi.*
13. Joachim Walther, *Sicherheitsbereich: Literatur, Schriftsteller und Staatssicherheit in der Deutschen Demokratischen Republik,* Berlin, 1996, p. 565.
14. *Ibid.,* p. 529.
15. *Ibid.,* p. 565.
16. *Ibid.,* p. 567.
17. *Ibid.*
18. *Ibid.,* p. 286.
19. Dieter Hoffmann, 'Robert Havemann: Antifascist, Communist, Dissident', in Kristie Macrakis and Dieter Hoffmann (eds), *Science under Socialism: East Germany in Comparative Perspective,* Cambridge, MA, 1999.
20. Walther, *Sicherheitsbereich,* pp. 362–3.

21. Stefan Wolle, *Die heile Welt der Diktatur: Alltag und Herrschaft in der DDR 1971–1989*, Berlin, 1998, p. 261; Roger Woods, *Opposition in the GDR under Honecker 1971–85*, London, 1986, pp. 195–6.
22. Wolle, *Die heile Welt*, pp. 163–9, and the writer's own experiences in the GDR.
23. Krenz, p. 123 reported in *Der Spiegel*, 11 August 1997.
24. *Ibid.*, p. 124. The relationship between the Ministry for State Security and the SED is fully researched in Siegfried Suckut and Walter Süß (eds), *Staatspartei und Staatssicherheit: Zum Verhältnis von SED und MfS*, Berlin, 1997.
25. Thomas Auerbach, *Vorbereitung auf den Tag X: Die geplanten Isolierungslager des MfS*. (BstU), Berlin, 1995.
26. *Ibid.*, p. 95.
27. *Ibid.*, p. 23.
28. Ekkehard Kuhn, 'Wir Sind Das Volk!': Die friedliche Revolution in Leipzig, 9. Oktober 1989, Berlin/Frankfurt am Main, 1999, pp. 44–5.
29. Auerbach, *Vorbereitung auf den Tag X*, p. 133.

Chapter 4

Coping with Gorbachev

Honecker had seen Soviet leaders come and go. As a working-class youth and district leader of his regional Communist Youth organisation in the early 1930s he had been to the Soviet Homeland and had learned to love 'Uncle Joe'. As the leader of the post-war Free German Youth his admiration for Stalin had continued. Had not Stalin led the Soviet forces to victory over the Nazi Wehrmacht in 1945, which resulted in Honecker being released from a Nazi jail? After Stalin's death in 1953 came Malenkov, followed by Khrushchev. Honecker witnessed Khrushchev as a member of the SED Politburo. Khrushchev had made scenes both in East Berlin and elsewhere but he had secured Castro's Cuba from American aggression and, more importantly, had secured the GDR by giving the go-ahead for the building of the 'Anti-Fascist Protective Wall' in Berlin in 1961. He had put the Soviet Union on top in the space race. As First Secretary of the SED, Honecker witnessed Khrushchev's successor, Brezhnev. He had also witnessed the decline of Brezhnev, who in his last years was a living corpse.

Gorbachev, 'a sharp debater'

When Brezhnev finally died in 1982, Yuri Andropov, who had been chairman of the KGB since 1967, replaced him. The appointment of 68-year-old Andropov made clear just how the security apparatus had come to play a dominant role in the CPSU. If he was remembered at all, Andropov was remembered abroad as the butcher of Budapest who had smashed the Hungarian revolution. As General Secretary he was ridiculed, at home, for his unsuccessful anti-drink campaign. He took up a hard line position against the Solidarity free trade union in Poland.[1] A sick man when he took office, Andropov died of kidney failure in 1984. There was shock and despair at home and abroad when Konstantin Chernenko, an ailing 72-year-old, was named as Andropov's successor. He had clawed his way up the CPSU ladder and was a close associate of Brezhnev. The appointment of Andropov followed by Chernenko exposed the ossification of the CPSU leadership. Chernenko died before his 74th birthday and Mikhail Gorbachev, who had been groomed as his successor, took up the reins of power without a hitch.

Gorbachev was just 54 when he emerged as General Secretary of the CPSU on 11 March 1985. His illiterate Orthodox Christian mother and his Communist grandfather defined his childhood. Both his grandfathers suffered under Stalin. His father, also a peasant, served in the 'Great Patriotic War'. Mikhail Gorbachev graduated in law in Moscow and was appointed to a full-time post by the Komsomol (the communist youth movement). He married Raisa, a philosophy graduate. From the Komsomol he moved on to the CPSU apparatus. Gorbachev was lucky enough to be included on party delegations to both Soviet bloc and Western states. This gave him the opportunity to get at least a superficial view of the 'imperialist West'. He was disturbed to have to conclude that living standards were so much higher there and that political debates were so much more open than at home.[2] In 1978 Gorbachev moved to Moscow as CPSU secretary in charge of agriculture. This was a potentially dangerous job because the chances of failure were great, but he enjoyed the backing of Andropov and was promoted to the Politburo in 1980. Thus Gorbachev was associated with Moscow's interference in Poland, including the banning of Solidarity and the introduction of martial law there. When Andropov took over as General Secretary, Gorbachev was entrusted with all branches of the Soviet economy.

He first came to the attention of the world media when he headed a delegation to Britain in 1984. Prime Minister Thatcher found 'his personality could not have been more different from the wooden ventriloquism of the average Soviet *apparatchik*. He smiled, laughed, used his hands for emphasis, modulated his voice, followed an argument through and was a sharp debater . . . I found myself liking him.'[3] Nearer home, Boris Yeltsin, later Russian President, agreed, 'He operated with amazing finesse.'[4] Yeltsin was then First Secretary of the Moscow party organisation and he had witnessed how Gorbachev rapidly established his sway by promoting his allies and moving his critics. Gorbachev changed 14 of the 23 heads of the departments of the key CSPU secretariat within his first year and 39 of the 101 government ministers.[5]

Moscow, Bonn and East Berlin

In 1985 Gorbachev was a relaxed 54-year-old, Honecker was a rather wooden 70-year-old. This fact alone would have made their relations somewhat difficult, especially as the Soviet leader was boss. When he told Honecker not to go on a much-heralded visit to West Germany, planned for July 1986, Honecker felt he had to obey. The Soviet Union alone set the pace in relations between Bonn and East Berlin. Honecker was allowed to go in September 1987. But the damage had been done in the relations between the two leaders.[6] The visit was more surprising because, in a remarkable statement, in October 1986, Chancellor Kohl linked the public relations abilities of Gorbachev with those of Nazi propaganda minister Goebbels.[7] Kohl's gaffe did him no good with his NATO allies, let alone in Moscow. However, by the time Honecker reached Bonn, Soviet–West German relations had improved greatly. Federal President Richard von Weizsäcker paid a state visit to Moscow in July 1987 and had successful talks with both Gorbachev and Soviet President Andrei Gromyko. There followed successful visits by Soviet Foreign Minister Shevardnadze to Bonn and his West German counterpart, Hans-Dietrich Genscher, to Moscow in 1988. On 24–7 October 1988, Kohl paid an official visit to the Soviet Union and held ten hours of talks with Gorbachev, which went well.[8] On that visit Kohl made a personal appeal to Gorbachev as a man and a father. Gorbachev was moved,

> I must admit that I was impressed by Mr Kohl's approach, both from the personal and business points of view. . . . Without the good political and personal rapport that Helmut Kohl and I gradually established, it would have been more difficult to cope with the complex of problems which unexpectedly confronted us as a result of the grass-roots landslide towards unification of Germany.[9]

This personal rapport between Kohl and Gorbachev could only worry the SED leaders. They did not want Moscow–Bonn relations to freeze, but, equally, they did not want them to get too close. The SED leaders always had at the back of their minds the possibility of the Soviets selling them out. In this respect matters took a turn for the worse in February 1989 when Gorbachev and Kohl agreed to install a direct telephone link between the Kremlin and the Chancellor's office in Bonn. In June, Gorbachev undertook a four-day visit to West Germany, the first by a Soviet leader since Brezhnev's visit in 1981. Both sides regarded it as a great success. They issued a six-page joint declaration covering such areas as human rights, disarmament, Europe, economic and environmental co-operation. Eleven agreements on bilateral co-operation were also signed. The icing on the cake for Gorbachev, however, must have been the results of a survey published in the weekly *Der Spiegel* shortly before his visit, which revealed he was more popular with the German public than French President Mitterrand, US President Bush or British Prime Minister Thatcher.[10] Gorbachev was popular because news of his reform policies had reached the German public. Gorbachev has written about his visit to Bonn, 'We were literally overwhelmed by manifestations of goodwill and friendship, the cheering crowds expressing their support and solidarity. I remember some of the slogans people were shouting: "Gorby! Make love, not walls!" "Please, Gorbachev, stay the course!" '[11] As for his relations with Honecker, Gorbachev has commented, 'It was as if I had been speaking to a brick wall.'[12]

What were Gorbachev's views on Germany and its future? He had inherited a situation which he had done nothing to bring about. Like Kohl, his generation had not been responsible for the war and its aftermath. Kohl's predecessor, Schmidt, had fought as a young Wehrmacht officer. Honecker had been a prisoner of the Third Reich. And all previous Soviet leaders had been active in the war. Gorbachev was learning from his travels. He was able to establish he had to escape the drug of propaganda to which he had been subject to all his life on a daily basis. He learned the superiority of personal reconnaissance over reports compiled by others. The more he understood the breathtaking problems of the Soviet Union domestically, the more he realised how important it was to review his own and Soviet images of the West.

It would be a mistake to assume that he changed his total perception in one blinding flash. The June visit to Germany certainly produced intoxication, but back in Moscow, under other influences, some of the old stereotypes would have come into play once again, though with far less effect. Gorbachev was not alone among the Soviet élite in changing his image of Germany and the West, however. Certainly, at all levels of the Soviet foreign policy, foreign trade and cultural, technological and scientific élite, changes in outlook were under way. Thousands of members of the Soviet intelligentsia were spending time in the West and were revising their views on Western societies.

Like all the other leaders of both pacts, Gorbachev's priorities were to have civilised, friendly relations between the states of Europe, within existing boundaries, in what he called a 'common European house'. No one wanted to rock the boat by contemplating revolutionary changes like the restoration of German unity. Yet within Germany, as the fortieth anniversaries of the two German states approached in 1989, it was inevitable that Germans would take stock of their situation and ask themselves whether they were likely to come together in the medium to long term. On the way to those anniversaries there were other significant ones. The Martin Luther anniversary in 1983 and the 750th anniversary of the founding of Berlin in 1987 were the focus of celebrations in both parts of Germany. And in West Germany there was a gentle but persistent re-emphasis on 'the German Question' in conservative circles.

Perestroika and *glasnost*

Gorbachev gave the world two new Russian words to learn: *perestroika* (restructuring) and *glasnost* (freedom of expression). He soon realised that there was something radically wrong with the Soviet economy. However, the situation was far worse than he initially thought. Most aspects of Soviet life were taboo areas regarded as state secrets, including data on the economy, social questions, culture, demography and the standard of living. 'Information about crime and medical statistics was kept under lock and key. . . . It was unbelievably difficult to open such "closed zones." '[13] He hoped that by investing in modern equipment in certain key sectors and by attempts to move from command to motivation and incentives, the workforce would be more productive. The economy did not produce enough and what was produced was often second-rate, even unsaleable. It was heavily distorted by the Soviet leaders' obsession with armaments and the space race. The most talented of the Soviet technical intelligentsia were put to work in these fields. The Soviet defence burden was approximately four times that of the US.[14] 'Moreover, no-one knew that the growth rate of expenditure on defence in many years was one and one-half or two times greater than the planned and actual increases of national income!'[15] Consumer industries were the Cinderella sector of the economy. There, materials were in short supply, there was no incentive to innovate, and designs were hopelessly out of date. Gorbachev did not have any detailed plan for sweeping reforms and simply attempted to deal with problems as he stumbled into them. He certainly did not wish to see the destruction of the socialist dream; he hoped to realise it. Some thought he was beginning to do that when a Politburo resolution of 24 September 1987 permitted small shops to be run by individuals and co-operatives. This was not unusual in the other Soviet bloc states, including the GDR.

Reform of the media, which were unbelievably dull, uninformative and even downright misleading, was high on Gorbachev's agenda. To let a little fresh air into the closed Soviet system he gave up jamming Western broadcasts, starting with those of the BBC in January 1987. The practice of jamming reveals the mentality of the Soviet leaders, their fears that those of their own people who had radios powerful enough to receive foreign stations could not be trusted to use this facility 'responsibly'. Gorbachev also sought to reintegrate well-known dissidents into Soviet life and politics, and he invited nuclear scientist Andrei Sakharov to return to Moscow from his place of exile, Gorky.

A pragmatic appraisal of the weak state of the USSR dictated other areas of policy. Once Gorbachev realised the parlous state of the economy, and that so much of it was dominated by weapons production, he saw the importance of reaching agreement with NATO about arms reductions. One other incident brought home to him the desperate need for agreement over nuclear arms. This was the near catastrophe at the nuclear power station of Chernobyl in the Ukraine on 26 April 1986. Moreover, in April 1988, the Soviet Union and the US guaranteed agreements signed in Geneva ending the war in Afghanistan. This brought to a close an intervention, which had begun in 1979 and had cost the Soviets much in material, bad publicity and above all lives. Honecker and his colleagues were to doubt relieved to see the end of that war.

At the XIX CPSU conference in June/July Gorbachev advocated a presidential system for the Soviet Union and a Congress of People's Deputies elected by contested elections. This dramatic break with the past took place on 26 March 1989. Elections were held to the Congress, a kind of electoral college from which the deputies to the Supreme Soviet, the Soviet parliament, were elected. Although 750 of the 2,250 seats were reserved for the CPSU and other Communist-dominated bodies, some genuine independent candidates were elected. Among them were Sakarov and Yeltsin, by this time himself something of a rebel who wanted to move more swiftly along the reform path than Gorbachev. Yeltsin eventually made it to the 542-member Supreme Soviet, which, unlike its predecessor, became a place of lively debate.[16] At last the Soviet Union appeared to be on the road to democracy. This was the kind of parliament the SED leaders did not feel they could live with. What of the other Soviet bloc leaders?

All the geriatric leaders of the Soviet bloc were under pressure to follow the Gorbachev example. They were all failing to fulfil the aspirations of their peoples in terms of living standards and personal freedom. Far from Moscow, the semi-independent Romanians and Albanians were the most backward and most brutal. The Bulgarians were traditionally the closest to the Russians and knew their people were following events in the Soviet Union with great interest. Perhaps the Czech, Hungarian and Polish leaders were under the greatest pressure. To a degree, the people of Czechoslovakia and Hungary were more influenced by foreign tourists and by foreign (Austrian) television. The Poles had wide contacts especially with the many Polish communites abroad. It was the Hungarians, however, who had experimented most with their economy.

Hungary changes course

When János Kádár died in July 1989, aged 76, he was widely mourned.[17] He had been installed by the Soviets after the crushing of the Hungarian revolution in 1956 and, after a murderous start, had gone on to rule relatively benignly. He had given his country peace and a degree of stability. Foreign travel was far easier for Hungarians than for East Germans. Relative to the other Warsaw Pact states, Hungary had been an innovator in economic reform over a long period. Hungary had a small private sector in farming, services and construction. In 1987 Western-style banking had been introduced and in the following year this was joined by Western-type taxation. Foreign investors were encouraged, and from 1989, there was full repatriation of profits. Yet all was not well. By the late 1980s it was close to economic collapse. It was heavily in debt and its economy could not fulfil the demand for consumer goods. It suffered from population decline. Half the population felt it necessary to have two jobs to make ends meet. As in other Soviet bloc states, alcoholism and ill heath were common.

Inspired by developments in the Soviet Union, nationalistically inclined intellectuals established the Hungarian Democratic Forum (HDF) in September 1987. Other groups followed, including the Alliance of Democratic Youth (FIDESZ), a collection of intellectuals, environmentalists and long-time dissidents. All of them opted for peaceful change. A special Communist party conference was called, in May 1988, at which Karoly Grosz replaced Kádár, who, together with most of the old guard, was removed from the Politburo. Grosz, aged 58, a career Communist, thought that by better media management and a few reforms his party could hold on to power. By January 1989, however, he felt compelled to promise multi-party elections and a law legalising parties, trade unions and other bodies free of the control of the Communist party.

Thus the SED's traditional ally was racing ahead of the GDR in political as well as economic reforms. As Hungary was something of a Mecca for travel-hungry East Germans, the SED feared that returning tourists would bring back more than just holiday snaps from Budapest. Honecker and his colleagues were taken aback when, on 2 May 1989, Hungarian border guards began to dismantle the barbed wire and posts that marked the Hungarian–Austrian border. The 'Iron Curtain' was coming down. At the very least some East Germans vacationing in Hungary would attempt to leave the Soviet bloc through what had become an open frontier to the West. Under West German law, once in Austria they could demand passports of the Federal Republic of Germany. Of course, if caught, the East Germans would still have had to face the consequences of what remained an illegal act. On 11 September the Hungarian government took the momentous decision to permit visiting East Germans to cross the border into Austria. The importance of this to the GDR's situation is discussed below.

In October 1989 the Hungarian Communists repackaged their party as the Hungarian Socialist Party. In November 1988 the Alliance of Free Democrats was established as a party. In the same month the traditional Small-holders' Party was re-founded, and in January 1989, the Social Democrats. In the elections of March 1990, the HDF gained 25 per cent of the votes, thus putting it ahead of its rivals. In the second round in April it won a majority of seats and formed a government with the Smallholders and the Christian Democratic People's Party. Less than half the electorate had voted in the decisive second round, during which the HDF used traditional fear of the Jews to gain advantage.[18] The Free Democrats, the former Communists and FIDESZ formed the parliamentary opposition. Like the other new governments in Eastern Europe, the Budapest government faced the high expectations of the electorate, who thought that by changing the political system they could get immediate economic benefits. In fact, price increases and unemployment followed. As elsewhere, privatisation also proved controversial in that state assets were undersold and the few benefited at the expense of the many.

Solidarity wins in Poland

General Jaruzelski, Polish Communist party leader since October 1981, attempted to combine being a Polish patriot with being a man Moscow trusted. In December 1981 he introduced martial law to crush the pro-democracy, independent trade union Solidarity. Honecker and his colleagues applauded him. He later claimed he had to take such steps to avoid a Soviet invasion of Poland. With Gorbachev in power in the Kremlin, the General helped the Soviet leader understand John Paul II, the Polish Pope, who was a key figure in the fall of Communism. Gorbachev helped Jaruzelski to create the conditions for a settlement with Solidarity, which, with help from the Catholic Church and the USA, had maintained an underground existence after being banned. Like the rest of the Soviet bloc, Poland was heavily in debt, and attempts at price increases and other reforms brought strikes in the spring and summer of 1988. Former electrician Lech Wałęsa, founder and leader of Solidarity, overcame the militant wing of his trade union, which opposed negotiations. Jaruzelski used the threat of resignation to persuade his colleagues to agree to the lifting of the ban on Solidarity. Negotiations ended on 5 April 1989 with an agreement to abrogate the bans on Solidarity and Rural Solidarity. It was also agreed to hold elections, in June 1989, in which 35 per cent of seats would be open to the opposition. The Politburo of the SED looked on in dismay. On a turnout of 62.1 per cent Solidarity won, in the first round, 92 of the 100 Senate seats and 160 of the 161 Sejm (parliament) seats available for contests. In the second round Solidarity gained roughly 65 per cent of the votes cast and 40 per cent of the total electorate. Help from the Catholic Church and the USA[19] was vital to give Solidarity a fighting chance against the powerful Communist apparatus. Wałęsa refused the offer to participate in a Communist-led coalition of 'socialist pluralism' and countered with the view that Solidarity should form a government itself. After tense negotiations, Jaruzelski, as President, invited Solidarity's nominee, Tadeusz Mazowiecki, a lawyer and editor of Solidarity's weekly, to form a government. Thus Mazowiecki emerged as the country's first non-Communist head of government in forty years. He had to put up with the defence and interior portfolios remaining in Communist hands. In addition, Communist satellite parties took six of the other ministries, with Solidarity taking over the remaining six. In the GDR some in the SED studied these developments carefully as a possible method of holding on to power.

Early in 1990 the Polish Communist Party dissolved itself. Its remnants then formed two parties calling themselves the Social Democratic Party of the Polish Republic and the Union of Social Democrats.

Poland's post-Communist governments, like their predecessors, had to grapple with massive economic problems. The smoke-stack industries were unprofitable, many consumer goods were of poor quality, agriculture was inefficient, the transport system and telecommunications were antiquated. Market reforms caused inflation and unemployment, which helps to explain why the former Communists could soon celebrate a revival.

In Prague a 'velvet revolution'

Under Communist tutelage Czechoslovakia declined from being a complex modern economy to being on the verge of bankruptcy kept going by arms shipments to the Third World and sales of cheap obsolete vehicles to the West. In theory a federal state, Czechoslovakia remained torn by tensions between Czechs and Slovaks. Like Honecker, the Prague Communist leadership thought they could prevent an outbreak of the Gorbachev sickness. In 1987, Gustáv Husák, who had headed the Communist Party since 1968 when the 'Prague Spring' was crushed, found himself forced to step down in favour of Miloš Jakeš. Politically there was little to chose between them. In January 1989, the riot police brutally smashed demonstrations commemorating the twentieth anniversary of dissident Jan Palach's public self-immolation. Václav Havel, famous dissident playwright and co-founder of Charter 77, the human rights monitoring organisation, was one of the 14 arrested and held for several months.

The fall of the Berlin Wall gave new impetus to the movement for change. On 19 November Havel established Civic Forum. In Slovakia the Public Against Violence movement was formed. Only days later massive demonstrations in Prague demanded the resignation of the Communist leaders and the end of one-party rule. After a two-hour general strike on 27 November the Communist leaders were forced to recognise that they lacked support among the industrial workers. They resigned *en masse*. The new Communist leaders clung to power, but on 10 December they were forced to acknowledge defeat. A non-Communist government was set up in which Civic Forum and the other non-Communists formed the majority. This new federal government started to prepare democratic elections and begin the introduction of a market economy. In the Czech Republic and Slovakia similar governments were set up. Alexander Dubček, the hero of 1968, was brought out of retirement to serve as the Chairman of the Federal Assembly and Havel was elected its president on 29 December. On New Year's Day the new President announced an amnesty for over 16,000 political prisoners. The secret police were officially disbanded one day later.[20] In June 1990 Civic Forum and Public Against Violence won the elections and formed a federal government. The Communists won 13 per cent. The peaceful nature of these dramatic events led to them being dubbed the 'velvet revolution'. Because of the close ties between East German dissidents and their Czech counterparts Czechoslovakia had been a factor in the GDR's internal development. The improving relations between Bonn and Prague over a long period also helped the changes in the GDR. With the election of Havel as President, Germany had another friend sympathetic to the restoration of German unity.

Ceauşescu goes in Romania

In neighbouring Romania Nicolae Ceauşescu attempted to shore up his personal regime by stoking up nationalism, by keeping his people isolated and, above all, by deployment of his feared security service. However, Voice of America, the BBC and other foreign radio broadcasts were able to inform at least a minority of Romanians. There had been strikes of industrial workers in Romania in the 1970s and 1980s as living standards worsened. Many basic foods were rationed in the 1980s. In 1989, demonstrations broke out in Timisoara, populated by members of Romania's Hungarian minority. Sadly, these ended in bloodshed on 17 December 1989. The demonstrations were sparked by Securitate attempts to arrest the Hungarian Protestant pastor Laszlo Tokes. More remarkable was what happened in Bucharest on 21 December. There security police opened fire when crowds called to support the dictator started to boo him. Unusually, the event was broadcast live on television. Ceauşescu was forced to make his getaway in a helicopter the following day from the Communist HQ. The secret police sought to keep matters under control and fighting went on for some days, but when the army defected to the demonstrators they knew they had lost. After a brief trial, which was broadcast later, Ceauşescu and his wife were shot on Christmas Day. Whether this was done to ensure there would be no revival of his dictatorship or simply to save others from embarrassment is not clear.

In Romania the Communists were quick to distance themselves from the late dictator and represented themselves as reformers, nationalists or democratic socialists. Like their comrades in rest of the 'socialist camp', the Communists enjoyed great advantages over the opposition. In their hands had been the administration, business, the media and the police. They knew how they functioned and many of them would be needed whatever the political complexion of the government. They controlled hidden funds from the old days. They were more likely to speak foreign languages and could, therefore, get themselves across to foreign journalists. In a country with little experience of democratic politics they succeeded in retaining power as the National Salvation Front led by Ion Illiescu, a former Communist Secretary for Agitation and Propaganda. The Front won again in 1992 by a lesser margin.

In Bulgaria, another Honecker ally was in trouble. Although, unlike the Romanians, the Bulgarians were pro-Russian, their leader since 1954, Todor Zhivkov, fought to avoid Gorbachev-style reforms. But the day after the Berlin Wall was opened, Zhivkov had to step down from office. Later he faced charges of gross embezzlement and was condemned to eight years' imprisonment in 1992. Like his Romanian neighbour, he had employed nationalist rhetoric to prop up his crumbling dictatorship, scapegoating the ethnic Turks and Gypsies. Petur Mladenov, who replaced Zhivkov as Communist leader, changed the party name to the Bulgarian Socialist Party and succeeded in winning a narrow victory in June 1990. After widespread strikes, the Union of Democratic Forces (UDF) and the Movement for Rights and Freedom (MRF), mainly representing the Turkish minority, soon forced the BSP to relinquish government.

China resists democracy

Like the two German states, the People's Republic of China was celebrating forty years of existence in 1989. In 1949 Mao Zedong's Communists had beaten American-backed nationalists led by Chiang Kai-shek and taken power. After following the Soviet Stalinist model, the Chinese decided to go their own way in the 1960s. This led to a sharp deterioration in relations with the Soviet Union. China's 'Great Leap Forward' in 1959 was an economic failure. The so-called 'Cultural Revolution' from 1965 to 1971 led to chaos and terror. Following the dramatic visit of President Richard Nixon to Beijing in 1972 there occurred a change for the better in Sino-US relations that helped to end the Vietnam War. Nixon's visit also gave a signal to Western industrial and financial institutions that China could be considered a reliable partner. The death of Mao in 1976 brought hopes for a gradual improvement in conditions in China itself. After an interregnum China underwent a remarkable series of changes in the 1980s under the leadership of the pragmatic Deng Xiaoping. His catch-phrase was 'Poverty is not Socialism'[21] and he sought modernisation and economic growth. The 'responsibility system' was introduced in the vast countryside under which, although the land still belonged to the state, peasant families became responsible for cultivation and reaped any profits. The earlier system of communes was gradually made redundant. Small private businesses were encouraged in the urban areas and the number registered increased from 100,000 in 1978 to 17 million in 1985.[22] Special trade zones in the coastal areas were set up in an effort to attract foreign investment with abundant cheap labour and tax concessions. Elsewhere in China state enterprises were subject to the profit motive. All these reforms led to disparities between regions and within them. Increasing inequality appeared, unemployment returned and beggars re-appeared on the streets. Much of what the Chinese did during this period Gorbachev studied in the hope of achieving an economic turnaround for the stagnating Soviet economy.

The comrades of the SED had admired Mao in the beginning because he had brought the world's most populous state into the 'socialist camp' and had been given Stalin's blessing. The GDR even issued a large postage stamp, one of the very few outside China, to honour Mao. Chinese volunteers saved North Korea from American/UN occupation in the Korean War, 1950–53, and the Chinese proved they could master modern technology by detonating their own nuclear devices. Unlike Khrushchev, Mao never denounced Stalin. As Sino-Soviet relations deteriorated, so did those between Beijing and East Berlin. This was especially so during the Cultural Revolution period. SED propagandists accused Beijing of hegemonic great-power ambitions. The Soviet–Chinese split in the early 1960s dismayed many members of the SED, coming as it did not long after the denunciation of Stalin. Relations between China and the GDR improved subsequently and party and state delegations were exchanged. Honecker had started very soon to rebuild contacts with China. The high point of these contacts was the state visit by Honecker to China in 1986 and a return visit by the Chinese.[23]

On 3–4 June 1989 Chinese troops and tanks were ordered to clear Tiananmen Square, where many thousands of students, workers and others were demonstrating for greater freedom, including free trade unions. Bloodshed followed as between 600 and 1,200 died and many times those numbers were injured.[24] The SED leaders appeared to endorse this (see below).

Notes

1. Carl Bernstein and Marco Politi, *His Holiness John Paul II and the Hidden History of Our Time*, London, 1997, p. 431.
2. Martin McCauley, *Gorbachev*, 1998, pp. 30–1.
3. Margaret Thatcher, *The Downing Street Years*, London, 1993, p. 461.
4. Quoted in McCauley, 1998, p. 52.
5. *Ibid.*, p. 54.

6. Hans-Hermann Hertle, *Der Fall der Mauer*, Opladen, 1996, p. 58.
7. Avril Pittman, *From Ostpolitik to Reunification: West German–Soviet Political Relations Since 1974*, Cambridge, 1992, p. 158.
8. *Ibid.*, p. 159.
9. Mikhail Gorbachev, *Memoirs*, London, 1997, pp. 670–1.
10. Pittman, *From Ostpolitik to Reunification*, p. 159.
11. Gorbachev, *Memoirs*, p. 671.
12. *Ibid.*, p. 675.
13. *Ibid.*, p. 263.
14. McCauley (1998), p. 66.
15. Gorbachev, *Memoirs*, p. 263.
16. J. N. Westwood, *Endurance and Endeavour: Russian History 1812–1992*, London, 1993, p. 508.
17. Mark Frankland, *The Patriots' Revolution*, Chicago, 1992, p. 104.
18. *Ibid.*, pp. 210–11.
19. Bernstein and Politi (*His Holiness John Paul II*, p. 373) state that the US spent over $50 million to keep Solidarity alive between 1992 and 1990.
20. I. R. Crampton, *Eastern Europe in the Twentieth Century and After*, London, 1992, p. 399.
21. Alan Lawrance, *China under Communism*, London, 1998, p. 107.
22. *Ibid.*, p. 110.
23. Krenz, p. 130.
24. Lawrance, *China under Communism*, p. 120.

Chapter 5

Gorbachev 1989: 'Life punishes those who come too late'

During the dreary, smog-laden days of January 1989 all seemed normal and quiet on the vast 'socialist' housing estate in East Berlin's Marzahn and in the old tenements of Hohenschönhausen. In the old flats in Leipzig's Beethoven Straße and in the newer flats of the Gabelsberger Straße 'socialist' law and order prevailed. It prevailed from Rostock in the north to Suhl in the south. As they travelled to work in their crowded trams, buses or on the S-Bahn many East Germans probably day-dreamed about their summer holidays. Would they be lucky enough to get away on a 'package' for a few days in sunny Bulgaria or Romania? Or should they try for a private holiday in the relative sophistication of Prague or Budapest? Or would another camping site on the Baltic await them? How great it would be to go on one of those trips to Spain, Greece or Italy advertised just now on West German television. Those were countries they were unlikely ever to see despite the GDR's ever-widening international contacts. Trips to the capitalist world were only for the chosen few.

Few were likely to have paid much attention to the visit of Swedish Prime Minister Ingvar Carlsson to East Berlin on 23 January or to that of Björn Engholm, Prime Minister of Schleswig-Holstein, on 31 January, or later, that of Lothar Späth, Prime Minister of Baden-Württemberg, on 23 February. Such occasions had become routine. Some East Germans privately criticised them, believing they simply gave credibility to bankrupt leaders like Honecker and Stoph who hoodwinked the visitors. Most hoped earnestly that the guests would be the heralds of better times, but little seemed to be happening. Bavarian leader Franz Josef Strauß had been warmly welcomed by ordinary East Germans, including some SED members,[1] on trips to the GDR. The same was true of Professor Kurt Biedenkopf, the CDU politician, who was a frequent visitor in the 1980s.[2] Few, if any, East Germans would have mourned the death of Emperor Hirohito of Japan, who died in January after serving as head of state since 1926. Perhaps one or two thought that Erich Honecker had ambitions to rule over the GDR as long as Hirohito had ruled the Japanese. Though regarded as a war criminal by many, Hirohito was Honecker's 'friend'. He had received the GDR leader on a state visit to Japan in 1981. The GDR was hoping Japan would help it modernise its economy.

After a visit to the GDR in May 1989, Ernst Albrecht, Minister-President of Lower Saxony, stated in an official declaration that for him re-unification was not an illusion but an aim and a concrete hope. Gerhard Schröder, leader of the opposition SPD in Lower Saxony, and future Chancellor of a re-united Germany, rejected this, saying the CDU was holding on to long out-of-date formulas. German unity simply meant a common past and a common language and culture.[3] Sadly, Schröder's view was typical of that of many leading Social Democrats. Helmut Schmidt, former Chancellor, had, according to the *Financial Times* (7 July 1987), called on Chancellor Kohl to acknowledge GDR independence. He meant of course as a foreign state in the sense that Austria or France were foreign states to West Germany. The Federal Republic recognised the GDR as part of the German nation and therefore not foreign to it. Schmidt's proposal, backed by other Social Democrats, would, in theory, have made it more difficult for East Germans to seek assistance from West German embassies abroad or to claim West German passports as they had a right to do under current West German law. Honecker favoured the expression of such views but the East German people did not. The comments by Schröder and Schmidt and others were to influence East German opinion against the SPD.

For the pessimists among ordinary East Germans who believed nothing would change for the better, who believed 'Ivan will never leave',[4] there was new proof on 6 February 1989. GDR frontier troops shot the 20-year-old Chris Gueffroy, who was attempting to escape via the Berlin Wall. Most heard this news from the West German electronic media first. Even among those who swallowed the official line in such matters that Gueffroy and others like him were breaking the law, there was a sickening feeling that their state resorted to such methods to hold people against their will. Many others who thought such attempts were foolish had no sympathy at all for official arguments. They believed that the SED state was simply the tool of Moscow, the regime that had shot down a Korean airliner in 1983 with the loss of over 250 passengers and crew when the plane strayed into Soviet territory. A few hundred of the roughly 12 million East German adults joined groups which sought to change things. Hardly any of them believed the GDR would soon cease to exist, and they did not seek its end; they simply wanted to 'humanise' the so-called 'socialist' system. Such individuals watched with wonder the changes taking place under Mikhail Gorbachev in the Soviet Union.

Dissident groups continued to grow in the GDR in the late 1980s. The Stasi infiltrated them, arrested and imprisoned their members when it felt the time had come. Imitating the action of the previous year in Berlin, on 15 January 1989, in Leipzig, between 150 and 200 individuals attempted to hold a silent march commemorating the murder of Karl Liebknecht and

Rosa Luxemburg in 1919. Through leaflets they sought to remind their fellow-citizens that Luxemburg had supported free speech and the right to differ. According to the Stasi, 53 of them were arrested but later released.[5] Over half of those involved were already known to the police for their previous activities of this nature. Earlier in the month 11 others had been arrested and held in custody in connection with the Liebknecht–Luxemburg leaflets.[6] The confiscated leaflet was very moderate indeed, arguing,

> It is time to express our opinions openly and courageously. Finish with the indifference and apathy, which lames us. Let us join together for the right of free expression; for freedom of assembly and association; for press freedom and against the banning of the *Sputnik* magazine and critical Soviet films.[7]

It urged citizens to meet in front of the Altes Rathaus (Old Town Hall) and take part in a silent march according to articles 27 and 28 of the GDR constitution. The Stasi no doubt felt it had dealt with the attempted, unofficial march effectively and efficiently. For them these were people on the margins of society, a student, a church carer, a carpenter working for a private firm. They were not workers or employees of Leipzig's major industries. As there were no foreign press correspondents present, unlike Berlin in the previous year, it did not get as much attention outside the GDR.

Gorbachev: 'blatant . . . election fraud'

On 7 May 1989 the SED scored another own goal. It falsified the result of the single-list local elections. Although most voters obeyed the call of the SED to support the official candidates, as widely expected, a significant number rejected them. Foolishly the SED denied that this was the case. According to the election commission, the voters had given 98.85 per cent of the votes to the National Front candidates. Later no less a figure than Gorbachev was to describe this as being marked by 'the most blatant cases of election fraud'.[8] After his fall from power, Honecker denied any knowledge of any fraud, claiming, rightly so, that it would have served no purpose to conceal a 2 or 3 per cent lower turnout of voters and even a result that was 10 per cent worse than usual. Such falsification would only play into the hands of the enemies of socialism. He seemed to feel that some elements within the SED leadership were involved in irregularities as part of a campaign to bring him down.[9] Whatever the truth of the matter, protests followed and continued on the seventh day of every month thereafter. On 7 June, for instance, 160 protesters tried to complain to the Council of State, headed by Honecker, about the matter. The answer of the authorities was to prevent them from reaching the Council of State building or to arrest them. They could not, however, prevent a 'prayer for peace' meeting taking place in the Church of St Sophie on the same day, attended by about 300, at which protests were made about the conduct of the local elections. One of the key figures at the meeting was Martin-Michael Passauer, pastor in charge of the Church of St Sophie, who was well known to the Stasi as an activist of the unofficial peace movement. He played a key role in sustaining the protests about the local election fraud. As always, the Stasi had at least one of their informants at the meeting. The lawyer Wolfgang Schnur, who represented arrested members of the opposition and was later exposed as a Stasi agent, was recorded in the secret MfS report as having been present.[10]

On the day before, 6 June, the GDR media had given prominence to official statements by the Chinese Communist leadership justifying their use of force against students and other demonstrators demanding free speech in China. As Krenz later admitted, this, in effect, identified the SED leaders with the Chinese.[11] It could be interpreted as a threat to anyone in the GDR hoping that by peaceful demonstrations they could bring about a change. On 8 June the Volkskammer totally discredited itself by supporting the position of the Chinese leaders. Attending a conference in Saarbrücken, West Germany, Krenz was given the job by the Politburo of answering his host, Oskar Lafontaine, SPD leader and Prime Minister of the Saar, who had attacked the Chinese Communist leadership. Krenz later claimed that a statement read out over the television purporting to be his had not been written by him.[12] Whatever the truth, this tarnished Krenz's image irrecoverably.

Hungarians allow East Germans to go West

Krenz was more or less forced by Honecker to go on holiday in August 1989. He himself was going in hospital for a serious operation. Meanwhile, the running of the GDR would be left in the hands of Günter Mittag.[13] From his holiday resort, Dierhagen on the Baltic, Krenz heard that the West German diplomatic mission in East Berlin had been closed because it could not cope with East Germans seeking asylum. The same was happening in Prague and Budapest. GDR citizens on holiday in Hungary, Czechoslovakia and Poland sought asylum in the West German embassies in those countries. They wanted to abandon life in the GDR for life in West Germany. Over the 1980s increasing numbers of East Germans had sought by legal means to do this, most without success.[14] The Hungarians, who had started to dismantle the 'Iron Curtain' between Hungary and Austria in May, allowed several groups of East Germans to leave for Austria. Honecker felt betrayed when on 11 September Hungarian Foreign Minister Gyula Horn announced that Hungary would allow those East German tourists who wanted to cross the border to neutral Austria to do so. Tens of thousands took this option and then travelled from Vienna to West Germany.[15] Seen on television, their actions persuaded others to follow. Meanwhile, attempts had been made to establish new parties, starting with New Forum on 19 September, and followed by Democratic Awakening, the Social Democrats and the Greens. Also on 19 September the Synod of the Federation of Evangelical Churches, meeting in Eisenach, called for pluralism in the media, multiparty democracy, freedom to travel, the right to demonstrate and economic reform.[16]

To avoid further haemorrhage, the GDR closed its frontier with Czechoslovakia on 3 October. There were angry scenes as East Germans who had paid for plane or train tickets, paid for hotels or other accommodation found they could not travel and had lost their money. The day before, the GDR had agreed to allow 14,000 of its citizens camping in West German embassies in Warsaw and Prague to go West.[17] To save face, a statement on GDR television said the move was because children were involved, children who had been let down by the irresponsible actions of their parents.[18] A riot took place (4 October) in Dresden as 20,000 East Germans attempted to board slow-moving trains taking refugees from Prague to the West. It was the first large-scale street disturbance in the GDR since 1953. Those who had managed to turn a holiday into an emigration would have any property they left behind sold for the benefit of the state. The Czech frontier was closed to East Germans just as the frontier to West Germany was closed. The Polish frontier was still open, though difficult to cross even with a visa. East Germans without visas swam across the Oder at night from the GDR to Poland. If caught, they faced imprisonment and then were sent back.

Word of these events reached Krenz in Beijing. Back from holiday, he had been dispatched to Beijing to the celebrations marking the setting up of the People's Republic of China under Mao in October 1949. This was a further blow to Krenz's prestige and prevented him from agitating against the recovering Honecker. On the way back he worked on a text, which he hoped would be 'Die Wende'.[19]

'Gorby, help us'

Gorbachev visited the GDR to celebrate its fortieth anniversary on 7 October. Fearing the wrong kind of demonstrations, the GDR media did not publish the schedule.[20] Nevertheless, crowds lined the route from the airport, who, unlike in the past with other Soviet leaders, genuinely wanted to greet Gorbachev.[21] At the official parade of 100,000 hand-picked Free German Youth members on the evening of 6 October, according to Gorbachev's own account, 'Perestroika! Gorbachev! Help us!' was heard coming from their ranks.[22] Honecker believed the FDJ leaders themselves had turned the event into a march of triumph for 'Gorbi'.[23] Gorbachev claimed that Honecker behaved 'as if he were in a trance'.[24] All over the GDR, demonstrations were held demanding reforms. In Dresden there had been altercations between the police and demonstrators on 5 October and a demonstration in Magdeburg. A demonstration of some 30,000 in Dresden on 7 October demanding more freedom and democracy was brutally dispersed. On the same day similar demonstrations occurred in Leipzig, Plauen, Magdeburg, Karl-Marx-Stadt, Potsdam and Arnstadt. They were broken up by the police.[25] In Berlin, on the morning of 7 October, the usual military parade was held. This was something that many Berliners thought was no longer appropriate and could, therefore, be regarded as another 'own goal' for the SED.

Taking the salute with Honecker were his Politburo colleagues, the leaders of the satellite parties and friends from far and wide, like Nicolae Ceauşescu, Wojciech Jaruzelski and of course Gorbachev, and many others who would soon be in the 'dustbin of history'. The afternoon was devoted to officially organised 'people's festivals' in all parts of East Berlin. This was a traditional feature of the annual anniversary celebrations. At 17.00, a crowd gathered on Alexanderplatz and started shouting 'New Forum', the name of the new opposition group, and 'We are staying here' ('Wir bleiben hier'). These were individuals who wanted to stay in the GDR and improve things rather just leaving for the West. Plain-clothes Stasi officers made some arrests as the uniformed police just watched events. The crowd then moved off towards the Volkskammer building, Palast der Republik, not far away. Their columns grew on the way and they chanted, in English, 'Gorby, help us' and, in German, 'Keine Gewalt' ('no force') and 'New Forum'. They kept up this chanting close to the Palast and some sang 'The International'. Because of the presence of Western TV crews covering the official celebrations, the police did not use force in Berlin as they were doing in other towns. As darkness fell, however, they changed their tactics and masses of police with anti-riot equipment moved in.[26] The unofficial demonstration was broken up with force and the 16,000 police deployed made 1,047 arrests.[27] Many demonstrators, before and after arrest, suffered verbal abuse, gratuitous violence and humiliation during detention. They were released within days.

When, during his visit, Gorbachev was greeted with posters 'Gorby, help us.' He pointedly responded in the direction of the SED leadership, 'Life punishes those who come too late.' According to Krenz, this was the message he gave to the SED Politburo on 7 October when he met its members at his guest residence, Schloß Niederschönhausen, 'in a friendly atmosphere'.[28] Gorbachev held a long private conversation with Honecker but there was evidently no meeting of minds.[29] The day after Gorbachev left the

GDR, 8 October, 5,000 Dresdeners united in a sit-down. The city council agreed to talk to them and the demonstration ended peacefully. This was not the case in Berlin, where the police used force against demonstrators, making many arrests.[30]

Honecker: 'Don Quixote's futile charge'

The ailing Honecker could still pull a punch in political terms and fight off Krenz's attempt to bring about a change of direction. He was quoted by ADN, the official news agency, as having told the visiting Chinese Deputy Prime Minister, Yao Yilin, on 9 October,

'Any attempt by imperialism to destabilise socialist construction, and slander its achievements, is now and in the future nothing more than Don Quixote's futile charge against the steadily turning sails of a windmill.' The two Communist leaders agreed that 'there was evidence of a particularly aggressive anti-socialist action by imperialist class opponents with the aim of reversing socialist develop-ment. In this respect there is a fundamental lesson to be learnt from the counter-revolutionary unrest in Peking and the present campaign against the GDR and other socialist states.'[31]

According to a report of the MfS dated 8 October, many workers, 'in-cluding many members and functionaries of the Party, say quite openly that the Party and state leadership are no longer able to evaluate the situation realistically and to push through urgently need changes. Because of their age structure they can no longer react flexibly.' They were bitter that their leaders missed the chance to use the fortieth anniversary festivities of the founding of the GDR to speak clearly about the current situation and to indicate ways leading to appropriate solutions. They also criticised the passive and defensive nature of the mass media, which did not attempt to counter hostile propaganda. Party functionaries were unable to discuss and argue effectively and just used quotations to save the day. Sometimes those who asked awkward questions were threatened with party sanctions. The MfS report claimed among the demands of these 'progressive forces' were the introduction of modern and effective methods of economic leadership; more independence for enterprises; changes in the policy on subsidies; introduction of payment by result; improvement in socialist democracy; introduction of the principle of co-determination (*Mitbestimmung*) and co-responsibility (*Mitverantwortung*); more transparency in decision-making by central organs of party and state; accountability of party and state leadership to the people; changes in the media, including sincere exposure of all problems and difficulties, the end of 'court reports' and one-sided success reports. Inside the party itself they wanted openness so that all members could discuss problems frankly. The report stressed that their informants believed the socialist state and social order were in serious danger.[32]

When those critical and worried SED members opened their copies of *Neues Deutschland* on 9 October many must have been overcome by anger or despair. No fewer than 18 photographs of Honecker appeared over three pages. Everything appeared to be going on as before. The only, tiny, ray of hope was found in *Junge Welt*, the FDJ paper, on the same day. The paper published a letter from Hermann Kant, President of the GDR Writers' Association, a member of the SED's Central Committee, and usually regarded as a creature of the leadership. He wrote that the exodus of almost 50,000 GDR citizens could not be blamed on the 'wicked class enemy' in West Germany. He attacked the smug 'self-glorification of the GDR press and the bossiness of the system'. He appealed for social understanding through criticism and self-criticism.

'An unbridled campaign of agitation and slander'

As archive material reveals, the Stasi, in October 1989, were ready to jump on individuals under surveillance at the time as well as others on their lists. On 8 October Mielke sent a message to his commanders claiming that because 'of an unbridled campaign of agitation and slander by the enemy, and massive attempts at interference, the internal political situation of the GDR had been further intensified'.[33] He ordered his subordinates to be ready for immediate action and to have their weapons with them at all times. All informers were to be activated, but in such a way as not to make them uncertain. Their job in this situation was to clarify 'Who is who?' ('Wer ist wer?') by targeted assignment among those who had applied to leave the GDR, those who sympathised with opposition movements such as New Forum, all of whom represented a potential reservoir of support for these forces. Probably because he had dealt in violence all his life, but also to heighten the anxieties of his subordinates, Mielke warned about the possibility of violence from the opposition. 'By applying appropriate means, all attempts at terror and other use of force, especially against members of the SED and other progressive citizens, as well as against members of the security organs, including their buildings and other establishments, are to be prevented.'[34] The day after this message was sent a great demonstration was expected in Leipzig. There was great apprehension on both sides as to the outcome.

The 'miracle of Leipzig'

On the evening of 9 October 1989 between 70,000 and 100,000 citizens of Leipzig took to the streets. These Monday demonstrations were by then traditional but never before had so many taken part. There had been rumours that violence was expected. After all, there had been violence by the police two days before when some 200 demonstrators were taken into custody and held in horse stalls at an agricultural exhibition centre outside the city.[35] On this occassion, doctors and other medical personnel had been placed on call, blood banks had been built up and emergency wards prepared. In schools, universities, factories, workshops, offices and retail stores warnings were given to keep clear of the city centre.[36] Students and employees were given to understand by their Professors or bosses that the time had come to deal with 'political rowdies', 'asocial elements' and troublemakers. The situation looked as grim as the polluted grey skies above the city. Professor Kurt Masur, the much-respected conductor of the famous Gewandhaus Orchestra, recalled, 'I knew that leading SED members intended to crush the Leipzig rallies that Monday. Columns of tanks and trucks had been strategically placed. After rehearsing with my orchestra all morning, I called the SED Regional Secretary of Culture, Dr Kurt Meyer, and expressed my concerns.'[37] The result was that, in the afternoon, an appeal was broadcast over the local radio signed by Kurt Masur, Pastor Dr Peter Zimmermann, well known in church and civil-liberties circles, the cabarettist Bernd-Lutz Lange, and three members of the Leipzig SED leadership. It read,

> We all need the free exchange of opinions about the further development of socialism in our country. Therefore those named promise all citizens that they will use their energy and authority to see to it that this dialogue takes place not just in Leipzig but also with our government. We implore you to be level-headed so that the peaceful dialogue will be possible.[38]

The three local SED leaders were Kurt Meyer, Jochen Pommert and Roland Wötzel. As second in charge of the SED in Leipzig, Wötzel was potentially very important. It appears a very mild and vague statement today and one wonders what effect it really had. There were other factors and other actors at work. Two leaflets were distributed on that day calling both sides, demonstrators and representatives of the state, to avoid all provocative behaviour which could lead to violence. One of them was issued in the name of the United Left, and the other, more representative, by the Working Party for Justice, the Working Party for Human Rights and the Working Party for Environment.[39]

Another key figure in the outcome of the events that day was Professor Walter Friedrich. Friedrich had made Leipzig his home after leaving his native Silesia as a refugee in 1945. He also made it the home for his *Zentralinstitut für Jugendforschung*. This became important for the FDJ and the SED, the institute's research was an important barometer of just how successful they were in the battle to win the hearts and minds of the youth of the GDR. Friedrich had become friends with Krenz over the years as Krenz, a former head of the FDJ, still had responsibility for youth. As we saw in Chapter 2, Friedrich's reports in 1989 revealed that youth was less inclined to identify with the GDR than in earlier years. Krenz trusted the judgement of the Leipzig academic and SED loyalist.

Friedrich rose early on 9 October and drove to Berlin to a pre-arranged meeting with Krenz. The two met at just after 09.30 in the ZK building, where Friedrich gave his friend an analysis of the situation in Leipzig. According to Krenz, Friedrich was very excited and repeatedly stressed that no blood should be spilled in Leipzig that night.[40] He also advised Krenz that a change in the leadership of the SED was overdue. Krenz gave Friedrich an assurance that he would sort out matters before anything could happen that evening. Another actor in the drama, Major General Gerhard Straßenburg, commander of the People's Police and the factory militias in Leipzig, claims he spoke on the phone with Minister of Interior General Friedrich Dickel. The minister agreed with Straßenburg that his units should only use force to defend themselves.[41] The fact is the SED and the other authorities had not expected that so many people would take part in the demonstration. They soon realised that their forces would be overwhelmed by the sheer numbers involved.[42] The demonstration proceeded peacefully; the first miracle of Leipzig became a reality with Masur and other prominent individuals at the front of the 70,000 people. The following Monday more than 150,000 turned out for another peaceful demonstration.[43]

At the meeting of the Politburo on 10 October, Krenz was only partly successful in presenting a declaration he wanted adopted, which Honecker opposed. The text which appeared in the SED newspaper *Neues Deutschland* on 12 October would have been regarded by the few who bothered to read it as 'too little, too late'. It is true that it withdrew earlier remarks that the GDR would not shed a tear for those who had turned their backs on it. Now the Politburo was saying that the GDR needed everyone and could not be indifferent when its citizens left for good. It talked about 'democratic togetherness', a good assortment of consumer goods, pay which reflected effort, media in touch with life, the possibility to travel and a healthy environment. Few could believe that the old gang of Politburo members could bring about the necessary changes to satisfy the masses, however. On 16 October the Stasi produced a report about the reaction of the population to the Politburo declaration. This revealed that the extent and intensity of extremely critical views being expressed had grown. Such views were heard among artists, members of the intelligentsia and students, growing numbers of workers and others in the Combinates and factories, including 'long-term members of the SED and other progressive elements, as well as

73

including members and functionaries of the allied parties'.[44] The FDJ leaders advised Krenz on 11 October that this was the view of the youth of the GDR. When, on 12 October, Honecker met the first secretaries of the SED from the GDR's 15 *Bezirke* he was faced with critical voices and the call from Günther Jahn, the Potsdam SED boss, to resign. He refused to take the hint. The situation was increasingly desperate daily as more demonstrations took place and more citizens turned their backs on the socialist state. Time was fast running out for those who wanted to save SED leadership in the GDR and even the GDR itself.

Krenz went to Leipzig on 13 October to see the situation for himself. With him went the Secretary of the National Defence Council, Major General Fritz Streletz, Deputy Minister of State Security Colonel General Rudi Mittig, Deputy Minister of Interior General Wagner and, not least, Wolfgang Hörger, head of the Department for Security Questions of the ZK. SED eye-witnesses later recalled that Krenz and his colleagues did not give a very convincing impression of understanding the problems or having any answers.[45] One result of their visit was an order of 16 October that a direct deployment of the police should only take place in the case of attacks on individuals or property. The same order did, however, state that all appropriate methods should be used to attempt to keep meetings confined to the churches and ensure they did not turn into 'provocative demonstrations'.

On the day that Krenz was in Leipzig, Honecker was making what turned out to be his last official engagement. He met the leaders of the 'allied' parties and claimed,

> Everyone has his place in the GDR. . . . Socialism offers room for everyone to develop his personality. . . . We have a comprehensive system of socialist democracy, that makes it possible for everyone to take part in the discussion of the problems of society and to play a part in solving them.[46]

One other factor that the SED leaders had to consider was the attitude of the Soviet leadership to developments in the GDR. Was there any chance that the SED, whether it was led by Honecker, Krenz or Modrow, would be able to ask the Soviet forces in Germany for help to remain in power? Krenz denied that it was ever his intention to do so. He later claimed that his view was that any attempt to build socialism with bayonets was doomed to failure.[47] He also claimed that the idea that the Soviet armed forces had been given an order not to intervene was a legend.[48] Gerlach believed the opposite. He claimed the Soviet Ambassador told him in September 1989 that they could not count on the Soviet forces as in 1953. The Soviet German expert Valentin Falin reported that from August 1989 the Soviet forces had received an order not to intervene. He went further. In his view the GDR's own armed forces would not have acted without the backing of their Soviet colleagues.[49] The lack of Soviet support must have weighed heavily on the SED leadership when considering what to do about the, from their point of view, deteriorating situation in Leipzig, Berlin and elsewhere. The large number of demonstrators was another key factor. Deployment of inadequate forces in an aggressive way could easily have led to demoralisation, indiscipline and desertion. One final factor in the SED's reckoning was the attitude of the West German government. On 9 October Chancellor Kohl warned the SED leaders, 'Internal peace and stability cannot be guaranteed by force and by denying the people a voice.'[50] There was little the West Germans could do immediately except in financial and economic terms.

None of this detracts from the efforts of Masur, Friedrich and even Krenz to avoid bloodshed. Had Krenz not been determined to avoid a 'Chinese solution', who knows how the crisis would have ended. On the other side, the patient, peaceful approach of the demonstrators was of crucial importance in the achievement of the 'miracle of Leipzig'.

In Bonn the members of the government had their holidays disturbed by the reports arriving from East Berlin over the summer. Contrary to what some in the SED thought, they were not expecting or plotting to see Germany re-united in their lifetimes. Like their Social Democratic predecessors between 1969 and 1982, they still wanted gradual, well-disciplined reform in the GDR, small steps to make their Eastern neighbour a more civilised place to live. They were afraid of where the demonstrations in the GDR could lead. Despite Gorbachev's good intentions, could there be a military, Chinese-style crackdown in the GDR, they asked themselves? They would not deny refuge to East Germans reaching the West, but they were worried by the great rise in numbers, which put an increasing strain on public finances and could lead to a possible backlash against the outsiders. A total of 110,184 refugees reached West Germany between January and September. The figure for the entire previous year was only 40,000.

Notes

1. As told to author by Heide-Marie Lüth, PDS member of the Bundestag.
2. As witnessed by the author in Leipzig.
3. *Hannövische Allgemeine Zeiting*, 12 May 1989.
4. As put to the author by an East German chauffeur working for the University of Jena.
5. Armin Mitter and Stefan Wolle (eds), *Ich liebe euch doch alle!*, Berlin, 1990, p. 12.
6. *Ibid.*, p. 11.
7. *Ibid.*, p. 13.
8. Mikhail Gorbachev, *Memoirs*, London, 1997, p. 680.
9. Erich Honecker, *Moabiter Notizen*, Berlin, 1994, pp. 28–9.
10. Mitter and Wolle (eds), *Ich liebe euch doch alle!*, p. 73.

11. Krenz, p. 132.
12. *Ibid.*, p. 132.
13. *Ibid.*, p. 29.
14. *Ibid.*, p. 36.
15. Hans-Hermann Hertle, *Der Fall der Mauer*, Opladen, 1996, pp. 104–5.
16. Stefan Wolle, *Die heile Welt der Diktatur*, pp. 285–7.
17. Mitter and Wolle (eds), *Ich liebe euch doch alle!*, p. 108.
18. Spiegel TV Video.
19. Krenz, p. 31.
20. Cornelia Heins, *The Wall Falls: An Oral History of the Reunification of the Two Germanies*, London, 1994, p. 196.
21. Krenz, 86, Gorbachev, *Memoirs*, pp. 676–7.
22. Gorbachev, *Memoirs*, p. 676.
23. Honecker, *Moabiter Notizen*, p. 32.
24. Gorbachev, *Memoirs*, p. 677.
25. Wilfried Tieding, *Ein Volk im Aufbruch: Die DDR im Herbst '89*, Dresden, 1990, p. 11.
26. Spiegel TV Video.
27. Charles S. Maier, *Dissolution: The Crisis of Communism and the End of East Germany*, Princeton, NJ, 1997, p. 148.
28. Krenz, p. 87; Gorbachev, *Memoirs*, p. 677.
29. Gorbachev, *Memoirs*, p. 677. According to the Soviet leader, it was just with Honecker. According to Krenz, 86, Mittag was also present.
30. Tieding, p. 12.
31. *The Independent*, 10 October 1989.
32. Mitter and Wolle (eds), *Ich liebe euch doch alle!*, pp. 204–7.
33. Thomas Auerbach, 'Vorbereitung auf den Tag X: Die geplanten Isolierungslager des Mfs' (BstU), Berlin, 1995, p. 136.
34. *Ibid.*, p. 137.
35. Ekkehard Kuhn, *'Wir Sind Das Volk!': Die friedliche Revolution in Leipzig, 9. Oktober 1989*, Berlin/Frankfurt am Main, 1999, p. 62.
36. *Ibid.*, p. 75.
37. Masur in Heins, *The Wall Falls*, p. 228.
38. Kuhn, *'Wir Sind Das Volk!'*, pp. 126–7.
39. *Ibid.*, pp. 84–6.
40. Krenz in *ibid.*, p. 90.
41. Straßenberg in *ibid.*, p. 137.
42. Hannes Bahrmann and Christoph Links, *Chronik der Wende: Die Ereignisse in der DDR zwischen 7. Oktober 1989 und 18. März 1990*, Berlin, 1999, p. 20.
43. Masur in Heins, *The Wall Falls*, p. 229.
44. Mitter and Wolle (eds), *Ich liebe euch doch alle!*, p. 225.
45. Heide-Marie Lüth in conversation with the author.
46. Tieding, 14.
47. Krenz in Kuhn, *'Wir Sind Das Volk!'*, p. 90.
48. Krenze in *ibid.*, p. 31.
49. Falin in *ibid.*, p. 29.
50. *The Independent*, 10 October 1989.

Chapter 6

The birth of the opposition parties

New Forum

On 19 September 1989 New Forum (NF) applied to be registered as an organisation, *not*, it should be noted, as a party. The organisers of this group were Bärbel Bohley and Jutta Seidel. Bohley, a 44-year-old painter, had been arrested in 1988 and forced to spend some time in England. She had the courage to return to the GDR to set up NF. The foundation appeal of NF dated 10 September started from the assumption that 'In our country the communication between the state and society has apparently broken down.' The GDR's citizenry had either retreated into the private sphere or had taken to flight on a scale usually associated with privation, starvation or force. NF therefore sought to establish a political platform for the whole of the GDR that would make it possible for people from all professions, circles, parties, and groups to take part in the discussion about the key problems facing East German society. NF would be a legal body in the sense of article 29 of the constitution of the GDR. Its efforts were the expression of the desire for justice, democracy and peace as well as the protection of nature. At no point did the Appeal attack individuals or parties, let alone the leading role of the SED or the 'achievements of the GDR'.[1] On the face of it, NF had no desire to overthrow the SED or destroy the GDR. Had the Politburo been clever enough, they would have granted NF a legal status and sought to control it as they did all dissident groups. Instead, on 25 September, the Ministry of Interior informed Bohley and Seidel that NF would not be given legal status.

Democracy Now

Two days after the appeal of New Forum came the publication of a programme from Democracy Now (DJ or *Demokratie Jetzt*). DJ sought above all an alliance of Christians and critical Marxists to think about 'our future, about a society based on solidarity'. Although similar to NF, it went beyond NF in both its criticism and its organisational plans. 'The subjugation of the state to the Politburo with its institutionalised patronage of offices must be ended.' It called for an election law which guaranteed freedom to vote and secret ballot. 'It must be possible to decide between different political programmes and their representatives.' It proposed the invitation of UN observers to the next Volkskammer elections. DJ demanded independent, non-commercial media, independent schools and universities, scientific institutions, parties, organisations and trade unions. It called for an end to the 'command economy' and its replacement by loose framework planning. It approved the establishment of private co-operatives and private firms provided there was appropriate co-determination (*Mitbestimmung*) for their employees. DJ wanted an inaugural conference in January or February 1990 to set up an organisation which would put up its own candidates for the Volkskammer.[2] Its key spokespersons were Dr Wolfgang Ullmann (60), a Protestant church historian, Ulrike Poppe (37), a history lecturer with a background of dissidence, and Konrad Weiss (47), a documentary film director and active Catholic, all based in Berlin. Weiss claimed he and his colleagues wanted to 'save the Utopia of Socialism . . . although we believe that the concept of Socialism has been so discredited by forty years of GDR practice that one can only use it with reserve and very cautiously if one wishes to have any impact'.[3] He was critical of West Germany, 'For me the Federal Republic of Germany is no example. There is much in the Federal Republic, which has grown in the last forty years, that is worthy of recognition, that is exciting, but there is much which I do not like.'[4]

Social democracy re-appears

Because of the social democratic traditions of the area in towns like Berlin, Leipzig, Erfurt, Gotha, Magdeburg and Chemnitz, the SED had always feared the re-emergence of a social democratic opposition. For years after the war, the SPD had organised an underground assisted by the *Ostbüro* in Bonn. Any such group, it was thought, would benefit from local traditions and identification with such West German figures as Brandt and Schmidt, who were undoubtedly popular in the GDR. On 26 August a group calling itself the Initiative Group 'Social Democratic Party in the GDR' issued a declaration. It proclaimed, 'Things cannot continue like this. Many are waiting for a change but that is no longer enough!' It argued that the necessary democratisation of the GDR required a challenge to the claim to power of the ruling party, the SED. It wanted an ecologically orientated social democracy. It looked forward to the establishment of a Social Democratic Party. The official founding of the Social Democratic Party in the GDR (SDP) took place on 7 October 1989 in the parsonage in Schwante, near Berlin. At that stage the SDP was not aiming at German unity. On the contrary, Ibrahim Böhme, and his co-signatory, Markus Meckel, emphasised in interviews that they wanted a democratic GDR. Meckel said, 'We do not want to be simply integrated into the other German state. . . . We want something like Socialism . . . a second functioning capitalist German state at the side of the Federal Republic would be senseless.'[5] Both Meckel and Böhme claimed to identify more with Swedish social democracy rather than the West German SPD. Meckel appeared more left-wing than Böhme but Böhme still called himself a Marxist. Both stressed that they had received no help or encouragement from the SPD in Bonn. The signatories to the appeal were Martin Gutzeit, Arndt Noack, Markus Meckel and Ibrahim Böhme. Gutzeit (37) and Meckel (37) were the sons of pastors who had followed their fathers into the Evangelical Church. Böhme (44) was from very different circumstances.

It is not certain where Böhme was born on 18 November 1944. Some accounts say it was in the Soviet Union, others Mexico, yet others in southern France. His father is said to have been a Jewish lawyer who left Germany in 1938 for Czechoslovakia. His mother apparently died when Böhme was 5. He was brought up, near Leipzig, in the family of the SED functionary Kurt Böhme, a brother of the later GDR Minister of Higher Education, Hans-Joachim Böhme. Böhme joined the SED's youth movement, FDJ, and left school at 16 to take up an apprenticeship as a bricklayer at the Leuna-Werk. He gained his university matriculation certificate at night school and went on to enrol as a trainee teacher of German, Russian and history. In 1963 he was employed in this capacity at the apprentices' hostel of the Leuna-Werk. In 1965 he was briefly arrested because of his support for the SED dissident scientist Professor Robert Havemann. His studies were disrupted and he took up work as a youth club leader in Greiz. He was briefly arrested a second time in 1968 because of his opposition to the Warsaw Pact invasion of Czechoslovakia. Somehow he managed to complete his studies and was appointed secretary of the official League of Culture in Greiz. He was soon in trouble again, earning an official warning for supporting a concert by dissident musician Jürgen Fuchs, in Greiz. In 1976 Böhme left the SED, which he had joined in 1967. He was jailed, in 1977/78, for 15 months for 'anti-state agitation'. He was fired from his next job, at the Friedrich-Wolf-Theater in Neustrelitz, in 1981, for expressing support for Polish Solidarity. The next few years Böhme spent doing odd jobs, mainly for the churches, and it was during this time that he got to know Meckel, Gutzeit and other social democratically inclined churchmen.[6]

Democratic Awakening

Before September was out there were other calls and petitions from rock musicians, members of the Berliner Ensemble theatre and trade unionists.

In some ways the most remarkable deviation from the old SED line was the contribution by Dr Manfred Gerlach, Chairman of the LDPD and Deputy Chairman of the GDR's Council of State, published in his party's paper *Der Morgen* (30 September 1989). Gerlach had led his party as a satellite of the SED and was seen as its loyal creature. He admitted that the official presentation of the GDR in the media was a long way from the reality of the GDR and he criticised the tendency to marginalise loyal citizens who wanted to take part in the shaping of socialism. It is still not clear how Gerlach came to make these remarks. On 24 October his party demanded the right to travel in the West for all GDR citizens and free elections.

An attempt to found Democratic Awakening (DA) in Berlin was prevented by the Stasi on 1 October after 70 delegates had arrived from all parts of the GDR. The party was provisionally founded instead on 30 October. Its leading members were Wolfgang Schnur (40), a Rostock lawyer, Brigitta Kögler, a Jena lawyer, Rainer Eppelmann (46), a Berlin parson, and Erhard Neubert (49), a former CDU member, sociologist and pastor. Although its first messages were similar to those of the Social Democrats, being 'social and ecological', it later threw in its lot with the CDU (see Chapter 10).

Other opposition parties

The Green Party was established on 26 November 1989 by Carlo Jordan, Marianne Dörfer and 148 others. It too was vaguely socialist as well as ecological. Jordan (38), a baker's son, had trained as a building engineer. He had a long record of conflict with the SED and interest in ecological issues. In view of the influence of the West German Greens on the protest movement in the GDR, and in view of the catastrophic environmental situation in the GDR, the question can rightly be posed, 'Why did it take so long to form a green party?' It appears that its late formation was at least partly due to Stasi activities. Jordan had attempted on 5 November to establish *Die Grüne Partei* after a service in the Bekenntniskirche in Treptow, East Berlin. After a long debate his proposal was postponed. A key figure in the debate was Wolfgang Schnur, a Stasi informer, who mobilised the other secret Stasi forces at the meeting. At that time, many demonstrators carried banners demanding environment-friendly policies. By the end of the month, the emphasis was turning from that concern to the question of German unity.[7]

December saw the foundation of yet another party, this time in Leipzig, the Christian Social Party of Germany (CSPD). On 20 January 1990, with assistance from the Bavarian CSU, it merged with other parties such as the Progressive People's Party and the German Peace Union to become the

German Social Union (DSU).[8] Dr Peter-Michael Diestel (37) was a leading light in both and was elected DSU General Secretary. The son of an officer, Diestel had originally trained as a swimming instructor, but after qualifying as a lawyer he worked in the agricultural sector. The chairman of the DSU was Hans-Wilhelm Ebeling (55), a graduate engineer who went on to become pastor of the Thomaskirche in Leipzig. He had helped to set up the CSPD. Another well-known figure was Professor Joachim Nowack, a Leipzig physicist.

Except for the DSU the new parties of the GDR all seemed to be vaguely ecological and vaguely social democratic. Abolition of the GDR did not seem to be part of their aims. Most of their leaders were under 50 and were still the prisoners of their indoctrination in the institutions of the GDR. It was difficult for them to envisage a world without the GDR. To a degree, they were being influenced by Stasi informers within their ranks. We are never likely to know just how many of them there were still active during *Die Wende*. However, the head of the Stasi in Dresden, Horst Böhm, wrote in an internal paper on 30 November 1989 that he had 80 to 100 informers, some in leading positions, in the new groups and parties.[9] The amount of damage they could do at this stage was probably very limited. The SED and the Stasi were themselves in the process of disintegration and were being overtaken by events.

Notes

1. Charles Schüdderkopf (ed.) '*Wir sind das Volk!*': *Flugschristen, Aufrufe und Texte einer deutschen Revolution*, Reinbeh bei Hamburg, 1990, pp. 29–31.
2. *Ibid.*, pp. 32–8.
3. Gerhard Rein (ed.), *Die Opposition in der DDR*, Berlin, 1989, p. 70.
4. *Ibid.*, p. 71.
5. *Ibid.*, p. 95.
6. *Frankfurter Allgemeine Zeitung*, 23 November 1999; *Leipziger Volkszeitung*, 23 November 1999.
7. *Der Spiegel*, 1 November 1999, p. 102.
8. Peter Weilemann *et al.*, Parteien im Aufbruch: Nichthommunistische Parteien und Politische Vereinigungen in der DDR, St Augustin, 1990, p. 33.
9. Stefan Wolle, *Die heile Welt der Diktatur: Alltag und Herrschafh in der DDR 1971–1989*, Berlin, 1998, pp. 339–40.

Chapter 7

The fifty days of Egon Krenz

The over 200 members of the Central Committee of the SED must have been a little surprised, even apprehensive, and perhaps relieved, to get two invitations to attend a meeting of the ZK within days of each other. The first was dated 13 October and gave as the agenda preparations for the next, XII, party congress in 1990, the usual Politburo report and the strategy of the SED in the 1990s. The second invitation gave as the agenda simply 'the political situation'.[1] Both letters bore Honecker's signature. Depending on their temperaments, knowledge and personalities, some would have been relieved by the first invitation, which seemed to indicate that the leaders had everything under control. Others would have found it frightening, as it seemed to indicate that Honecker and the others were totally out of touch with the unfolding drama in the GDR. The second letter could only mean change, but what change?

'Stony-faced' Honecker replaced by Krenz

With demonstrations now taking place daily, Honecker was forced to resign by a unanimous vote of his colleagues on 17 October 1989. The crucial meeting opened normally with Honecker, as usual, in the chair asking for any additions to the routine agenda. Willi Stoph then made his dramatic move and proposed adding as first item on the agenda Honecker's removal and the election of Krenz as General Secretary. According to one eyewitness, Honecker took it calmly and opened the discussion.[2] Another of his colleagues present said he was stony-faced.[3] He was attacked by his erstwhile intimates Mittag and Mielke.[4] The following day he formally asked the ZK to release him from his positions on health grounds. This was plausible because he had just undergone an operation and was now 77 years old. One of those present voted against this move.[5] The move against Honecker had been planned by Krenz and Schabowski, who had consulted with others, including Stoph and Hager.[6] Ten to eleven members were involved in the plot.[7] Schabowski had also consulted the Soviet Ambassador about the situation but apparently he made no comment.[8] Honecker did not go alone. His comrades Mittag and Joachim Hermann also lost their places in the Politburo. Mittag was blamed for the precarious state of the economy. Hermann was held responsible for the failure of the GDR media to give a truthful picture of the problems of the GDR and present convincing SED arguments. Mielke did not go. It had been necessary to involve him in the plot to oust Honecker and, for the time being, he remained a powerful figure controlling a vast security apparatus.

Egon Krenz, aged 52, seen for many years as the crown prince, succeeded him. Much more than for Honecker, for Krenz the GDR was really his *Heimat*. He had been born in Kolberg, which, after the war, was taken over by Poland. He had very little experience outside the Soviet bloc. He lacked imagination at a time when it was desperately needed by the SED. When asked on television immediately after his election what he had to say, he could only reply, 'As I told our Central Committee, I am conscious that I have taken on a difficult task in a very complicated time and it means a lot of work and more work...'[9] The fact that he was seen as Honecker's crown prince was a disadvantage. Moreover, Krenz had been chairman of the election commission, which had presided over the falsification of the local election in May.[10] For ten years he had been the Central Committee secretary in charge of security – that too made people suspicious. Worse still, Krenz made the mistake of taking on all Honecker's positions as head of the SED, the Defence Council and head of state. On 24 October some members of the Volkskammer voted against this last appointment. Finally, as we have seen, Krenz was, rightly or wrongly, identified with repression in China. He did, however, introduce a small measure of unilateral GDR disarmament and re-opened the frontier to Czechoslovakia from 1 November. Once again thousands used this route to leave for West Germany. This was meant as a temporary measure until a new liberal travel law could be introduced.

1 November: Gorbachev's 'Judas kiss'

The Politburo was confronted on 31 October with an analysis by Gerhard Schürer, Politburo member responsible for planning, and Gerhard Beil, Minister for Foreign Trade, that the GDR was virtually bankrupt. For the GDR to begin to pay its way would need a fall in the standard of living of 25–30 per cent. They estimated that productivity in the GDR was 40 per cent lower than that of the Federal Republic.[11] This was clearly politically unacceptable. Gorbachev could offer no material help, as he told Krenz when the new GDR leader visited him on 1 November. During that trip Krenz was warned by high-level contacts that the Soviet Union's economic situation was worse than at any time since the October Revolution of 1917; it was therefore seeking rich friends, and in no position to subsidise its allies. The GDR's future was in jeopardy. Krenz left Moscow believing the SED could expect neither military nor economic help from Moscow. Those in his entourage interpreted the traditional kiss of greeting he had received from Gorbachev as the 'Judas kiss'.[12]

4 November: Alexanderplatz

An estimated one million people attended a demonstration co-ordinated by Henning Schaller of the Maxim-Gorki Theatre in East Berlin's main square, Alexanderplatz, on 4 November. The demonstrators, who had come from all over the GDR, carried a wide variety of banners. Among the slogans were: 'Freedom, equality, sincerity'; 'One lie kills a hundred truths'; 'Privileges for all'; 'Legal security is the best state security'; 'Don't give hatred of foreigners any chance'; 'Regression is progression'; 'For hard work, hard currency'; 'Cut down the functionaries not the trees'. There were also calls to make the Volkskammer a real parliament, and the popular slogan 'We are the people' was also to be seen. Among the crowd were countless well-known personalities, including writers Christoph Hein, Stefan Heym and Christa Wolf, Jen Reich of New Forum, Gregor Gysi, the bright SED loyalist and lawyer. Liberal Democrat Manfred Gerlach hit the right note when he called for the government to resign. Markus Wolf, until 1986 deputy Minister for State Security, was booed when he attempted to say that not all Stasi officials were criminals. Wolf had apparently seen a key role for himself in a reformed GDR. One of 27 speakers, he was forced to realise this was not to be and went away shocked and shaken.[13] The demonstration was broadcast live by GDR television – in itself a daring move. The Politburo feared the demonstrators would force a way through the Wall.[14] Günter Schabowski also turned up to brave the catcalls of the assembled crowd.

The demonstration is seen as another milestone in the downfall of the SED. It could have gone badly wrong but it all passed off remarkably peacefully. Meanwhile demonstrations continued in other towns and cities such as Altenburg, Dresden, Halle, Lauscha, Leipzig, Plauen, Potsdam, Rostock, Schwerin and many other towns. It appeared increasingly that no self-respecting town could not have a demonstration by this time. Free elections, press freedom, the resignation of the government and unrestricted travel were high on the agenda.

8 November: The Politburo resigns

Within the SED the calls for change became ever greater. This was spurred on by revelations in the GDR media about the privileges of the top party brass and their cronies. It started with the revelation in the *Berliner Zeitung* of the new home being built for Gerhard Nennstiel, Chairman of the trade union IG Metall. Workers from the Berlin underground railway using materials imported from West Germany were constructing the house. Nennstiel was forced to resign the same day, 1 November. It never occurred to most ordinary members of the SED that in the basement of the Central Committee headquarters in Berlin there was a store were the comrade functionaries could buy Western imports and other luxuries with GDR marks. This was true of all the mass organisations as well. Also revealed were the holiday homes on the Baltic Sea Island of Vilm, a place out of bounds for ordinary East Germans. Then there were the holidays in West for the chosen few and their friends. Many ordinary members became disillusioned: some stayed passively watching the unfolding drama; some turned to drink as they thought of the time and money they had wasted on the SED; others left the party and/or their trade union. No doubt some of these saw themselves as victims of political fraudsters. No doubt others had joined the SED to gain advantage and now realised its days were numbered. If the official figures are correct, in 1989, up to 8 November, 66,000 had left the SED, while only 36,000 had taken up membership. By the end of November 200,000 had returned their party documents.[15] As the old guard became more defensive under the impact of these exposures, those who wanted a Gorbachev-style change got bolder. Some really believed a new beginning was possible. A wave of resignations started. The first 'big fish' to go was Harry Tisch, Chairman of the trade union federation. He resigned under pressure on 2 November after he was told that a 'workers' revolt' was likely if he did not. Tisch was expelled from the union on 29 November and arrested on 3 December. Other less important resigners on 2 November were Gerald Götting, Chairman of the CDU, Heinrich Homann, Chairman of the NDPD, and Margot Honecker, Minister for People's Education. Götting and Homann were both expelled from the parties they had led and investigated for corruption.

On 8 November about 15,000 pro-reform SED members congregated in front of the ZK headquarters demanding changes at the top and policy changes. Dieter Klein, Michael and André Brie, Gregor Gysi and Markus Wolf had done their best to mobilise these members. Honecker later reflected that it appeared that a group of GDR Gorbachev-supporters with Stasi connections were attempting to decapitate the SED leadership.[16] The result of the demonstration was that the entire Politburo was forced to resign and the Central Committee elected a new one. Krenz retained his position. Including Krenz it consisted of 11 full and 6 candidate members. The leadership had taken another small step in the direction of renewal. With Krenz, 7 full members held on to their positions. General Heinz Keßler, Minister of Defence, Siegfried Lorenz and Werner Eberlein, all promoted by Honecker, were re-elected. Gerhard Schürer, who had been a candidate member since 1973, was retained, as was Werner Jarowinsky. The two long-serving women candidates were re-elected: Inge Lange (candidate since 1973) and Margarete Müller (candidate since 1963). Perhaps it was thought the SED leadership badly needed token women members and no others were on hand. Perhaps these women were regarded as harmless. The two most significant figures elected turned out to be Hans Modrow, a new member and long-serving SED First Secretary in Dresden, and Günter Schabowski, a full member since 1984 and SED Berlin First Secretary.

9 November: The Wall opened

Krenz had been discussing a new travel law since he took over but no one expected the events of 9 November. On that fateful night came the sensational opening of the Berlin Wall and the other frontiers of the GDR to the West. How did this come about? At 09.00 on 9 November two colonels from the MfS and from the Ministry of Interior met to discuss the proposed travel law. They were under orders to frame suitable regulations as quickly as possible so that they could be implemented the following day. Under their proposals, an East German citizen would have been able to visit the Federal Republic for a few days or permanently without having to justify the move. They would still need a passport and an exit visa. Unlike in the past, in most cases, the visa would be issued on a routine basis. Passport applications would take four to six weeks. These new arrangements were meant to be made public on the following day at 04.00. Stoph, as head of government, read out the new regulations to the ZK on the afternoon of 9 November. Schabowski was not present.[17] All those who needed to know in the SED and the appropriate ministries were given this information. However, Krenz made the mistake of asking Schabowski, as member of the Politburo now responsible for media relations, to give the news at a press conference following the ZK meeting on 9 November at 18.00. Apparently without discussing the issue, he simply gave him a piece of paper to read out.[18]

It was a minor sensation for the GDR viewers that a member of the Politburo was to hold a press conference to be broadcast live. This was a first for the GDR. Most of the conference was, as expected, devoted to the leadership changes in the SED. At the end of the conference, at about 19.00, a rather tired Schabowski dealt with the travel issue in a rather confused reply to an Italian journalist, Riccardo Ehrman. He said the SED leaders wanted to liberate the people from a situation of psychological pressure by legalising and simplifying migration (*Ausreise*).[19] Until the Volkskammer passed a new travel law there would be interim regulations which would enable all East Germans who wanted to leave the GDR to do so. When pressed as to when these regulations would come into force, he replied 'immediately', and 'without delay'.[20] He meant those who wanted to migrate, turn their backs on the GDR, not tourists. But it made no sense and was simply interpreted by the media. Schabowski repeated the same meaning immediately afterwards in an interview, in English, with the American television station NBC. He told Tom Brokaw that citizens of the GDR 'are not further forced to leave GDR by transit through another country'. Was this freedom to travel asked Brokaw? 'Yes. Of course. It is no question of tourism. It is a permission of leaving GDR.'[21]

There was confusion about the actual situation after the press conference. That evening the BBC World Service reported in its *Newshour* programme, the mounting tension between the USA and Panama over the Canal, the shooting by Israeli troops of a member of an extremist Palestinian group, and the announcement in Beijing of the retirement of veteran leader, Deng Xiaoping, from the Military Commission, his last post. Its main item of news was of course Schabowski's press conference. But when the programme started there was no indication of the dramatic events to follow. David Shuckman, reporting directly in front of the Brandenburg Gate, on the Western side, still thought that it would not be until the following day that East Berliners could apply for a visa to travel. Mike Hamburger of New Forum, in the same programme, commented that he had been 'flabbergasted' by the news, but pointed out that to leave permanently you just needed to go to a police station with your identity card to get an exist visa. To go on a visit, however, you needed a passport, which many East Germans did not have, 'You can't just walk across the border, but it's very easy to travel now.' Also in the programme, the present author thought the new regulations were 'too little too late' to satisfy the people. All were overtaken by the actual events. Thomas Kielinger, editor of the *Rheinischer Merkur*, speaking from Bonn, told the BBC's listeners that the first East Berliners had gone to the local police station, got visas, crossed the frontier and returned to East Berlin. They just wanted to test the situation. In the Bundestag in Bonn there was thunderous applause at the news. In West Berlin, Walter Momper, the Governing Mayor, was said to be 'stunned' by the announcement, but managed to say, 'This is an historic hour.' The BBC also reported that there were already fears in West Berlin about jobs and housing if East Germans took advantage of the easing of travel restrictions. Friedrich Bohl, the floor leader of the Christian Democrats in the Bundestag, told the BBC that he hoped West Germans would be clear about the duty to help the East Germans. He also hoped that the citizens of the GDR would ask themselves whether it was now absolutely necessary to leave. Nevertheless, all the people who came would be certain of help. Hamburger thought, 'I'm afraid that this rush to leave the country in the last few days has been getting rather irrational. It seems to be getting a bit of a hysterical touch.' The Soviet news agency Tass meanwhile reported the events without commentary.[22]

Those East Germans who watched GDR television news at 19.30 thought they only needed to show their identity cards, get them stamped and travel.[23] Confusion reigned in the Ministry of Interior and Ministry for State Security. Veteran Deputy Minister for State Security General Dr Gerhard Neiber called for the crowds to be kept back from reaching the Berlin 'frontier' crossing points, advice that, had it been needed, would likely have resulted in violence.[24] Failing higher orders, and afraid for their own safety, commanders at border crossings in Berlin simply gave in to the pressure from the awaiting crowds.[25] Many thousands crossed the frontier that very night. During the evening, as this was going on, GDR television gave confusing information that before anyone could travel they needed to request an exit visa at the local police station during office hours and get travel authorised.[26] The gathering masses at the various Berlin crossing points got increasing restless and started to shout, 'Open the gate, open the gate.' Already, before midnight, the police and frontier guards had to give up all attempts to control the crowds. Not open was the Wall in front of the famous Brandenburg Gate, but there East German crowds broke through the light barriers and went through the Gate to the Wall in front of it. Some climbed the Wall into the West. West Berliners climbed over into the East. A few minutes after midnight all the crossing points between East and West Berlin were open.[27] There was a night of informal festivities throughout Berlin. One eye-witness reported seeing East Berliners crossing in their night-clothes and bedroom slippers.[28] The frontier crossing points to West Germany were opened at 01.00. There it was the same story as thousands of East German motorists crossed in their shabby little Trabant cars to the West. The world held its breath in amazement.

On the following day, 10 November, people with pickaxes began to take chunks out of the Wall on the Western sides. No one intervened to stop them. On the first weekend over 800,000 East Germans crossed into West Berlin.[29] They were warmly welcomed, often receiving free soup, hamburgers, chocolate, fruit and Sekt. One eye-witness observed Westerners handing out money to complete strangers and guiding them around the city.[30] The West Berlin Senate provided free street maps and free public transport. There was also free beer, free souvenirs, free football matches and even free accommodation. Those from the GDR were able to get 100 marks 'welcome money' courtesy of the Federal Republic. Those wishing to change their GDR marks for German marks had to do so at private banks at a rate of 10 to 1. Many were prepared to spend their hard-earned savings in this way. Within the first four days 4.3 million people – a quarter of the GDR population – had crossed the frontier. At a rally in front of the West Berlin City Hall, Mayor Momper admitted that,

> some people here in our part of the city are afraid of the rapid changes, and they fear the problems and burdens that we will have to face. I beseech all Berliners to remember always the happy hours of this day, and I beseech all of us to ever be mindful of the grief that the Wall has symbolised for us.

He asked East Germans who were considering leaving to think about whether they could not now have more faith in the renewal process in the GDR. West Berliners supported the reform movement in the GDR, the call for free elections and free travel. Momper saw Modrow's nomination as new head of government as a sign that the SED was ready for a new beginning. However, 'The SED must give up its claim to leadership because, in all reality, it lost that claim a long time ago.'[31]

The SED had hoped to stabilise the situation by opening its frontiers; in fact it had lost control. Through the increased migration and absenteeism the pressure on the economy and services increased. Moreover, for hundreds of thousands of East Germans their joy at being able at last to travel soon turned to anger. Many found the prosperity in the West was even greater than they had gleaned from watching Western television. They felt they had been cheated by the SED rulers, even denied a life.

In an effort to stabilise the situation, a new government headed by reform Communist Hans Modrow was formed on 18 November. Less than two weeks later the Volkskammer struck the 'leading role' of the SED off the GDR constitution. As Krenz himself rationalised the situation, it was easy enough to have the leading role written into a constitution, but that did not mean people had been convinced. For that a great deal of political work was needed to earn the right to lead. Despite his brave words, he was unable to stabilise the situation even within his own party. The lower ranks of the SED demanded an extraordinary party congress to decide the future direction of the SED. After opposing it, offering a lesser conference instead, the Politburo accepted a congress putting this to a hastily recalled Central Committee. Having agreed the congress, the Central Committee was devastated to learn that the GDR was as good as bankrupt. They heard from Günter Ehrensperger, Schürer and Jarowinsky that this was so, and they were the three in their ranks most likely to know.[32] Weary and angry, the Central Committee members felt the old Honecker Politburo had betrayed them and that they had allowed this to happen. In theory the Politburo was the servant of the Central Committee. In practice this had never been so.

Over the weeks of November the SED grassroots members had been asserting themselves, for the first time in the history of their party. All the first secretaries of the 15 *Bezirke* had been forced out of office and replaced by reform-minded comrades. They had contacted Krenz and urged the Central Committee and Politburo to go to save the party. Another meeting of the Central Committee was called for 3 December. The members of the ZK had to do two things: expel Honecker, Krolikowski, Mielke, Sindermann, Stoph and Tisch and six of their colleagues from the SED; and resign themselves from the ZK. In a separate action on the same day, the state prosecutor's office ordered the immediate arrest of Günter Mittag, Harry Tisch, formerly Chairman of the GDR trades union federation (FDGB), and other top officials for misusing their functions and damaging the GDR economy. Honecker and fellow former Politburo member Hermann Axen avoided arrest because of the state of their health. These were Krenz's last acts as SED leader. Krenz surrendered his posts as head of state and head of the Defence Council on 6 December. The SED continued to lose members. In the first half of December membership was estimated at 1.7 million. This meant it had lost about 600,000 since the dramatic changes began.[33] Could the party be saved by Modrow, who had attempted to distance himself from Krenz and the old Politburo members?

Despite Krenz's limitations, much had been achieved without violence by the East masses and very little violence from the side of the SED regime. Why was this so? Krenz certainly deserves some of the credit. It was against his inclinations to use force. In any case, the SED leaders knew that without Soviet military help they could not hold their people in check. The GDR military feared for their own lives if they used force, as they knew they would ultimately lose. The SED and MfS had prepared to defend their regime against armed opponents. They were at a loss to know how to deal with unarmed peaceful demonstrators. As for the forces around New Forum, they had learned to protest from the West German Greens and anti-nuclear Christians.

Notes

1. Egon Krenz, *Wenn Mauern fallen*, Vienna, 1990, p. 11.
2. *Ibid.*, p. 144.
3. Schabowski, p. 105.
4. *Ibid.*
5. Krenz, p. 19.
6. Schabowski, p. 100.
7. *Ibid.*, p. 100.
8. *Ibid.*, p. 101.
9. Spiegel TV video.
10. For Krenz's version see, pp. 125–6.
11. Hans-Hermann Hertle, *Der Fall der Mauer*, Opladen, 1996, p. 145.
12. *Der Spiegel*, 1 November 1999.
13. Wolf (1998), p. 443; Ralf Reuth and Andreas Bönte, *Das Komplott: Wie es wirklich zur deutschen Einheit kam*, Munich, 1995, p. 149; *Der Spiegel*, 1 November 1999,

pp. 98–100. Alexander Reichenbach (*Chef der Spione: Die Markus-Wolf-Story*, Stuttgart, 1998, pp. 199–200) has Wolf shocked and shaken. There are conflicting estimates of how many attended the demonstration. Reichenbach claims 'over 500,000'. Hannes Bahrmann and Christoph Links (*Chronik der Wende: Die Ereignisse in der DDR zwischen 7. October 1989 und 18. März 1990*, Berlin, 1999, p. 61) write that later official estimates put the figure at nearly a million.

14. Hertle, *Der Fall der Mauer*, p. 104.
15. Heinrich Bortfeldt, *Von der SED zur PDS: Wandlung zur Demokratie?*, Berlin, 1991, p. 104.
16. Erich Honecker, *Moabiter Notizen*, Berlin, 1994, p. 35.
17. Hertle, *Der Fall der Mauer*, p. 167.
18. *Ibid.*, p. 168.
19. *Ibid.*, p. 170.
20. *Ibid.*, p. 171.
21. *Ibid.*, p. 173.
22. This paragraph is based on the recording of the BBC broadcast in the author's archive.
23. Hertle, *Der Fall der Mauer*, p. 177.
24. *Ibid.*
25. *Ibid.*, p. 230.
26. *Ibid.*, p. 187.
27. *Ibid.*, p. 188.
28. Alexandra Richie, *Faust's Metropolis: A History of Berlin*, London, 1998, p. 835.
29. *Ibid.*, p. 837.
30. *Ibid.*
31. Harold James and Marla Stone (eds), *When the Wall Came Down: Reactions to German Unification*, New York, 1992, p. 47.
32. Bortfeldt, *Von der SED zur PDS*, pp. 111–12.
33. *Ibid.*, p. 125.

Chapter 8

International reactions to events in the GDR

Thatcher: 'rather apprehensive'

In September 1989, Margaret Thatcher, who enjoyed a large following around the world as Britain's first woman Prime Minister, as a champion of freedom in the Soviet bloc, and as a protagonist of the free market economy, called on Gorbachev in Moscow. She was on her way home from Tokyo. According to her own testimony, 'I explained to him that although NATO had traditionally made statements supporting Germany's aspiration to be reunited, in practice we were rather apprehensive.' She told the Soviet leader that François Mitterrand shared her apprehensions. Gorbachev, according to Thatcher, confirmed that the Soviet Union did not want German re-unification either. She went on, 'This reinforced me in my resolve to slow up the already heady pace of developments.' She did not want the East Germans to live under Communism. But she wanted a truly democratic East German state to emerge before the question of the future of Germany was put on the agenda.[1]

By the end of the month, on a visit to Nottingham University, she felt able to praise the achievements of West Germany. However, she did not want 'the German Question' raised. For her there was no German Question.[2] This remained her position, but pressure of events meant there was little she could do to oppose it. By November, Thatcher thought she was in danger of being outmanoeuvred in the European community by a 'Franco-German Axis'. Kohl had telephoned her on 10 November just after the Wall was opened. 'He was clearly buoyed up by the scenes he had witnessed: what German would not have been?'[3]

Many members of the British foreign policy élite looked more favourably on the Germans than did Mrs Thatcher. However, there was a widespread feeling that most Germans in West and East were not really after the unification of their two states. As Professor William Wallace wrote in *The Independent* (14 June 1989),

> Most West Germans would like closer and more open relations with their Eastern neighbours, fewer troops on their territory . . . but what they are motivated by is the desire for a peaceful life, not for overcoming the present order in Europe, with all the risks and costs which that would entail.

An expert of the older generation, Hugh Trevor-Roper, communicated his doubts about the practicalities of any future German reunification in *The Independent Magazine* (17 June 1989). He asked,

> How then would reunification begin? An alliance? A federation? A coalition? Have such experiments between capitalist and communist states or parties ever worked? History provides no trustworthy precedent.

Kohl's ten points

Thatcher had not expected the proposals in Kohl's Bundestag speech of 28 November, in which he outlined a ten-point plan for a confederation of the two German states. In the circumstances, this could be seen as a very moderate speech, rather than as the international sensation which many, including Thatcher, saw it as.[4] Kohl did not seem to be laying out a schedule for the immediate restoration of German unity. Rather, in points one to four, he offered financial and political support for reform in the GDR, if the new leaders, Modrow and Krenz, were genuine about their readiness to introduce democracy and market reforms. Points six to nine dealt with the European context. Kohl declared that, 'The development of inter-German relations remains embedded in the common European process. . . .' Kohl's final point contained his reference to German unity, which remained the aim of the Federal Government. He did not set down any timetable; on the contrary, he saw this as raising a question which could not be answered. He recognised that it could only be achieved within the context of European security. Overcoming the division of Germany and of Europe were two parts of the same task. It was point five which contained the explosive phrase 'konföderative Strukturen' ('confederational structures'). 'We are also ready to take a more decisive step, that is, to develop confederational structures between both states in Germany with the aim of creating, in Germany, a federation, that is, a federal state order. But that presupposes a legitimate, democratic government in the GDR.'[5]

The fact is that most, even better informed, people did not realise the immense pressure Kohl and his colleagues were under. In West Germany itself, the far right so-called Republicans had made progress with their anti-immigrant rhetoric, and German re-unification was high on their list of campaigning slogans. Kohl was also under some pressure from the Bavarian CSU. He faced elections in 1990 and could not appear to be doing nothing to ameliorate the East German crisis. In November 133,000 East Germans presented themselves as refugees in West Germany. They were taking no chances of a reversal to the old situation. After all, the SED was still at the heart of power backed by a massive military and security apparatus. Behind them stood the Soviet armed forces in Germany if they chose to intervene. On a yearly basis the November refugees represented a rate of loss for the GDR of a tenth of the population.[6] East German society would soon collapse at this rate and West Germany would face great problems in attempting to deal with the sudden influx. The SED itself was bleeding to death, having been reduced from 2.3 million members before the crisis started in the summer to around 600,000. Kohl needed, with his speech, to give hope to ordinary East Germans. On 17 November demonstrators in Leipzig had dispensed with the GDR flag and displayed the simple black–red–gold tricolour, which was the flag of democratic Weimar Germany, the original GDR flag and the flag of the Federal Republic. They chanted, 'Germany, united Fatherland'. The words were from the original GDR national anthem of 1949. Honecker had in effect banned the words of the anthem in the early 1970s. The demonstrators' desires and sympathies could not have been clearer.[7] At the same time, Kohl, with his speech, had to assuage the possible fears of Germany's neighbours and ex-enemies. His Foreign Minister, Hans-Dietrich Genscher, had been putting more emphasis on this than on the question of German unity. In an interview with the French newspaper *Le Figaro* (2 November 1989) shortly before the opening of the GDR's frontiers, he had emphasised the issue of European *rapprochement*. He also went on record emphasising the right of the GDR's citizens to determine their own place on the continent by freely expressing their own opinions in their own state. Genscher, himself a refugee from the GDR, rightly did not want to be seen as railroading the East Germans into unity. They had to be convinced they wanted it themselves.

Poland: 'The wheel of history will not be turned back'

The neighbour that more than any other needed re-assurance was Poland. The older generations of Poles still remembered the horrors of the war, first the German and then, slightly later, the Soviet invasion, and the final 'liberation' by the Soviets in 1944. They remembered also the evils of the Nazi occupation. In their attempts to gain a modicum of popularity, successive Communist leaders, since 1945, had played on fears of German revanchism. Millions of Poles had been settled, some of them forcibly, in the former German areas of East Prussia and Silesia, from Danzig (Gdansk), Kolberg (Kolobrzeg), Stettin (Szczecin), Thorn (Torun), Wollin (Wolin) to Allenstein (Olsztyn), Breslau (Wrocław) and Gleiwitz (Gliwice). Millions of Germans had fled or been expelled from these areas, and a German minority still lived there. After years of improvement following Chancellor Willy Brandt's mission to Warsaw in 1970, relations between Poland and West Germany deteriorated in 1980–81. This was the result of the suppression of the free trade unions of Solidarity, led by Lech Wałęsa. German Foreign Minister

Genscher's visit to Warsaw in January 1988, and the Polish Prime Minister's visit to Bonn in January 1989, marked a positive turning point. Speaking at the UN on 24 September 1989 Genscher attempted to re-assure the Polish people of their right to live with secure frontiers, which the Germans 'now or in the future' would not question.

GDR leader Krenz had also visited his Polish neighbours. On 2 November 1989, he met Communist President Jaruzelski, who attempted to re-assure him that Thatcher, Mitterrand and Italy's Giulio Andreotti were against German re-unification. Krenz also met the non-Communist Prime Minister Tadeusz Mazowiecki and other politicians. He left Warsaw with the impression that, whatever their ideological differences, the Poles saw the GDR as a bulwark against any revanchist endeavours from West Germany. No doubt there was truth in this feeling, but many Poles were also coming to the conclusion was the GDR was like a dyke which had been breached perhaps irreparably.[8]

Kohl's visit to Poland on 9 and 14 November 1989 saw the conclusion of 11 agreements and a joint communiqué on the 'firm foundation' of the 1970 Warsaw Treaty. These were based on the underlying policy of continuing German economic help, civilised treatment for the German minority in Poland (which had been deprived of its cultural freedom) and recognition of the Polish–German frontier. This visit was cut short by events in the GDR, which caused Kohl to take flight to Berlin. By this time the Communist era was virtually at an end in Poland. Party boss General Wojciech Jaruzelski had initiated Round Table Talks with Solidarity and the Catholic Church in 1988 which had led to elections in the summer of 1989. As a result of these elections, Mazowiecki became Prime Minister. In November 1989 Jaruzelski was still presiding over the state. The German Bundestag sought to give Poland re-assurance by its resolution of 8 November 1989 when it declared, 'The wheel of history will not be turned back. We want to work with Poland for a better Europe. The inviolability of frontiers is the basis for peaceful living together in Europe.' Nevertheless, the Poles felt aggrieved that in his ten-point plan of 28 November Kohl had found no space to mention the frontier issue. This was, of course, not an accident.

Washington: 'profoundly uneasy with the idea'

Early in 1989, Professor George Kennan, former Director of the US State Department's Policy Planning Staff and former Ambassador to the Soviet Union, set down his thoughts on the German problem for the prestigious American Institute for Contemporary German Studies in Washington, DC. Of the East Germans he wrote,

It would be an exaggeration to say that 40 years of separation from the rest of Germany and subjection to the discipline of a Leninist-communist regime have created in the people of East Germany a new sense of nationality. They remain Germans. Nonetheless, these long years of separation unquestionably have affected them in many ways – in their habits, their outlooks, and their tastes and preferences. In certain respects, to be sure, they envy their West German cousins the conditions in which the latter live; but there are other aspects of West German life that they would not find entirely congenial and where they would prefer to preserve habits, outlooks, and, in some instances, even institutions to which they have grown accustomed. . . . German unification would not be as simple today as it might have been four decades ago.

He did not believe that the demand for unification within Germany was so great as many Western commentators assumed. Its achievement could not be 'a serious immediate aim of West German or NATO policy'. He expected relations between the two German states to improve via 'a long series of practical measures'. As for Berlin and its Wall, he could conceive of its dismantlement in the not-too-distant future without serious consequences for the East German side provided the West did not use this event to humiliate the East German authorities. The only hopeful resolution of the Berlin problem was by 'eventual Europeanization of the city'. Kennan's view was that of a well-informed, enlightened intellectual and diplomat who regarded himself as a realist and was so regarded. Some of his former State Department colleagues thought that his essay was a sensible summing up. Others probably thought he was being a little bit too optimistic. During the months that followed State Department officials were forced to conclude that Kennan had been too cautious and pessimistic.

In August 1989, writing in Bonn, Ann Philips, a Ford Foundation Fellow, who had interviewed many in the SED, SPD and American experts, believed, 'Reunification of the two Germanies "on FRG soil" is not possible and reunification of the two states is not desired. This may prove to be an invaluable, if ironic, trump for the SED. . . . Washington is no more favourably disposed . . . than the Soviet Union, Poland, France, or Great Britain.'[9]

There had been vague talk about German re-unification in Washington before October 1989. By October, however, as *The Wall Street Journal* reported (8 October 1989), State Department officials saw Germany's future as an issue demanding more attention. They apparently thought that German re-unification would not 'happen tomorrow', but 'we may have to respond sooner than we thought'. The United States remained formally pledged to support German re-unification, as long as it occurred democratically. 'But U.S. officials actually are profoundly uneasy with the idea. Only a few weeks ago . . . Secretary of State James Baker was ducking the issue.' He told the Senate Foreign Relations Committee that he preferred to speak of it in terms of normalisation of relations between the two Germanys on the basis of Western values. In other words, even in a Europe where 'Western values' prevail, there still would be two Germanys. Federal German President Richard von Weizsäcker attempted to re-assure Americans by saying that Germany would stay on the solid ground of the NATO alliance and European Community 'to strengthen those partnerships which we have been lucky enough to find after a more-than-terrible past'. *The Wall Street Journal* commented that the arguments had fallen on 'friendly but sceptical ears'. American officials believed that the EC was still largely an economic organisation, years or even decades away from holding the kind of power that could curb nationalist sentiments in its largest member. Moreover, West Germany was already the dominant power in the EC. The paper concluded that the 'German question' was 'a hot potato nobody wants to handle but which will be increasingly hard to avoid'.

This was the situation when Kohl's ten-point bombshell exploded. Although President Bush and his colleagues had not been notified beforehand of Kohl's initiative, they soon concluded they did not want to do anything to harm Kohl. They regarded the Chancellor as their most reliable ally in Bonn. Accordingly, a day after Kohl's speech, Secretary of State James Baker gave a press conference at which he dealt with Kohl's initiative. He laid down four principles concerning German re-unification. Firstly, self-determination had to be realised without pre-determining the end result. That meant that the parties involved should not bind themselves to a specific form of unity and exclude other perspectives. Unity could mean many things – it could mean a single federal state, it could mean a confederation, or it could mean something else. The second principle was that unity should be within the context of continuing German membership of NATO and growing European integration. Thirdly, unity should be achieved by a peaceful, gradual and step-by-step process. Finally, it should be based on the Helsinki Final Act regarding frontiers in Europe.[10] President George Bush reiterated these conditions in his speech to the NATO council on 4 December.

Mitterrand: 'I am not afraid of German re-unification'

For the French, events in the GDR and Eastern Europe came at an inopportune moment. They were engaged in the bicentennial celebrations of the French Revolution of 1789. For three days, 13–16 July, Paris had been transformed into the diplomatic capital of the world, when the celebrations were combined with the G7 meeting of the leaders of the world's top industrial nations,[11] and Mitterrand held forth on human rights.[12] From August on, however, world attention shifted from Paris to East Europe. Since the Franco-West German Treaty of 1963 there had been close co-operation between Federal Germany and France. There was a tacit agreement that German economic power was counterbalanced by French political supremacy. The prospect of German re-unification threatened to shatter this delicate balance. Six days after the opening of the Berlin Wall, Roland Dumas, French Foreign Minister, asserted that German re-unification was 'not an issue of current concern'.[13] By 12 December he admitted that for the first time since the end of the war there was the chance that the self-determination was not just a theoretical right for the German People. However, he emphasised that certain realities could not be ignored. These were the existence of two internationally recognised German states belonging to two different alliances. He also stressed that for France the final character of Poland's Western frontier must be recognised without any reservations.[14]

Mitterrand had made the famous statement, 'I am not afraid of re-unification', and added that the German striving for re-unification was legitimate 'if they want it and if they can get it'. This was on 3 November 1989 at a joint press conference with Kohl at the conclusion of the Franco-German summit.[15] Yet in response to Kohl's November speech, Mitterrand seemed to be heading in the opposite direction of his erstwhile German ally. The French President, like the British Prime Minister, was offended that Kohl had not given him prior intelligence of his ten-point plan. On 6 December he and Gorbachev made public a joint declaration in Kiev which stipulated that any changes to European frontiers would be premature and would have a destabilising effect.[16] The French President also visited Warsaw and East Berlin. In December (20–2) 1989, Mitterrand gave legitimacy to the new, but unelected, East German leader, Hans Modrow, saying he was destined to play a vital role in the construction of Europe. Mitterrand also made an unfortunate appearance on GDR television in which he played up the idea of an East German identity. French trade ministers also conferred with their East German opposite numbers. This was interpreted as France's attempt to ensure that its industry gained contracts in the GDR rather than just leaving this virgin territory to the West Germans.[17] Remarkably, in certain respects, Mitterrand was at odds with French public opinion, which, as surveys revealed, was strongly in favour of German re-unification. Instead Mitterrand pushed for the strengthening of the European Community. In Strasbourg on 9 December, he stressed that 'it would be wise to develop, strengthen and accelerate the structures of the Community before any further steps'.[18]

Gorbachev: 'We had finally crossed the Rubicon'

More important than France or Britain remained the Soviet Union and the United States. Gorbachev was surprised by Kohl's ten points and felt they were not an appropriate answer to the situation. He had a frank 'and rather sharp' exchange of views about them with Genscher in early December on the West German Foreign Minister's visit to Moscow.[19]

A few days earlier on 2–3 December, Presidents Gorbachev and Bush had held talks by turns on the Soviet warship *Slava* and USS *Belknap*. This was their first meeting and many issues were discussed, including, of course, the situation in Germany. At the end of their talks Bush declared that he expected German unity to be the final result of the process now in motion. For his part, Gorbachev insisted that the situation in Germany was the result of the Second World War. The reality was that we had two German states both sovereign and members of the UN. 'History has decided so.' He warned against attempts to speed up the process of change, which would only make it more difficult for many European states. However, he did not condemn the changes in the GDR nor did he deny the right of Germans to self-determination.[20] Gorbachev wrote in his memoirs that, 'The Malta summit convinced me that we had finally crossed the Rubicon. For the first time since the Second World War, the political barometer of East–West relations stopped skipping back and forth to steady on "fair".'[21]

The North Atlantic Council, to which all NATO member states belong, issued a balanced statement after its meeting, in Brussels, on 14–15 December. It stressed that NATO would not seek one-sided advantages from the reform process taking place in East Europe, that it would keep to international agreements, and that it wished that the reform process would, by peaceful and democratic means, be successful. The same was true for the achievement of German unity. It had to be reached by peaceful and democratic means and on the basis of international treaties.[22]

One of the last contributions to the debate over the future of Germany was made by Eduard Shevardnadze on 19 December. He had been Communist Party boss in the Soviet Republic of Georgia, and since taking over as Soviet Foreign Minister in 1985 had gained widespread respect for his efforts to ease Cold War tensions. On this occasion, his speech to the Political Committee of the European Parliament appeared to be putting a damper on hopes for German unity. 'Recently the question of self-determination of both German states has been at the centre of heated discussions. Appeals for the GDR to link up with the Federal Republic have produced worries not only among the political parties and the population of the GDR.' The neighbours of the Federal Republic and the GDR were also worried. And one could understand this, he continued. Clarity was needed on many practical issues. He raised the issue of frontiers, military alliances and foreign troops on German soil, and so on. He also warned about the ghosts of political extremism, which, in his view, were haunting Europe.[23]

As the momentous year of 1989 drew to a close, there appeared to be wide international consensus that no one wanted to disturb the peace of

Europe for the sake of German unity. Most West European leaders welcomed peaceful change in the GDR but were reluctant to see German unity restored. The Soviet Union's leaders continued to express their doubts and fears about it. The Americans, on the other hand, although stressing the need for peaceful change, appeared the least opposed to German unity.

Within the GDR itself the process of decay went hand in hand with the renewal process. During December 1989 and January 1990 the GDR was losing more than 2,250 of its citizens daily. In 1989, 343,854 East Germans had moved West. Over 116,000 had left between 9 November and 31 December. In 1988 just under 40,000 had turned their backs on the GDR.[24] Often it was the younger and better-qualified GDR citizens who were leaving. But they could not be found work, housing, furniture and other assistance immediately. Emergency camps had to be set up for them. Meanwhile thousands of foreigners were seeking asylum in West Germany. In this climate the SPD leader Oskar Lafontaine proposed restrictions on emigration from the GDR.[25] This was quite impractical and would have required West Germany to build some kind of wall between itself and the GDR. It was also a disastrous move undermining the prospects for the new Social Democratic Party in the GDR. To anyone seeing the unfolding events in the GDR in December 1989 it seemed a race against time. Could the East German people be convinced that a better future was theirs, including unity with West Germany? Could reforms be carried through speedily yet orderly enough to avoid a horrific collapse into anarchy? 'Chaos within Germany was imminent. A quick solution was absolutely essential.'[26] Or as Gorbachev later wrote, based on all his sources of information, the GDR 'was on the verge of social chaos and complete political and economic collapse'.[27]

Notes

1. Margaret Thatcher, *The Downing Street Years*, London, 1993, p. 792.
2. In conversation with the author, 29 September 1989.
3. Thatcher, *The Downing Street Years*, p. 793.
4. Karl Kaiser, *Deutschlands Vereinigung: Die internationalen Aspekte*, Bergisch Gladbach, 1991, p. 37.
5. *Ibid.*, pp. 158–68 for text.
6. *Ibid.*, p. 37.
7. The author was in Leipzig later in the month and experienced the demonstration and talked with some of those on the march.
8. Krenz, p. 224. For Jaruzelski's remarks about Thatcher, Mitterrand and Andreotti, see *Der Spiegel*, 1 November 1999.
9. Ann L. Philips, *Seeds of Change in the German Democratic Republic: The SED–SPD Dialogue*, Washington, DC, December 1989, p. 54.
10. Kaiser, *Deutschlands Vereinigung*, p. 169.
11. Alistair Cole, *François Mitterrand*, London, 1997, p. 151.

12. Thatcher, *The Downing Street Years*, p. 754.
13. Cole, *François Mitterrand*, p. 153.
14. Kaiser, *Deutschlands Vereinigung*, p. 175.
15. Renata Fritsch-Bournazel, *Europe and German Unification*, New York/Oxford, 1992, p. 172.
16. Cole, *François Mitterrand*, p. 154.
17. Christa Luft, *Zwischen Wende und Ende Eindrüche: Erlebnisse, Erfahrungen eines Mitglieds der Modrow-Regierung*, Berlin, 1992 and 1999, p. 121.
18. Fritsch-Bournazel, *Europe and German Unification*, p. 174.
19. Gorbachev, *Memoirs*, p. 681.
20. Kaiser, *Deutschlands Vereinigung*, pp. 170–1.
21. Gorbachev, *Memoirs*, p. 666.
22. Kaiser, *Deutschlands Vereinigung*, p. 180.
23. *Ibid.*, pp. 182–3.
24. Bark and Gress, Vol. 2, p. 711.
25. *Ibid.*
26. Immanuel Geiss, *The Question of German Unification, 1806–1996*, London, 1997, p. 106. The author was in the GDR in December 1989 and this was his conclusion also.
27. Gorbachev, *Memoirs*, p. 680.

Chapter 9

Modrow's fight to save the GDR

On 7 November 1989 the GDR's government resigned. It remained in office according to article 50 of the constitution until a new government could take over. The outgoing government of Willi Stoph had been largely the creature of the Politburo led by Honecker. On the following day the SED's Central Committee elected a new Politburo and confirmed Krenz as General Secretary. The Volkskammer only came into session on 13 November. It elected, for the first time, a non-SED member, Günther Maleuda, Chairman of the Democratic Farmers' Party (DBD), as President of the Volkskammer, replacing Horst Sindermann of the SED. Surprisingly, there were five candidates for the Presidency. The Volkskammer broke new ground by holding a secret ballot. Also surprisingly, Maleuda, always a tame SED creature, beat Manfred Gerlach (LDPD), who had spoken up recently in criticism of his SED friends, by 246 votes to 230.

The Volkskammer, meeting for the first time in extraordinary session, also invited Dr Hans Modrow to head a new coalition government. By this time Modrow was quite well known. The Western media had given him publicity as a Gorbachev reformer at a time when he was virtually unknown to the GDR public outside the Dresden *Bezirk*, where he had been SED first secretary since 1973. Aged 61, he was a recently elected member of the Politburo. He presented himself as a modest man who did not seek the trappings of power. He was reported to have lived like the other citizens of his fiefdom in an ordinary block of flats. But he was no great orator like some Western politicians. Western attention had undoubtedly helped his career. A bitter and angry Honecker was later to write that Modrow was a key figure in a plan of Gorbachev, Krenz, Markus Wolf and Harry Tisch to bring about *Die Wende* in the GDR.[1]

Modrow's coalition government

Modrow carried on real negotiations with the erstwhile satellite parties, now with new leaders, under the watchful eye of Krenz,[2] who remained head of state. These led to a five-party government, which was confirmed by the Volkskammer on 18 November. Against previous practice, five members voted against and six abstained. The new government had only 28 ministers as against 44 in the previous administration. It was meant to be streamlined, lean and fit to deal with the not fully understood horrendous problems of the GDR. The previous eight industrial ministries were reduced to three, for example. Eight ministers had served in Stoph's government. Among them was Oskar Fischer, who had been Stoph's Foreign Minister, and Gerhard Schürer, who retained his position as Chairman of the State Planning Commission. Schürer was the longest serving minister, having held his position since 1966! Eleven of the portfolios went to non-SED members. Of these, four were from the LDPD, three were CDU and the NDPD and DBD each got two ministers. No fewer than seven of the non-SED members were, or had been, Stasi informers.[3] Among the ministries to go was the Ministry for State Security. Modrow announced its abolition on 17 November. At the same time, he announced that an Office for National Security would replace it. General Wolfgang Schwanitz headed the new office, and he was included as a minister in the government. This was certainly a mistake. Many people thought this was just a cosmetic change introduced to disguise the reality that the SED intended to go on using the old Stasi cadre to control the GDR. Schwanitz's military rank did not help him, nor did his membership of the SED's Central Committee. More importantly, he had been Deputy Minister for State Security under Mielke from 1986 onwards and was thus totally compromised. Modrow's common sense should have suggested that a civilian not associated with the SED should have been appointed to head this highly sensitive office. The SED also retained the Interior Ministry under General of the People's Police Lothar Arendt. He had been its deputy head since 1984.[4] Professor Christa Luft of the SED was one of three women members of the new government; she was Minister for Economic Questions and one of three Deputy Chairpersons. The other two deputies were Lothar de Maizière (CDU) and Peter Moreth (LDPD). Moreth had been in the Volkskammer since 1986 and was a member of the Council of State. He was a former deputy mayor of Karl-Marx-Stadt and held a doctorate in economics from Leipzig University. Modrow was clearly the most experienced of the four politically. Luft later wrote that, although the ministers had ability and experience, it was doubtful that such a group of long-serving state functionaries could inspire the confidence of the population.[5]

Clearly, the SED was still trying to hold on to power and save what it could. The pressure for change was, however, building up. On 1 December the Volkskammer, still made up entirely of SED-approved members 'elected' at the unfree 'elections' of June 1986, decided to cancel article 1 of the constitution which enshrined the right of the Marxist-Leninist party, the SED, to lead the GDR. This was on the initiative of the Liberal Democratic members. At the same session the Volkskammer apologised to the peoples of Czechoslovakia for the GDR's part in the Warsaw Pact invasion of their country. Five days later, following a demand by the CDU faction of the Volkskammer, Egon Krenz felt obliged to surrender his positions as head of state and Chairman of the National Defence Council. Accordingly, Dr Manfred Gerlach (LDPD) took over under article 69 of the constitution. In his letter of resignation Krenz admitted that his many years in the Council of State and Politburo under Honecker had reduced his credibility in the eyes of many GDR citizens.[6] By this time Krenz was already finished politically.

As we saw above, arrests were the order of the day. Mielke, Stoph and former CDU Chairman Gerald Götting were among those placed under arrest on 8 December. Earlier, on 1 December, the former leader of the DBD, Ernst Goldenbaum, and NDPD leader Heinrich Homann resigned from the Volkskammer. Both had been closely identified with Honecker and the SED. The remaining leaders must have asked themselves, 'Where will it all end? Will I be on the next list of those to be expelled and arrested?'

Demonstrations continue

All of these changes must be seen against a background of continuing mass demonstrations on the streets of many GDR towns and cities. On 4 December, over 150,000 demonstrated in Leipzig. Over 60,000 demonstrators in Karl-Marx-Stadt demanded that the town regain its old name of Chemnitz and that the *Kampfgruppen* should be disbanded. A similar number of demonstrators in Magdeburg demanded the end of the Stasi and the SED. In Dresden, 60,000 demanded an end to the destruction of the Stasi files. About 10,000 demonstrators in Schwerin called for the punishment of corrupt SED officials. Several thousand women in Cottbus wanted changes to family policy and education policy. In Halle, where 20,000 took to the streets, the main theme of the demonstration was environmental protection.[7] There were other demonstrations in East Berlin, Potsdam, Suhl and Frankfurt an der Oder. The day after this (5 December) most of the senior officials of the new Office for National Security resigned. The buildings were taken over by the regular police to prevent the unauthorised removal of documents. It was also announced that the para-military 'Factory Fighting Groups' (*Kampfgruppen*) of the SED were to be disarmed immediately and disbanded. On 6 December the Council of State announced an amnesty aimed mainly at political prisoners. Earlier, on the day that Modrow was asked to form a government, 200,000 participants at the regular Monday demonstration in Leipzig demanded free elections, guaranteed right to travel, renunciation by the SED of its right to lead, and the resignation of corrupt functionaries.[8] The demonstrations in turn were stoked up by the increasing revelations about the luxurious life-style enjoyed by the Politburo members under Honecker, the activities of the now dissolved Stasi and the appalling state of the GDR economy. Obviously, they were also encouraged by the success they were achieving in forcing one concession after another from the SED regime.

Round Table talks

In an effort to prevent the GDR from becoming ungovernable, Modrow attempted to use the Round Table process already functioning in neighbouring states. On 7 December the first of a series of discussions took place between the government and representatives of parties and groups. These included New Forum, the SDP, DA, DJ, the Green Party, the United Left and the Initiative Peace and Human Rights. The old political forces and the new each had 15 votes at the Round Table discussions. This was later increased to 19 as other groups were brought in on both sides. This meant that, initially, the SED had three votes, as did the CDU, LDPD, NDPD and DBD. The theologian Dr Wolfgang Ullmann of Democracy Now (DJ) took the chair. He played a decisive part in holding things together and getting the election process under way.

The Round Table, which met 16 times from December 1989 to March 1990, also started work on a new constitution for the GDR. Similar 'round tables' were set up in many towns, replacing the old SED-dominated local government structures. From the SED's point of view the new arrangement had the advantage of drawing all the opposition groups into the process of government. The leaders of these groups had little or no experience of government and initially lacked all the paraphernalia of government available to normal ministers. The ministers from the four bloc parties also enjoyed the advantages of experience and organisation over the new opposition, although they were being implicitly downgraded in that they had to share their 'power' with the opposition as well as with the still powerful SED. Some of them resented these individuals elected only by a handful of people making demands on the government. They knew of course that their own legitimacy was questionable. Despite its attempt at being all-inclusive, the Round Table was unrepresentative of the mood of the mass of GDR voters, as the elections would show. The SED hoped that with so many divisions and personal rivalries among its opponents it could still dominate the government and win time to stage a counter-offensive later. This is not to suggest that Modrow and his colleagues would have wanted to return to the conditions prevailing under Honecker.

Exit the SED, enter the SED–PDS

After the Politburo and Central Committee had committed political sui-
cide, the future of the SED was left to a shadowy body, a working committee (*Arbeitsausschuß*) of 25, which was entrusted with preparing an
extraordinary party congress. Lothar Bisky and Gregor Gysi were the most
significant members of this committee. Professor Bisky, Rector of the University for Television in Potsdam-Babelsberg, had been appointed head of
the ZK's cultural department in November. Gysi, son of former Minister of
Culture Klaus Gysi, was a lawyer. Feverish efforts were made to organise
the congress. Finally, it opened in the Dynamo Sports Hall in Berlin-
Weißensee on 8 December. The 2,753 delegates debated for seventeen hours.
Many of them were without political experience at this level. Because of the
lack of experience, relatively poor organisation and the weighty decisions
the delegates had to take, it was decided to divide the congress into two.
The first sessions were followed by others on 16 and 17 December.

Previous SED congresses were completely disciplined affairs with the
leaders taking up most of the time, and their followers, if they spoke at all,
simply endorsing their leaders' policies. The delegates were given presents
for their loyalty. On this occasion it was quite different. Outside, there
were young men handing out Trotskyite leaflets near the entrance to the
Dynamo Sports Hall. Inside, it was more like old-fashioned British Labour
or West German SPD conferences with vitriolic, sarcastic or tearful speeches
from the floor. The hall looked relatively shabby. One thing which was
different from Western conferences, however, was the large number of
military uniforms. Every branch of the armed forces and police of the
GDR seemed to be well represented. If the SED was looking for a fresh
start, surely this was a mistake? Some members of the old Politburo like
Schürer and Hager were present but they were not permitted to address
the congress. They moved around like ghosts and were more than happy
to talk to anyone who approached them.[9] Once that happened they were
soon surrounded by ordinary delegates and visitors who wanted to hear
their explanations, pleas of ignorance, indignation and even warnings about
the future. In conversation Schürer was quite prepared to admit his part in
the collective ruination of the GDR. Hager was more indignant, shocked
and angry. The whole atmosphere of the congress brought to mind John
Reed's *Ten Days That Shook the World*, which describes the Bolshevik
take-over of Russia in 1917.

At the session on 8 December Gregor Gysi was elected to lead the party
as Chairman, a new position. He was the only candidate and was supported with a 95.3 per cent vote.[10] Of Jewish background, he revealed
himself to be a witty, self-assured intellectual, at home on television chat

shows and at political mass meetings. Modrow, Wolfgang Berghofer, Mayor of Dresden, and Wolfgang Pohl, First Secretary of the SED in Magdeburg, were elected as deputy chairmen. An Executive Committee (*Vorstand*), rather than a Central Committee, was elected as the party's governing body. The word *Vorstand* was that used by West German parties. Of the 101 members elected to the *Vorstand*, only four, including Modrow, had belonged to the previous Central Committee. The Politburo was replaced by a Presidium, to which belonged Gysi, his deputies, and five others who headed party commissions. When the SED congress reconvened on 16 December there was much discussion about the party's name. Many veteran members did not wish to change it. Many younger ones felt it was an impediment to renewal. In the end, on the recommendation of Gysi, the SED became the SED–PDS (Party of Democratic Socialism). It gave up its organisations in the armed forces, police, and so on, like Western political parties, and would concentrate in future on organising in electoral constituencies. Looking back, the congress was a great success for the SED camp. If the old guard had somehow managed to thwart the reformers, the SED would have been virtually destroyed in the elections which followed. On the other hand, had the reformers gone too far, the party would have split, like the neighbouring Polish United Workers' Party or the Hungarian Communist Party. As it was, Gysi was able to hold the disparate factions together and mount an effective election campaign. It was then in a better position to secure a place for itself in the political landscape of a united Germany.

On that same weekend, 15/16 December, in another part of East Berlin, the CDU of the GDR was holding its congress. Although it was largely ignored by the foreign press, it was to prove as important as the SED–PDS gathering. The congress confirmed Lothar de Maizière as Chairman. He was elected with 714 of the 759 votes cast. Martin Kirchner, a lawyer and Evangelical Church leader, was elected as General Secretary. Kirchner had been an early advocate of a change of direction in the CDU. A new *Vorstand* was elected replacing the previous discredited body. The congress revealed the anger and passion for change of many provincial CDU activists, about half of whom were untainted by the party's part role as an SED satellite. Typical of this group was Bernd Beck, recently elected Mayor of Heiligenstadt, a small town on the East–West German frontier. He spoke with conviction, demanding a total break with the past, the introduction of the social market economy, free elections and early union with the Federal Republic on the basis of acceptance of its Basic Law. In October 1989 the CDU wanted 'Democratic Socialism' as opposed to the previous SED pseudo-socialism'. Now it dispensed with socialism altogether. It advocated a return to the GDR's non-socialist 1949 constitution, including the re-establishment of the five regions abolished in 1952 and a federal structure. In the end the

800 or so delegates accepted the proposals of de Maizière, which fell short of Bernd Beck's hopes. The CDU called for an early economic, currency and energy union with West Germany and a German confederation in a united Europe.[11]

Public opinion tested

What did the GDR people think about their leaders and would-be leaders at the end of this momentous year of 1989? The West German weekly *Der Spiegel* commissioned a public opinion poll in the GDR in December. The results were published on 18 December. A representative sample were asked about their views of 11 GDR politicians. Hans Modrow topped the list with a positive evaluation of 97 per cent of those asked. Günther Maleuda, leader of the former SED satellite Democratic Farmers' Party (DBD), followed him on 75 per cent. Maleuda was at this point the President of the Volkskammer. Up to very recently he had served Honecker's SED very loyally. Wolfgang Berghofer of the SED came third, with a positive evaluation of 59 per cent. It should be mentioned that 33 per cent of those asked did not know who he was. On fourth place was Manfred Gerlach, who, as mentioned above, was the first leader of a satellite party, the LDPD, to step out of line. Far more convincing than Maleuda, he scored 58 per cent positive, 28 per cent negative and was not known by 6 per cent. Bärbel Bohley, who had done so much for freedom and reform in the GDR, took fifth place with 45 per cent positive, 30 per cent negative and 14 per cent saying they did not know her. Next in line was Günter Schabowski. He scored 39 per cent positive evaluation, 47 per cent negative and 3 per cent did not know him. Rainer Eppelmann of Democratic Awakening (DA) followed Schabowski. He received a positive evaluation by 35 per cent of those asked, 7 per cent negative and was unknown to 48 per cent. Lothar de Maizière, leader of the CDU and Deputy Minister-President in the Modrow government, attracted a positive evaluation by 33 per cent, negative by 10 and was unknown to 44 per cent. What of Krenz? Only 32 per cent gave him a positive evaluation, as against 54 per cent who saw him in a negative light. Everyone of course knew him. The final two on the list were Günter Hartmann, the new leader of the NDPD, and Ibrahim Böhme, leader of the new Social Democratic Party. Most people did not know them. They received positive evaluations from 19 and 12 per cent respectively. Both got negative evaluations from 5 per cent of those questioned.

The poll results reveal the influence of the media. In the days and weeks before the poll, Modrow and, to a much lesser extent, Maleuda, Berghofer, Gerlach and Bohley had received favourable publicity in both the GDR and West German media. Few realised at that time that de Maizière was going to have his moment of glory and play a prominent role in the moves towards integrating the GDR into the Federal Republic. When asked about their views on seven West German politicians, Walter Momper, Mayor of West Berlin and a Social Democrat, was most popular, followed by Federal President Richard von Weizsäcker (CDU), Willy Brandt (SPD), Hans-Dietrich Genscher (FDP) and Hans-Joachim Vogel (SPD), with Helmut Kohl trailing in sixth position. Theo Waigel (CSU) came bottom of the list. This reflected fairly accurately the sympathetic involvement of those politicians with the GDR's problems up to that point. It was of course to change. Mikhail Gorbachev was, according to this survey, more popular than any of the German politicians, East or West. When they were asked about their party preferences, only about half admitted a preference. The SED claimed 17 per cent; the new SDP came second with 7 per cent. This was five months before the elections promised for 6 May. Those polled were also asked about how they viewed the West German parties. They put the SPD first, followed, in order, by the Free Democrats, Greens, CDU and, well behind, the far-right Republicans.[12] On the crucial question of German unity, only 27 per cent said they were for the two German states building a united state. This sounds a conservative estimate at that stage, although it must be said that many East Germans, whatever their political views, were in a state of shock and were almost afraid of thinking ahead too much. Many too had a feeling of pride and did not want to be begging to be let into the home of their rich big brother.

What were West Germans thinking at the time? How did they view their politicians? According to *Der Spiegel*'s monthly opinion poll published on 27 November 1989, Hans-Dietrich Genscher, the Foreign Minister of the Federal Republic, who had done so much to achieve better relations with the Soviet Union and the GDR, was receiving the recognition he deserved in terms of public esteem. He stood at the head of *Der Spiegel*'s monthly list of politicians preferred by a representative sample of West German voters. He was followed by Rita Süssmuth (CDU), President of the Bundestag, Lothar Späth (CDU) and the SPD leaders Hans-Jochen Vogel, Oskar Lafontaine, Bjön Engholm and Johannes Rau. Federal Chancellor Helmut Kohl was on tenth place, on a par with Walter Momper, SPD Mayor of West Berlin. Momper had been much in the limelight since the fall of the Berlin Wall.

The Brandenburg Gate opened

Whatever his inclinations, genuinely democratic or not, Modrow was under pressure from both below and without to act in a democratic manner. He needed high-profile foreign visitors to bolster his regime. Many of those visitors were likely to advise him to stick with democracy. Modrow was in something of a daze. Only weeks before he had been just another GDR provincial politician, who, unlike Western politicians, was not used to the cut and thrust of democratic debate. Suddenly he had become the centre of German and even international attention. It was difficult to know whom to turn to for help and whom to trust as all the old structures crumbled and so many new actors appeared on the political stage. In the midst of all the turmoil in Berlin and elsewhere he found himself being courted by international figures whose faces were only familiar to him, if at all, from television.

The new GDR leader was being re-assured on all sides that no one wanted the GDR to fall and be united with West Germany. Walther Leisler Kiep, CDU Treasurer, member of the board of Volkswagen, Deutsche Bank and many other bodies, and confidant of Helmut Kohl, was among them. He had long been interested in Poland and the GDR and, unlike most of his party, had voted in favour of the Brandt government's treaties with these countries in 1971. He told Modrow's adviser Günter Rettner that re-unification was unrealistic and not wanted by the majority of West Germans.[13] His job was to prepare the ground for Rudolf Seiters, Federal Minister for Special Tasks and Kohl's representative, with whom Modrow had early discussions. Modrow also had talks with James Baker, US Secretary of State (12 December), and with lesser figures such as Austrian Chancellor Franz Vranitzky (24 November) and the Minister-President of Hesse, Dr Walter Wallmann (24 November). The day after his SED–PDS congress he met Federal President Richard von Weizsäcker, who also talked to Gerlach and de Maizière. On 19 December Modrow held talks with Helmut Kohl in Dresden. As mentioned in Chapter 8, Mitterrand flew to Berlin to bolster the new regime.

Finally, on 22 December Modrow stood with Kohl, the East Berlin Mayor, Erhard Krack, and the Governing Mayor of West Berlin, Walter Momper, as Berlin's symbolic Brandenburg Gate was opened for the first time in twenty-eight years. Kohl and Modrow gave a carefully stage-managed handshake in front of the world's television cameras. Speeches were made about the historic moment, division and unity, despair and hope. 'There was enough hermeneutics to make your head spin, if you were listening.'[14] Was this a new beginning for the GDR and the SED, Modrow must have asked himself? Or was it just the beginning of the end?[15] The crowds just enjoyed the moment. They rushed forward from both sides, West and East. As on that earlier, more truly historic occasion, they celebrated. Champagne, Sekt, beer, were drunk. The souvenir photographs were taken. Those East German border guards not called upon to have their photographs taken or take a glass looked on in amazement, still dazed by the dream-like quality of the event. The more thoughtful of them must have realised that their days were numbered. Two days earlier it was announced that the visa requirement for West Germans and West Berliners visiting the GDR had been abolished. The currency regulation requiring them to change a minimum amount of West German money into GDR marks was also abolished. Earlier, on 14 December, the Office for National Security, which had only recently replaced the dreaded MfS, was dissolved. The Office was to be replaced by West German-style internal security and external intelligence-gathering bodies subject to parliamentary control. There was talk of discipline breaking down among the conscripts in the GDR's armed forces.[16] By that time the crowds on the streets of many towns were calling for German unity. They had been encouraged by Kohl's ten-point plan of 28 November with its reference to a possible German confederation, which in turn led to the 20 December agreement between Modrow and Kohl to begin negotiations for a treaty of community (*Vertragsgemeinschaft*) between the two German states.[17] Yet no one realised how fast the pace would be. At this time Willy Brandt was proposing that a joint parliamentary assembly drawn from both German states should act as a kind of watchdog over the political changes taking place in the GDR. Within the GDR itself, Manfred Gerlach proposed that the West German President, Richard von Weizsäcker, should be elected president of the two German states to chair the unification process. Both these original proposals had some merit but were completely unrealistic in the circumstances. Another proposal, which was outlandish as well as rather insulting to the Germans, was made by Soviet Foreign Minister Eduard Shevardnadze. This was that Germany's neighbours should determine the fate of German unity by referenda. Had this been taken seriously, it would at least have slowed down the unification process.

The SED–PDS dissolving?

The year 1990 had not started too badly for the SED–PDS. On 3 January it had played a decisive part in a demonstration of around 250,000 Berliners. This had been organised against the 'threat' from the far right. Great play had been made about the damaging of the Soviet War Memorial in Treptow Park, Berlin. It was also alleged that members of the far right Republicans had been handing out material to demonstrators in Leipzig.[18] This looked very much like the SED–PDS's attempt to frighten not only Germans East and West, but also Germany's neighbours and the USA with the fear of revived Nazism. Despite this momentary success, the resignations from the party continued. Since the extraordinary congress in December, another 250,000 comrades had turned their backs on the party. At the beginning of January the SED–PDS claimed 1,463,000 members, which represented a loss of 900,000 since the autumn.[19] The party was also developing into

Communist, Social Democratic and 'third way' factions. When the Presidium met on 18 January, Gysi reported a further decline in party membership to 1.2 million. He also reported that of the 855 full-time officials who had worked for the old Central Committee, 233 had left. Only 11 of the old departmental heads out of 40 were still in office.[20] At the lower levels of the party administration the changes had been even more dramatic. There were many voices raised both inside the party and outside against calling for its abolition. The party suffered a serious blow when Vice-Chairman Wolfgang Berghofer resigned. With Berghofer went 39 other prominent Dresden members. They called for the SED–PDS to go into voluntary liquidation. Their argument was that its continued existence frightened people that there could be a restoration of the old SED to power.[21] They also feared for the safety of their members in a growingly hostile environment. Some of course hoped that by ditching the party they would be able to hold on to their posts in industry, universities or in local government. In Magdeburg, Karl-Marx-Stadt and Leipzig there were also manifestations of the party dissolving itself.

Modrow's 'government of national responsibility'

On 3 January the Round Table called for a 'grand coalition of reason' until the new Volkskammer elections on 6 May. However, on 24 January the CDU decided to withdraw its ministers from the government. Two days later it changed its mind.[22] The problem was that the old bloc parties needed to distance themselves as much as possible from the former SED and their past collaboration with it. However, there was also the fear that if the government disintegrated, chaos would reign, and perhaps the Soviets would be forced to intervene. No one really wanted this. The new parties were worried, however, that if they were seen too often in the company of Modrow, they could be tarred with the same brush and lose their credibility. The Round Table proposed in this situation to hold the elections two months earlier, on 18 March. On 29 January Modrow told the Volkskammer of the desperate situation faced by the GDR, including strikes and the collapse of local government due to the lack of confidence in them. The Volkskammer responded to these developments by agreeing to hold the elections on the earlier date. The opposition groups then agreed to serve in the government on condition that Modrow and his colleagues cut their alignment with the former SED. On 5 February, the Volkskammer elected eight new ministers without portfolios to be part of Modrow's expanded 'government of national responsibility'. They were drawn from the eight groups, which were part of the Round Table. They included Dr Wolfgang Ullmann, Rainer Eppelmann, Sebastian Pflugbeil, Gerd Poppe (IFM), Konrad Weiß and Dr Walter

Romberg of the SPD. Their brief was to shadow the normal ministers. Power was slipping away from Modrow and the former SED step by step.

On the day that Modrow announced his expanded coalition, Honecker tottered out of hospital 'visibly disorientated'.[23] The 77-year-old had survived three cancer operations and the shock not only of falling from power but of being disowned by his erstwhile comrades and expelled from the party he had helped to establish. He was forced to find sanctuary for a time in the home of a Protestant minister whose children he and his wife Margot (for many years Minister of People's Education) had deprived of higher education.[24] He was briefly held on charges of misuse of office and corruption before being released as unfit. He showed a remarkable zeal to survive ordeals which would have killed off most normal people. Later he took refuge in a Soviet military hospital before being spirited away to Moscow.

One of the curious anomalies was ended in January 1990 when Modrow's government re-instated the words of the GDR national anthem. In a way, the banning of the words by Honecker in early 1970s, leaving his subjects with no text to sing, revealed the inability of the regime to cope and made it a laughing stock. Two or three of the many talented GDR text writers could easily have written an alternative in secret before the original text by Communist poet and the GDR's first Minister of Culture, Johannes R. Becher, was withdrawn. As it was, many embarrassments were caused. The reason for this unprecedented situation was that the text referred to 'Germany, united Fatherland' ('Einig Deutsches Vaterland'), three words that demonstrators in Leipzig and elsewhere chanted. Sixteen years earlier, in 1974, Honecker's SED wanted to emphasise that it had no such aspiration for a united Germany, socialist or otherwise. Becher's text was not heard again and was not reprinted. Like pornography, as far as possible, it was removed from bookshops and libraries. Under Modrow, however, as in the early days of the GDR, Becher's words were heard over the GDR's electronic media. Modrow's ending of the embarrassment, on 5 January, gave a little hope to those already wanting re-unification, and even found favour with many SED veterans from the old days. They wanted to claim that they had never wanted Germany divided in the first place. They were proud of 'their' anthem:

> Reborn out of the ruins
> turning to the future
> let us serve you as we may
> Germany, united Fatherland.
> All constraint to overcome
> and overcome we shall together
> since some day we must succeed
> to make the sun as never yet
> shine over Germany.

The Round Table held its final session on 12 March, when a draft constitution was discussed. It was agreed that the draft would be discussed by the
newly elected Volkskammer and put to the GDR electorate in a referendum
on 17 June 1990. This underlines how divorced these well-intended ministers were from their fellow-citizens. At this same final session the SPD
criticised a law approved by the Volkskammer on 6–7 March, which laid
down that publicly owned enterprises and institutions should be turned
into joint-stock companies. A decision (*Beschluß*) of the Modrow government had established an *Anstalt zur treuhänderischen Verwaltung des
Volkseigentums* (*Treuhandanstalt*) on 1 March. This 'trusteeship body' was
to administer the People's Property. This meant those industrial enterprises
run directly by ministries, which constituted the bulk of the economy. Its first
job was the *Wahrung* (protection) of the People's Property. On the same day,
by order in council, these assets were to be transformed into commercial
companies. This left open their future as publicly owned, private or mixed
companies.[25] The SPD warned against speedy privatisation of public assets.

Gorbachev seals the GDR's fate

Modrow kept in close contact with Moscow, but he found his influence
was in steep decline with his Soviet comrades. At this critical time Gorbachev
was himself under pressure from both conservatives and reformers in the
CPSU. It was a haggard-looking Gorbachev, not seen in public for ten days,
who met Modrow on 30 January.[26] He told Modrow, 'The majority of
people in the German Democratic Republic no longer support the idea of
two German states . . . and it seems it has become impossible to preserve
the republic.'[27] According to *Neues Deutschland* (31 January 1990), he was
told by Gorbachev that there was a certain agreement between the Germans in the East and in the West and the Four Powers that the unity of the
Germans was not, in principle, in doubt. This sealed the fate of the GDR.
Two days later Modrow released his conception for 'Germany, united
Fatherland'. This looked like a surrender, even treason, to some SED
stalwarts, and there were more resignations. The party Presidium attempted
to come to terms with the situation and on 1 February came out for a 'progressive, social, democratic, humanist Germany'.[28] Meeting on 4 February
the *Vorstand* called a party congress for 24/5 February and dropped the
SED from the party title, leaving it as the 'Party of Democratic Socialism'
(*Partei des Demokratischen Sozialismus*, PDS). This was to emphasise its
break with the structure and methods of the SED and the SED's desire to
enjoy a monopoly of power. The *Vorstand* also announced it was handing
over 3,041,000,000 marks to the state from its coffers. This did not please
all the members, who felt they had not been consulted.[29] Some felt they

should have had their members' subscriptions returned to them. More members left the party. By mid-February membership stood at about 700,000. Among the 595 delegates at the first PDS congress were many young members and many women. Gysi took his party into the election battle as an opposition party to the left of the SPD.

Modrow, meanwhile, in a last-ditch attempt to save what he could, put forward a proposal for 'Germany, united Fatherland'. This was a four-stage plan which envisaged: (1) the conclusion of a co-operation treaty, including economic, currency and transport union and legal alignment; (2) the formation of a confederation of the two German states; (3) the transference of sovereignty to the confederation; and (4) the creation of a German Federation or Alliance after elections to a unified parliament which would decide on a constitution and government with its seat in Berlin. Modrow's plan foresaw military neutrality for Germany and was reminiscent of Stalin's 1952 plan. It was rejected by Kohl, who insisted that he would wait until the outcome of the GDR elections before going into talks on unity. The French paper *Le Monde* (3 February 1990) rightly described the 'sudden conversion' of Modrow to German unity as a reaction to the rising demands for unification from the masses and the continuing exodus of East Germans to the West.

Notes

1. Erich Honecker, *Moabiter Notizen*, Berlin, 1994, p. 34.
2. Krenz, p. 233.
3. According to *Der Spiegel* (15 November 1999, pp. 177, 188–90), half of the members of Modrow's government were, or had been Stasi informers, including Frau Luft.
4. *Die Welt*, 18 November 1989.
5. Christa Luft, *Zwischen Wende und Ende Eindrücke: Erlebnisse, Erfahrungen eines Mitglieds der Modrow-Regierung*, Berlin, 1992 and 1999, p. 47.
6. Krenz, p. 243.
7. Hannes Bahrmann and Christoph Links, *Chronik der Wende: Die Ereignisse in der DDR Zwischen 7. Oktober 1989 und 18. März 1990*, Berlin, 1990, p. 115.
8. Wilfried Tieding (ed.), *Ein Volk im Aufbruch: Die DDR im Herbst '89*, Dresden, 1990, p. 26.
9. The author attended on 16/17 December and spoke to Hager and Schürer.
10. Bortfeldt (1992), p. 138.
11. The author was present at the CDU conference. Much later he interviewed Lothar de Maizière. The CDU's proposals are found in Peter R. Weilemann *et al.*, *Parteien im Aufbruch: Nichtkommunistische Parteien und politische Vereinigungen in der DDR*, St Augustin, 1990, pp. 20–3.
12. These findings about party preferences and the popularity of West German politicians were similar to those produced by a small survey carried out by the author in Leipzig on 18 December.

13. *Der Spiegel*, 15 November 1999, p. 182.
14. Robert Darnton, *Berlin Journal, 1989–1990*, New York, 1993, p. 108.
15. The author interviewed Modrow later.
16. The sight of totally drunken GDR troops on Berlin-Lichtenberg station and a conversation with one of them on the way to Leipzig was an eye-opener for the author.
17. Karl Kaiser, *Deutschlands Vereinigung: Die internationalen Aspekte*, Bergisch Gladbach, 1991, p. 186.
18. Bortfeldt, p. 152.
19. *Ibid.*, p. 155.
20. *Ibid.*, p. 159.
21. *Ibid.*, p. 167.
22. Darnton, *Berlin Journal*, p. 226.
23. *Ibid.*, p. 224.
24. Cornelia Heins, *The Wall Falls: An Oral History of the Reunification of the Two Germanies*, London, 1994, p. 345.
25. Birgit Breuel (ed.), *Treuhand intern Tagebuch*, Frankfurt am Main, 1993, pp. 30–3.
26. Dusko Doder and Louise Brancoe, *Gorbachev: Heretic in the Kremlin*, London, 1990, p. 417.
27. Mikhail Gorbachev, *Memoirs*, London, 1997, p. 681.
28. Bortfeldt (1992), p. 172.
29. Bortfeldt (1992), p. 174.

Chapter 10

The free elections of March 1990

As we saw in the previous chapter, it was originally agreed by the old Volkskammer that Western-style elections to a new Volkskammer would take place on 6 May 1990. As the population haemorrhage continued daily, public services of all kinds – medical, local government, mail, schools and colleges, transport – came under increasing pressure. Even private services – shops and handicrafts – were becoming less reliable. In general, absenteeism was growing. The Stasi was being disbanded and in the armed services discipline was weakening. The deteriorating situation made it urgent to carry through elections as soon as possible to give hope of better things to come. On 28 January Modrow and the representatives of the 'Round Table' agreed that they should be integrated into the government and that the new elections should take place on 18 March. How prepared were the parties for such early elections?

Gysi: 'A strong opposition for the weak'

The SED had many advantages over its rivals, especially over the new parties. It had a GDR-wide organisation with many thousands of full-time officials anxious to hold on to their jobs. In addition to the GDR's main daily paper, *Neues Deutschland*, and local papers, it owned many other publications and retail outlets. Virtually all those working in the mass media were SED members. It controlled *de facto* what was left of the Stasi apparatus. Most state employees, including the police, were SED members anxious about their future. The government was still in its hands, with leading members like Hans Modrow getting the lion's share of the publicity, much of it favourable. In the weeks up to the election the new leader of the PDS, Gregor Gysi, gave a good performance. The Western media, as well as those of the GDR, gave him ample opportunity to get himself across. He denounced the crimes and mistakes of the Honecker era, attempted to put a gloss on the early founding period of the GDR, and played on the doubts and fears of the electorate. Having changed its name on 4 February to simply PDS, the party presented itself as the main defender of the weak and the underprivileged in the GDR against the coming onslaught of West

German capitalism. Without it, workers would lose their jobs, collective farmers their farms, women the right to work, working mothers their kindergarten, householders their properties to former owners now in West Germany or overseas. The fear of German revanchism was played upon both in the GDR and outside it. A re-united Germany would be too strong and potentially a danger to Europe. At its last major rally on Alexanderplatz in Berlin, Gysi reinforced one of the main slogans of the PDS. His party represented 'a strong opposition for the weak'.[1]

Against the SED's experienced cadre, the opposition politicians were amateurs. They had no organisation, no funds, and no means of getting their message across. Even with members' donations, they found it difficult to get such things as office equipment, stationery and transport or have their literature printed. They were in desperate need of outside help if they were to mount campaigns in anyway matching the SED's efforts. The four former 'allied' parties were all well organised and each had its own daily paper and other publications. They too had experienced organisers. Like their former master, the SED, they were discredited among the electorate as a whole. However, a considerable number of their members remained loyal. Some of them were fearful about the future. They were either full-time officials or held jobs dependent on their party affiliation, or they had joined to gain enough respectability in the eyes of the SED to be able to pursue their careers. Many felt guilty about these associations. Many small traders, independent artisans, and the like, had joined to be able to obtain or retain licences to open businesses.

The Alliance for Germany formed

As we have seen, the leader of the LDPD, Manfred Gerlach, had been the first to challenge Honecker's policies when it was still relatively dangerous to do so. That subsequently helped him to survive. His party found its long-standing contacts with the West German FDP very useful in gaining financial and other material assistance. The CDU was the first to rid itself of its discredited leader, Gerald Götting. On 8 December it held an extraordinary congress at which it broke with its past and revealed that it had swept aside many of the old leaders at all levels of the party. Since 10 November its new leader was Lothar de Maizière (50), who, although he had been a member since 1956, had never held office. He was a lawyer and musician and member of the Evangelical Church synod. Through his service as deputy Prime Minister in Modrow's government he had become relatively well known. His party came out clearly for German re-unification and the social market economy. It suffered initially by not being backed by the West German CDU. It had been a satellite for virtually the whole of the existence of the GDR, but a considerable number of voters had probably not even noticed it as the SED stood out as *the* party. The CDU's very name was an advantage in that many associated it not so much with the old SED but with Kohl's successful party. And Kohl was on hand to help.

At first, however, the West German CDU and Kohl were uncertain about the GDR party bearing the same name. This party had long ago been purged, infiltrated, bribed and undermined by the SED and the Stasi and had danced to their tunes. On his visit to Dresden in 1989, Kohl had rebuffed de Maizière's requests for an audience, choosing to talk to Modrow instead. De Maizière tried again in January, however, and a number of secret meetings took place between him and Kohl. The East German CDU leaders knew that they were in great danger if they went into the election without Kohl's blessing and other assistance. There were other parties competing for their constituency and there was the SDP/SPD, which already enjoyed the backing of the West German Social Democrats. For his part, Kohl knew his party needed a partner in the East. He could not stand aloof and just let things happen. In the unlikely event that national unity was still far off, the Federal Republic needed a GDR government with which it could co-operate easily, and the East German CDU now had new leaders and a programme that was compatible with the principles of the Bonn party. If unity was just around the corner, Kohl needed to convince the East German voters that he cared about them because they would soon be voters in a united Germany.

On 1 February 1990 Kohl came together with the leaders of the East German CDU and of the parties which sought to ally themselves with it. These were Democratic Awakening (DA), the German Social Union (DSU) and the German Forum Party (the latter eventually deciding to link up with the liberals instead). According to Kohl,[2] it was a difficult meeting, with the leaders of the different parties jockeying for position and anything but united on aims or policy or who should do what. All believed that in the event of victory their man should head the government. The small, new parties greatly overestimated their own strength and, like so many others, found it difficult to believe that the old East German CDU would make a major impact in the short time available. Kohl and his colleagues might have opted to give most of their support to the DSU as they still mistrusted the old satellite CDU, but the new DSU was heavily dependent on the Bavarian CSU, which was often at odds with Kohl and his CDU in Bonn.

There was also a problem of what to call the group of parties fighting the right-of-centre corner together. A number of suggestions were made, including the Democratic Union of Germany and the Alliance of the Middle. In the end, on 5 February, after hard bargaining and some disappointment, they decided on the Alliance for Germany (*Allianz für Deutschland*). Some thought this sounded like an insurance company rather than a political alliance (there was a famous German insurance company called *Allianz*). Perhaps this was no bad thing, as so many voters, especially the older ones, wanted the security we are supposed to get from a policy with a good insurance company.

What position did the other two parties of the Alliance represent? As we saw in Chapter 6, Democratic Awakening was founded originally in Berlin in October. On 16–17 December it was formally inaugurated as a political party at a congress in Leipzig in the presence of a glittering array of prominent West German politicians. Among them were Foreign Minister Hans-Dietrich Genscher, Bundestag President Rita Süssmuth, and representatives of the SPD and the Greens. DA, which had been a loose movement to this point, presented itself as 'social and ecological', for German unity and for the social market economy. Wolfgang Schnur, a Rostock lawyer who had defended dissidents, was elected Chairman. He claimed the party was made up of socialists, social democrats, Christians and 'social ecologists'. On 12 March, six days before the election, Schnur was forced to resign after admitting he had worked as an informer for the Stasi. This greatly weakened DA's credibility and could have been a disaster for the Alliance for Germany. Pastor Rainer Eppelmann, a civil rights activist and foundation member, took over the chairmanship. The two deputies to Eppelmann were Dr Brigitta Kögler and Dr Bernd Findeis, both from Jena. The party had about 40,000 members.[3]

As we also saw above, on 20 January 1990, also meeting at Leipzig, the German Social Union was established as a political party. Hans-Wilhelm Ebeling, the Leipzig parson, was elected Chairman. The DSU wanted German unity 'as soon as possible' and backed the social market economy. It criticised the CDU of the GDR for its past collaboration with the SED. This was a just criticism and for a short period it looked possible that the DSU would become the authentic right-of-centre party of the GDR. Its election slogan was 'Freedom instead of socialism', which was Kohl's CDU slogan in the 1976 election in West Germany.

The programme of the *Allianz*, published in early March under the heading 'Freedom and Prosperity – Never Again Socialism', had 13 points.

1. We strive for the unity of Germany on the basis of the Basic Law [of the Federal Republic].
2. We advocate the immediate introduction of the German mark.
3. We back private property and unrestricted freedom to do business.
4. There must be no obstacles for investors from the Federal Republic or abroad.
5. Help from the Federal Republic to build up a system of unemployment insurance.
6. The building up of a system of social insurance.

7. Pensioners and pensions will be especially secured.
8. An immediate programme for the environment and energy supply.
9. The legal system must be brought in line with that of the Federal Republic.
10. A register of cultural monuments.
11. Educational reform in connection with the re-establishment of the regional states [*Länder*].
12. State-financed nurseries and kindergartens.
13. Unlimited press freedom.

Although the programme contained a number of items that were of special interest to GDR voters, like points 8 and 12, it was a programme to the right of the CDU in West Germany. There was no mention of trade union rights and co-determination (*Mitbestimmung*), which had always been fundamental to the West German Christian Democrats. Nor was there any mention of women's rights, a growing issue in West Germany. Finally, nothing was said about the problems or prospects of youth. Usually, all German parties paid lip service to this segment of voters.

Kohl: 'We will build a flourishing land together'

Whatever his reservations about his new political friends, Kohl threw himself into the fight to get them elected. He campaigned in Erfurt, where he was introduced as the Chancellor of our German Fatherland. That went down well with the 130,000 people present. He told the admiring crowd, 'We will shape the future as one people in one Germany.' His audience responded with, 'Germany, united Fatherland!' This was the first of six speeches delivered by Kohl during the run-up to polling day. He struck a chord wherever he went. He had three main themes: unification, prosperity and the danger represented by the SPD, as the former East German SDP now called itself (see below). He unfairly attacked the SPD as partners with the Communists.[4] In fact the SPD under Kurt Schumacher had fought the Communists even after the forced merger with them to form the SED. Kohl promised his audiences, if they went down the way trodden by West Germany, 'We will build a flourishing land together'.[5]

In his sixth and final campaign speech on 13 March in Cottbus, Kohl promised, 'We want savers to know that when the change in currency comes it will be at one-for-one for them. This will be valid for small savers but not for the whole currency. It is crucial that those who deserve our support and solidarity should not be disadvantaged.'[6] This was a bold commitment by Kohl. He ignored the advice of the German Federal Bank, the Bundesbank, and earned the criticism of the SPD, PDS and other opposition groups that he was attempting to bribe the electorate. His promise gave ordinary East Germans hope of better times, however, and that is what they were desperately short of.

The leaders of the Alliance for Germany, the CDU, DA and DSU, were secondary to Kohl, who officially was not even a candidate. Lothar de Maizière of the CDU appeared an honest, cultured, almost non-political, figure. His message was simple. He had three wishes: firstly, that his children would no longer have to lie at school; secondly, that his wife would be the only one to listen when he telephoned her; thirdly, that the only persons to enter his apartment would be invited guests.[7] The crowds understood very well what he was talking about.

The NDPD also embraced German unity and the social market economy. It identified itself at its pre-election congress in January 1990 as a party of the middle, 'against right-wing nationalism and left-wing radicalism'. It claimed to have lost only about 10 per cent of its membership. After its leader Heinrich Homann (78) was expelled, on 10 December 1989, for bringing the party into disrepute, the NDPD went through a leadership crisis. Homann's deputy, Günter Hartmann (49), was Chairman from November 1989 to January 1990. He was then deposed and Wolfgang Glaeser (50), a teacher, was elected, only to resign two days later. Glaeser's replacement was Wolfgang Rauls (41), a full-time politician working in the Magdeburg city administration. He had been a party member since 1968. The NDPD had hardly made any impact in the past in the GDR and badly needed a partner in the election. Unlike the CDU, the LDPD and the new SDP, it could not appeal to a sister party in West Germany. It foolishly rejected an alliance with the LDPD.

Also presenting itself as the party of German unity and the social market economy was the DBD, which retained a well-organised machine in the rural areas. It stressed the rights of collective farmers and wanted the state to continue to play a dominant role in agriculture. At its congress on 27–8 January it re-elected, as chairman, Günther Maleuda (58), whose membership went back to 1950 and whose career was entirely in the DBD. He had gained valuable publicity since November 1989 as Chairman of the Volkskammer. All four former satellites of the SED – CDU, LDPD, NDPD, DBD – declared themselves against future coalitions with the PDS, but, in the case of the DBD, there was no clear water separating it from its past association with the SED.

Brandt: 'What belongs together will grow together'

What of the GDR's new parties? By the end of January 1990 the Social Democrats appeared to be in the lead. They had been greatly encouraged by their recognition by the West German SPD in the previous October.

Their representatives were received with enthusiasm by the SPD congress held in West Berlin in December 1989. Willy Brandt campaigned for them in the GDR and was joined by some of his leading colleagues. The GDR Social Democrats changed their name from the SDP to the SPD on 13 January to identify themselves more closely with their West German comrades, and with German unity, which the East German party strongly supported. Their leaders in the election were Ibrahim Böhme (Chairman) and Markus Meckel, Angelika Barbe and Karl-August Kamilli (Deputy Chairpersons).[8] Lacking the experience and resources of their West German comrades, it was perhaps inevitable that the GDR Social Democrats should allow themselves to be overruled by a more cautious Bonn on the question of re-unification.

At the SPD's pre-election congress in Leipzig on 24 February, Willy Brandt received a standing ovation after telling the delegates, 'What belongs together will grow together.' At a mass rally he told cheering spectators, 'The train of unification is gathering steam. Now we must make sure that no one falls under the wheels. It is more important to prevent that than to assure the comfort of those who are travelling first class.'[9] What did it all mean in plain language? It meant that the West German SPD leaders had opted for unification by gradual and carefully negotiated stages. If this policy had been adopted, the restoration of Germany unity could have taken years. Oskar Lafontaine even argued against accepting East Germans into West Germany who had not already got a job and a place of residence in the Federal Republic. He also opposed Böhme's plea for the introduction of the West German mark to replace the GDR's currency by 1 July 1990. It was in some ways surprising to find Brandt supporting this view. Brandt made the point that an SPD government would defend the subsidies and social welfare legislation that protected East Germans from the worst abuses of a market economy. The GDR SPD adopted a policy which promised, if it formed a government, to negotiate with Bonn on the creation of a Council for German Unity, to be composed of representatives from both German states under the chairmanship of Brandt. The Council, deliberating with commissions from the Volkskammer and the Bundestag, would propose a constitution for a united Germany. This constitution would be put to referenda in East and West; if approved, it would go into effect after the election of a common parliament. During this lengthy process the two economies would be adjusted to each other and negotiations would be carried on with the four Allied powers to integrate Germany into the European order. The present frontiers of Germany would be guaranteed.[10]

This sounded all very sensible and reasonable but it was not what the impatient East German masses wanted to hear. The more they saw of the Federal Republic of Germany, the more they wanted to be part of it. Whether the West German SPD leaders had their attention on their own voters in the Federal Republic rather than those of the GDR is not clear. Voting was scheduled in West Germany for December 1990. Perhaps they thought they could stop any potential slippage of votes to the right, to the Republicans, by a cautious policy on German unity. There were signs that West German electors were worried about the increasing numbers of East Germans crossing over. Whatever their motives, they greatly underestimated the mood of the East Germans and ability of the German administrations to bring about a speedy and orderly unification of the two states.

Grass: 'There can be no demand for ... a unified nation'

It is worth mentioning here that a number of West German intellectuals associated with the SPD also put a damper on an early restoration of German unity. Best known of them was Günter Grass, famous author of *The Tin Drum*, *Dog Years* and other novels and essays. Grass told readers of the *New York Times* (7 January 1990) that

> no one of sound mind and memory can ever again permit such a concentration of power in the heart of Europe. Certainly the great powers, with the accent now on victorious powers, cannot; nor can the Poles, the French, the Dutch, the Danes. But neither can we Germans. Because there can be no demand for a new version of a unified nation that in the course of barely 75 years, though under several managements, filled the history books ... with suffering, rubble, defeat, millions of refugees, millions of dead, and the burden of crimes that can never be undone.

Grass had no sympathy for the old Stalinists of the SED, and much admiration for the East Germans who went on to the streets and, unlike West Germans, 'had to wrest their freedom from an all-embracing system'. But he would reward them by supporting Modrow! He wanted to help the GDR by cutting West Germany's defence budget and 'imposing on every West German citizen a surtax commensurate with his or her income'. This recipe would appeal to certain political circles in New York and to some on the left in both parts of Germany and elsewhere. But it overlooked the fact that it was not what the voters of the GDR wanted.

Genscher pulls centre together

As the election approached, many of the parties and groups realised they could achieve little by themselves and they therefore looked for possible alliance partners. They were unknown quantities and their leaders were unknown. They seemed in many cases to be saying the same things. As we saw, West German Christian Democrats had with difficulty been instrumental in the formation of an alliance on the right of centre. What of the centre itself? West German FDP leader, Foreign Minister and Vice-Chancellor Hans-Dietrich Genscher had worked hard to try to unite the Liberals in the GDR and prepare them for the election. He had a strong personal interest as he himself was from Halle and had been a member of the LDPD before leaving for the West. He attended the pre-election conference at Leipzig on 10 February, where the LDPD modified its name dropping the 'D' for *Deutschland* from its title. Thus it reverted to its original title Liberal Democratic Party (LDP). The 'D' had been foisted on it by the SED in a foolish attempt to pass it off as a party speaking for all Liberals West as well as East. While retaining the apparatus of the old LDPD and, so it hoped, its members, it sought to present itself as a new party. It elected a new leader, Rainer Ortlieb (46), a professor of shipbuilding at Rostock University. On 12 February, the League of Free Democrats comprising the LDP, the Free Democrats (FDP) and the German Forum Party (DFP), a splinter group from New Forum, was presented to the media.

Bündnis 90 and other groups

New Forum, which had been the biggest of the new groups established, had been courted by the Western media since its foundation in September 1989, but it was soon overshadowed by the SDP/SPD. NF moved slowly towards supporting German unity and a market economy in the months before the election. It still put strongly the view that the GDR should not be simply 'sold out' to West Germany. Nor should it be part of NATO. In fact, a united Germany should be demilitarised. Declining almost daily in importance, New Forum cobbled together an alliance with Democracy Now (DJ) and the Initiative for Peace and Human Rights (IFM). This was known as *Bündnis 90* (Alliance 90). Democracy Now (DJ) warned against a speedy re-unification of the two German states and advocated a decentralised democracy. The Initiative for Peace and Human Rights (IFM), which stood for a lengthy process leading to eventual restoration of German unity and the abolition of both the Warsaw Pact and NATO. Finally the Green Party teamed up with the Independent Women's League and the United Left (UL), who wanted to maintain an anti-fascist GDR, linked with the reformed FDJ to form the Action Alliance United Left (AVL). In spite of these alliances, the electorate was presented with a ballot paper with the names of the 24 parties on it.

On the eve of the election there were roughly three political camps in the GDR. Firstly, completely isolated, there was the PDS. It proclaimed the virtues of socialism and wanted to believe that the GDR had achieved a great deal, but was anxious to distance itself from the mistakes and crimes of the old leaders Ulbricht and Honecker. PDS supporters drawn more from the academic professions than from the working class, comprised a small number who genuinely believed in the party's virtues, and a far larger number who feared for their present jobs and their futures should German unity be restored. Secondly, there were the supporters of *Bündnis 90* and the small parties close to it. They too wanted to hold on to certain GDR traditions, believing that the blatant consumerism of West Germany would destroy them. They had no truck with the PDS, with its claims to be the interpreter and guardian of these positive GDR traditions. The third, much larger camp, consisted of the main GDR parties in the Alliance for Germany, the League of Free Democrats and the SPD. They saw in West Germany's political, social and economic achievements the route to a better life for their own people. They disagreed only on the details of how to establish West Germany's norms in the GDR and on the procedure leading them to unity with the Bonn republic.

The key issue of the election was how to achieve German unity. The Alliance for Germany and the League of Free Democrats favoured the fastest practical route. This meant the GDR becoming part of the Federal Republic of (West) Germany under article 23 of its Basic Law. By re-establishing the GDR's five *Länder*, abolished in 1952, they would have the means. The *Länder* would only have to decide to adopt the Basic Law to accede to the Federal Republic. No great debate would be needed and no lengthy ratification or administrative process. As we saw above, the SPD wanted a new constitution, which would be placed before the two parliaments for ratification. This seemed a slow and complicated route.

Electoral law

The election law was agreed on 20 February and voters had one vote for one of the listed parties. Candidates' names were not listed. There were 15 electoral districts based on the 15 *Bezirke* of the GDR. The number of members of the Volkskammer depended on the population size of each. Given the GDR's undemocratic past and the number of competing parties, it was essential to ensure that the new Volkskammer reflected as wide a range of views as possible. The parties were allocated seats on the basis of the proportion of votes they attracted. According to the Hare–Niemeyer system, to win one of the 400 seats in the chamber a vote of only 0.25 per cent was necessary. There was no postal vote, but those on the electoral register who were away from home on polling day could get a polling card enabling them to vote anywhere in the GDR. This had been a feature of the GDR's previous election law. Also from the past was the rule that groups or parties pursuing fascist, militarist or anti-humanist aims or which advocated hatred on religious, racial or ethnic grounds were debarred from taking part in the election. A five-man election commission decided such prohibitions. The far-right West German *Republikaner* had been prevented from establishing a presence in the GDR.

The East German voters were bombarded by the electronic media and the press with election news. One feature of the campaign was the many reports of GDR events by the West German media, which were seen by most East Germans. The smaller parties gained in that, lacking their own press and organisations, television gave them valuable publicity. Nevertheless, the big parties had the overall advantage through press, radio and television. They also had the funds to put on mass rallies addressed by top West German politicians such as Kohl, Genscher and Brandt. CSU Chairman Theo Waigel left Bavaria and crossed the frontier to campaign for the DSU. Although the GDR was still a sovereign independent state, there appeared to be little opposition to West German politicians getting directly involved in the campaign. Most East Germans had seen them on television over the years and some felt it gave them new dignity to have these important personalities vying for their votes. As the head of the GDR government, Modrow got even more publicity than the other politicians did, and this undoubtedly helped his party, the PDS.

In addition to the media, the electors faced a mass of propaganda from the parties and alliances. There were large and small posters everywhere. A key CDU poster depicted Lothar de Maizière against a background of the German black, red and gold tricolour with the words ' "Prosperity for All" – Ludwig Erhard,' and ' "We are *one* People" – Lothar de Maizière.' The CDU was banking on most voters remembering Erhard as the 'father' of West Germany's economic miracle. However, if they did, they would have known he was dead and buried and could not help them. The poster also carried the words 'CDU '90 Future – only together'. *Bündnis 90*'s slogan was 'citizens for citizens'. The PDS made heavy use of Modrow, with the slogan, 'PDS. Forwards but don't forget. A new party goes on its way.' It was not quite clear what voters were supposed to forget. Another favourite PDS slogan was 'Sooner a glass of Gorbachev than a bowl of Kohl soup', playing on the fact that Kohl means cabbage in German. The PDS worked hard to present itself as a party of youth. One widely used poster depicted a teenage couple kissing, with the young man wearing a baseball cap. The slogan was, 'Close your eyes when kissing, open them when you vote. The first time. PDS.' The big parties followed the West German tradition of offering free badges, pencils, biros, matches, bottle openers, car stickers, paper flags, posters and other trinkets suitably adorned with their party logos. Money did not seem to be a problem for the PDS or the CDU.

127

According to *Die Welt* (19 March 1990), the PDS admitted spending 5.5 million GDR marks on its campaign. This compared with 0.5 million spent by the SPD. The CDU was estimated to have spent 1.5 million and *Bündnis 90* 1 million. It seems unlikely that these figures include gifts from West German organisations, which greatly helped the CDU, DSU, SPD and the Liberals.

According to German tradition, election day was a Sunday, with polling stations open from 7 a.m. to 6 p.m. The same facilities, mainly schools, which had been used in the discredited previous GDR 'elections' were made available for these dramatic but peaceful free elections. Weather conditions were perfect. Despite the short distance, in most cases, to the polling stations, this was slightly more important than it would have been in West Germany because of the fewer motor vehicles available in the GDR. The PDS probably enjoyed a small advantage in this respect because its officials and supporters were more likely to be motorised. The PDS also enjoyed a residual advantage in that many of the previous electoral officials in the polling stations were the same people who had done this job for the SED. In Leipzig the author found a considerable minority of voters emerging from the polling stations reluctant to divulge their party preferences. The great majority of those asked were prepared to condemn the previous SED-run 'elections'. With few exceptions, fear was given as the reason for voting in these phoney elections. One professor of architecture, when questioned, said he had thought the previous elections were democratic. The count was open for anyone to observe. In Leipzig the author detected a tendency to reject ballot papers clearly marked for one or other party, other than the PDS, if they were slightly unusual. Nevertheless, the election appeared to be well run throughout the GDR with few complaints. The excellent weather probably marginally increased the customary high turnout at German elections. In the first really free election in this part of Germany since 1932 the 93.4 per cent turnout was higher than that at any West German election since 1945.

Results: some surprises

The results of the March election came as a surprise in all camps. The influential West German paper *Die Welt* (19 March 1990) headline was, 'Sensational Victory of the CDU and DSU. Quick steps to unification awaited.' The equally influential *Frankfurter Allgemeine Zeitung* (19 March 1990) reported, 'Alliance for Germany ahead in the GDR election. The SPD unexpectedly weak. The old SED stronger than expected. The Liberals around 5 per cent. High poll.' *Der Spiegel* (19 March 1990), not one of Kohl's best friends, called the *Allianz* victory 'a dream result for Chancellor Kohl'. The modest de Maizière himself, reported *Der Spiegel*, looked pale

Table 10.1 Opinion Polls Nov/Dec 1989 and Jan/Feb 1990

	CDU	LDPD	SED/PDS	NDPD	DBD	SPD	NF	DA	Greens	DSU	DJ
I	10	23	31	3	5	–	17	–	–	–	–
II	13	3	12	1	4	53	3	2	2	2	1

Source: *Das Parlament*, 9 March 1990.

and exhausted and simply told his colleagues it was an unexpectedly good result. As for Kohl, according to *Der Spiegel*, it was a 'super result', 'a historic result', and he could hardly take in the triumph. Kohl had other reasons to be happy on that night. In the Bavarian local elections, held on the same day, the CSU had held on to its leading position despite some SPD gains, and the dreaded right-wing Republicans had been stopped in their tracks. The failure of the Liberals in the GDR election meant that the FDP, Kohl's coalition partners, would have to take up a more modest posture. In the opposition camp there was naturally dismay and despondency. Stefan Heym, critical GDR loyalist, concluded, 'There won't be a GDR any more.' His despondency, if that's what it was, was shared by the members of New Forum and the other groups in *Bündnis 90*. They had done so much to bring about the situation which led up to the free elections and yet they got so little support. Social Democratic leader Böhme said he would not join a coalition but he urged his party to do so. Modrow and Gysi knew their PDS could not win but were pleasantly surprised by their result. The public opinion pollsters were embarrassed. Some thought it was their Waterloo. Earlier opinion polls, like the *Spiegel* poll mentioned above (Chapter 9) had put the SPD ahead. Table 10.1 the results of a poll at the end of November/ beginning of December 1989 (I) and of a second poll conducted at the end of January/beginning of February (II). These were the work of the *Zentralinstitut für Jugendforschung* and *Institut für Marktforschung*, both in Leipzig.

According to the second poll, the SPD was likely to get 60 per cent of the votes of the workers. Those in favour of unity were more likely to vote CDU, and 71 per cent of those totally against would vote PDS. The poll also found the voters fairly certain about their preferences. Very certain were 42 per cent, relatively certain 43 per cent. Why were these polls and others so far out? When these polls were taken, the electorate had not yet been exposed to the full charm offensive by Helmut Kohl and his lieutenants. They were also uncertain and confused as for most of them this was a totally new experience. The underestimate for the PDS was probably due to some of its supporters feeling intimidated, being afraid to identify with a sinking ship, lost cause or an outfit regarded by many as a criminal conspiracy.

Table 10.2   Results of March 1990 Volkskammer election

	Votes	%	Seats
CDU*	4,710,598	40.8	163
SPD	2,525,534	21.8	88
PDS	1,892,381	16.4	66
DSU*	727,730	6.3	25
BFD	608,935	5.3	21
Bündnis 90	336,074	3.0	12
DBD	251,226	2.2	9
Greens/UFV	226,932	2.0	8
DA*	106,146	1.0	4
NDPD	44,292	0.4	2
DFD	38,192	0.3	1
AVL	20,342	0.2	1
Others	53,733	0.5	–

* Alliance for Germany

Source: Die Volkskammer der Deutschen Demokratischen Republik 10. Wahlperiode: Die Abgeordneten der Volkskammer nach den Wahlen vom 18. März 1990, Staatsverlag der DDR, 1990.

Some perhaps turned back to the PDS in desperation fearing what would happen to them when Germany was again united. Finally, perhaps, there was an element of unconscious bias on the part of the interviewers, who took for granted that the old pre-Hitler SPD strongholds were still social democratic-orientated. Commentators had overestimated the so-called 'GDR identity', which, had it been stronger, would have led more voters to vote for parties other than the CDU or even the SPD. As always, the activists on the streets were not completely representative of the voters as a whole. Many old people who never went to a demonstration, particularly old women, were more inclined to the Alliance for Germany.

As it turned out, the overwhelming victory of the Alliance, and of the CDU within it, was totally unexpected. The second surprise was the defeat of the SPD and the third was the *relatively* large vote for the PDS (see Table 10.2). The election result was widely interpreted as an endorsement of Helmut Kohl and his values. He had entered into the campaign relatively late, but by the end of it had addressed over a million people in six GDR towns and was much better known than the leaders of the Alliance for Germany, which he was supporting. Within the Alliance, the old CDU triumphed rather than the new DA or DSU. Here again the association of the initials CDU with Kohl's CDU must have been an important factor. The CDU's better organisation than its partners in the Alliance had also helped. Clearly, most GDR voters wanted the fastest possible route to German re-unification, and the Alliance, backed by Kohl's government, seemed to be the vehicle best equipped to achieve that goal. The Alliance had received its best results in the southern industrial towns, which suffered most from pollution, poor housing and poor health facilities. There were some smiles when it became clear that it had gained its best result in Karl-Marx-Stadt (Chemnitz). Its lowest vote was in Berlin (21.5 per cent). It came first in 12 of the GDR's 15 administrative districts. It appeared to have gained support from men and women in roughly equal proportions. According to figures given by the Friedrich-Ebert-Stiftung, the Alliance gained the votes of 58 per cent of the industrial workers, 47 per cent of white-collar employees, 43 per cent of pensioners, but only 32 per cent of graduates.

After an early lead the SPD had been punished for the hesitation and doubts of the West German SPD's leaders, above all Oskar Lafontaine. The party was also hampered by poor organisation, despite West German help. The Social Democrats came first in three areas, including Berlin, where they scored their highest vote of 34.8 per cent, and second in ten others. Its lowest percentage, 9.7, was in Dresden.

Apart from a few old Communists who were living in a fantasy world of illusions, most former SED members expected the new PDS to be virtually annihilated. This turned out not to be the case. The convictions of the few and the fear of the many had served the PDS well. It best result was in Berlin, home of so many of the GDR's political, administrative, military and cultural élites. They provided the party with 30.2 per cent of the vote in East Berlin, where it came second to the SPD. It also came second in Dresden and Neu Brandenburg. Its poorest result was in Erfurt, with 9.9 per cent. The PDS obviously benefited from its huge funds, good organisation and desperate determination to save as much as possible or go down fighting.

With 10 per cent, the League of Free Democrats scored its best result in Halle, the hometown of West German Foreign Minister Hans-Dietrich Genscher. The League did not appear to gain much reflected glory from Genscher's many services to East–West relations and wide international reputation. It suffered from its late formation and the squabbling which had preceded it. A better strategy for the Liberals would have been simply to call themselves the FDP, as most GDR voters had orientated themselves to the political scene in West Germany.

Although with hindsight it seemed inevitable, the low vote of *Bündnis 90* was something of a shock and seemed unfair. The truth is that it had little or no organisation and had rather despised the publicity machines of the major players. Its image was rather austere and its policies not entirely clear to most voters. It suffered from not being readily identifiable with a West German political product seen on television for so many years. Its best result, 6.3 per cent, was gained in Berlin. In Leipzig and Dresden, the scene of so many mass demonstrations, it recorded votes of 3.3 and 3.6 per cent respectively. Had the parties campaigning as part of *Bündnis 90* agreed to fight as New Forum, a much better known label, it would probably have ended up with a few more percentage points. As it was, it lost votes to all sides, including some to the PDS among those who really believed it was different from the old SED.

Half the parties contesting the elections failed to gain representation in the Volkskammer. At the head were the Alternative Youth List, itself an alliance of four groups, which scored 14,616 votes. The Christian League, with 10,691 votes, followed it. There were groups with left-wing names such as the Communist Party of Germany (KPD), which attracted 8,819 votes, gained throughout the GDR except for Halle, New Brandenburg and Suhl. It had nothing to do with earlier Communist parties bearing that name. The Independent Social Democratic Party, with 3,891 votes, owed nothing to the party of the early Weimar period of the same name. It was not organised throughout the GDR and mustered its votes in Magdeburg, New Brandenburg, Potsdam, Rostock and Suhl. The European Federalist Party won 3,363 votes, the Independent People's Party 3,007 and the German Beer Drinkers' Union 2,534, all of them in Rostock! The Spartacist Workers' Party only attracted 2,417 votes, gaining them in Berlin, Cottbus, Halle, Leipzig and Rostock. Unity Now collected 2,396 and the League of Socialist Workers 386 votes. With only 380 votes, gained in Berlin and Leipzig, the Association of Working Circles for Employees and Democracy came next to the bottom. Finally, the European Union of the GDR had the distinction of attracting no votes!

The CDU was victorious once more on 6 May 1990 in the GDR's first democratic local elections. True, its vote declined from 40.8 per cent to 34.4 per cent, but it emerged as the biggest single party. Its greatest success was once again recorded in Chemnitz. The SPD's percentage declined slightly to 21.3 and the PDS to 14.6. The Free Democrats came out slightly better than before, achieving 6.7 per cent. The DSU vote collapsed to 3.4 per cent, while New Forum, fighting the election alone in many areas, gained 2.4 per cent. New Forum won seats throughout the GDR in some cases in harness with Democracy Now or the Initiative for Freedom and Human Rights. The Greens were also elected to a number of town halls. Although considerably lower than turnout in March, the 75 per cent turnout revealed that the citizens of the GDR were taking their newfound freedom seriously.

It is astonishing that ten years later there should be those who question that election, who claim the voters were not voting for re-unification, that only an élite wanted this. This view was put to Olga Frenkel of the BBC when she visited Chemnitz in November 1999.[11] The Green interviewee also claimed that, although there had been election fraud by the SED under the old regime, most people had voted for the official candidates. But why had they done so? I interviewed 50 voters as they left the polling station on that day in March 1990. Most had little hesitation in saying they had previously voted out of fear. They voted in March 1990 not for the Greens or the SPD, who were ambivalent about re-unification, but for the parties most clearly identified with it and all things Western.

Notes

1. Peter Thompson, 'The GDR Election: An Eyewitness Account from Berlin', *Politics and Society in Germany, Austria and Switzerland*, Vol. 2, No. 3, Summer 1990, p. 83.
2. Peter Joachim Lapp, *Ausverkauf: Das Ende der Blockparteien*, Berlin, 1998, p. 91.
3. Peter R. Weilemann *et al.*, *Parteien im Aufbruch: Nichthommunistische Parteien und politische Vereinigungen in der DDR*, St Augustin, 1990, pp. 24–5.
4. Robert Darnton, *Berlin Journal, 1989–90*, New York, 1993, p. 239.
5. *Ibid.*
6. *Keesing's Record of World Events*, News Digest for March 1990, 37301.
7. Darnton, *Berlin Journal*, p. 240.
8. Weilemann *et al.*, *Parteien im Aufbruch*, p. 71.
9. Darnton, *Berlin Journal*, p. 241.
10. *Ibid.*, pp. 242–3.
11. *Newsnight*, 3 November 1989.

Chapter 11

German unity achieved

The grand coalition

Having won a remarkable victory, the Alliance for Germany claimed the right to head the first, and last, democratically elected government of the GDR. Lothar de Maizière was, therefore, duly elected head of government or Minister-President. The idea was to have a government which represented, as far as possible, all shades of democratic opinion. Difficult negotiations followed and a grand coalition was formed on 9 April. (Before this happened the SPD received an apology from the DSU for part of its electoral propaganda which suggested that the SPD were Communists in disguise.) The grand coalition commanded 301 of the 400 seats in the new Volkskammer. The new government was made up as shown in Table 11.1.

Most of the ministers were not well known and the majority of them faded into obscurity after October 1990. Only six of them remained in the Bundestag elected in December 1990. Romberg went on to serve as a Member of the European Parliament. At ministerial level, the most experienced was Kurt Wünsche, who had served under Stoph as a Deputy Chairman of the Council of Ministers, 1965–72, and Minister of Justice, 1967–72 and again from January 1990. He had been a member of the Volkskammer since 1954! His colleague, Economics Minister Gerhard Pohl, had been a member of the Volkskammer since 1981.

Who were the Volkskammer members?

What of the members of the new, democratic Volkskammer? They were well educated and younger than those of most other European parliaments, and certainly than those of the previous Volkskammer. The average age was 41.8 years old. The youngest member was 19-year-old Kay Reiman of the CDU, the oldest a SPD member, Dr Günter Kilias, aged 64. Kilias, a forestry engineer from Cottbus, was followed by Lothar Piche (DSU), an electrician from Karl-Marx-Stadt, who was just under 64.[1] By contrast, in the West German Bundestag elected in 1987, the oldest member was Willy Brandt, aged 74, and the youngest was Frau Verena Krieger of the Greens,

Table 11.1 The grand coalition

Office	Office-holder	Party
Minister-President	Lothar de Maizière	CDU
Chief of Minister-President's staff	Klaus Reichenbach	CDU
Deputy Prime Minister & Minister of Interior	Peter-Michael Diestel	DSU
Foreign Minister	Pastor Markus Meckel	SPD
Regional & Local Affairs	Manfred Preiss	BFD
Economy	Gerhard Pohl	CDU
Finance	Walter Romberg	SPD
Trade & Tourism	Sybille Reider	SPD
Justice	Kurt Wünsche	BFD
Food, Agriculture & Forestry	Peter Pollack	Non-party
Labour & Social Affairs	Regine Hildebrandt	SPD
Disarmament & Defence	Rainer Eppelmann	DA
Youth & Sport	Cordula Schubert	CDU
Family & Women	Christa Schmidt	CDU
Health	Jürgen Kleditzsch	CDU
Transport	Horst Gibtner	CDU
Environment, Nature Conservancy, Energy & Reactor Safety	Karl-Hermann Steinberg	CDU
Post & Telecommunications	Emil Schnell	SPD
Construction, Urban Development & Housing	Axel Viehweger	BFD
Research & Technology	Frank Terpe	SPD
Education & Science	Hans-Joachim Meyer	Non-party
Culture	Herbert Schirmer	CDU
Media	Gottfried Müller	CDU
Economic Co-operation	Pastor Hans-Wilhelm Ebeling	DSU
Government Spokesman	Matthias Gehler	Non-party
Parliamentary State Secretary in Minister-President's Office	Günther Krause	CDU

Sources: *Neues Deutschland*, 14–15 April 1990; *Neue Zeit*, 14 April 1990.

aged 26. The largest age group in the Volkskammer was the 40 to 50 year olds, of whom there 178. They were truly children of the GDR. Relatively few women were elected to the Volkskammer. Altogether there were 83 of them, 20.8 per cent. Nevertheless, although low by Scandinavian standards, this percentage was higher than that of the Bundestag or the British House of Commons. In the 1987 Bundestag there were 80 women, that is, 15.4 per cent. In the British House of Commons a record number of women had been elected in 1987, but they represented only 6.3 per cent. The PDS group boasted the highest number of women. In the BFD there were no women at all. Of the 400 members of the Volkskammer, 143 had obtained a doctorate and 18 of these were professors. The main groups were engineers, educationalists, medical practitioners and economists. In the Bundestag, by contrast, graduates were more likely to be lawyers followed by educationalists. Medical practitioners were hardly represented. The difference between the two democratic parliaments was that in the Bundestag there were far more professional politicians. Most of those in the Volkskammer were amateurs. Most of the Volkskammer members had attempted to keep clear of politics in the past by choosing medical, technical or natural science-based careers. Among them was Dr Sabine Bergmann-Pohl, a specialist in respiratory diseases, who joined the CDU in 1981. She was elected President of the Volkskammer, thus becoming the last head of state of the GDR. Only 12 of the 400 members of the newly elected Volkskammer had served in the old undemocratic Volkskammer. Six of them belonged to the PDS, 2 to the CDU, 2 to the DBD and 2 were former NDPD members who had joined the BFD. Religion was well represented in the Volkskammer. No less than 27 evangelical pastors were elected. Of these, 14 were SPD members, 9 belonged to the Alliance for Germany, 3 to *Bündnis 90*/the Greens, and 1 belonged to the BFD.

Hans Modrow was the most prominent of the SED politicians to make the transition to the democratic Volkskammer. He had been a member of the Volkskammer since 1958. His PDS colleague Kätie Niederkirchner, a medical practitioner, had been a member since 1967, and in that limited sense vied with Kurt Wünsche as the most experienced politician in the new Volkskammer. Another prominent PDS member elected was Professor Lothar Bisky, who had played a major role in the transition from the SED to the PDS and in planning the party's media strategy. In 1993 he was elected Chairman of the PDS. Gregor Gysi, Chairman of the PDS in 1990, was also elected and was to go on to serve the party in the Bundestag. Modrow's government colleague Professor Christa Luft was also elected to the Volkskammer. She was elected to the Bundestag in 1994 and re-elected in 1998 on the PDS list. The most remarkable old Volkskammer member, who had served the SED well, was Günther Maleuda, who, as Chairman of the DBD, had been in the chamber since 1981. He had served as a Deputy Chairman of Honecker's Council of State, and was the Chairman of the Volkskammer in the *Wende* period. He was elected PDS candidate to the Bundestag in 1994.

Among the GDR dissidents elected were Joachim Gauck, Gerd Poppe, Werner Schulz, Konrad Weiß and Vera Wollenberger of *Bündnis 90*/the Greens. Poppe, Schulz and Wollenberger went on to serve in the Bundestag. Wollenberger eventually joined the CDU. She had been arrested in connection with the Liebkneckt–Luxemburg demonstration in 1988. Schulz had lost his job for protesting against the Soviet invasion of Afghanistan. Dr Thomas Klein, elected for the United Left (VL), had earned his spurs in

Bautzen jail for 'illegal contacts' with West Germany. He later served briefly as a PDS member of the Bundestag. The physicist Günter Nooke and theologian Dr Wolfgang Ullmann were elected as DJ members. They joined *Bündnis 90*/the Greens. Dr Ullmann went on to serve in the Bundestag and the European Parliament. Professor of molecular biology Jens Reich was demoted because he refused to break off West German contacts. Elected as a New Forum candidate in the *Bündnis 90*/Greens group, he went on to serve in the Bundestag. The pictures of individual members did not betray their party affiliation as they often did in the case of the House of Commons at that time. Beards and thick pullovers, sensible haircuts and collars and ties were not the preserve of any one party.

'We ask the Jews . . . for pardon'

Top on the agenda of the new Volkskammer was a statement agreed unanimously on 12 April. This recognised the responsibility of the GDR Germans for 'their history and their future'. During the National Socialist era, immeasurable suffering was inflicted by Germans on the peoples of the world. Nationalism and racial fanaticism led to genocide, especially against the Jews from all European states, against the peoples of the Soviet Union, the Polish people and the Sintis and Romanies. It recognised joint responsibility for the humiliation, expulsion and murder of Jewish women, men and children.

> We feel sadness and shame and recognise this burden of German history. We ask the Jews all over the world for pardon. We ask the people of Israel for forgiveness for the hypocrisy and hostility of official GDR policy towards the state of Israel and for the persecution and degradation of Jewish fellow-citizens in our country since 1945.

The Volkskammer members saw as a special task the education of youth to have respect for the Jewish religion, traditions and culture. The declaration called for the establishment of diplomatic relations with Israel. The declaration was also aimed at the Soviet Union. 'We have not forgotten the terrible suffering inflicted by the Germans on the people of the Soviet Union in the Second World War. . . . We want to intensify the process of reconciliation between our peoples.' It recognised that without the New Thinking and the *perestroika* in the Soviet Union, the transformation of the GDR would have been impossible. The Volkskammer members thanked the citizens of the Soviet Union for the stimulus in this direction. They admitted shared guilt for the crushing of the 'Prague Spring' in 1968, 'which had put back the democratisation in Eastern Europe by 20 years'. They accused themselves for doing nothing about it. Finally, the statement re-affirmed the Oder–Neisse frontier with Poland as 'inviolable' and as basis for the peaceful co-operation of the two peoples in a 'common European House'.[2] No one could say that the members of the Volkskammer were not prepared to face the past at the same time as they were looking to a better future.

The Volkskammer, and the government it had just elected, received encouragement from the European Community. Meeting in Dublin on 28 April, the Council of Heads of State and Heads of Government warmly greeted the unification of Germany, which it saw as a positive factor in the development of Europe in general and of the European Community in particular. The political leaders of the EC promised to ensure that the integration of the territory of the GDR into the Community would be carried through harmoniously and without a hitch. Until unification took place, the GDR would have full and total access to all the credit facilities of the EC.

Professors of Marxism–Leninism retired

The democratically elected Volkskammer also wanted to 'clean out the stables' left behind by Honecker and Krenz. This meant removing political appointees at all levels and employing people for their professional skills and qualifications rather than their *Weltanschauung*. Many organisations would have to be restructured to conform to democratic or commercial norms or would be closed down. Among those who were to find life a little more difficult were the 6,700 school directors of the GDR. Towards the end of May it was announced that they would all be dismissed.[3] Virtually all of them were SED members. They could apply for their old jobs, which were being advertised. Alternatively, they could apply to take early retirement. Also facing the sack were 550 professors and lecturers in the field of Marxism-Leninism. Their posts were simply to disappear. In the same month, Economics Minister Gerhard Pohl announced that all the industrial chieftains of the GDR, the so-called 'General Directors', would lose their jobs. In future, the new supervisory boards, modelled on those of West German firms, would appoint the heads of GDR businesses. The general directors had all been SED members, some of them serving on the ZK of the party. Judges and lawyers were another group needing urgent attention. The great majority of them were total subjects of the ruling Politburo. Yet it would have been both undesirable and impracticable to attempt to replace them with West Germans or untrained East Germans. Also to go were the functionaries of the FDJ, which had shrunk from around 2 million members to 20,000 within a few months. Among the bodies on the demolition list was the secret *Institut für Jugendforschung* in Leipzig founded in 1966. The Institute, which had a staff of 90, had provided secret reports on the mood of GDR youth to the FDJ, SED and government. Its Director, Professor Walter Friedrich, was informed in September that it was to be closed on

2 October. In this case those over 50 would receive nine months' severance pay.[4] With the dismantling of the SED state, many tens of thousands more would find themselves going to the new job centres. They would form the hardcore of PDS voters. PDS members in Berlin took to the streets on 2 June to protest against legislation to determine the value of the assets of parties which were in existence on 7 October 1989. They faced expropriation of their properties.

Monetary, economic and social union

All parties represented in the government were agreed on the aim of the restoration of German unity, though they were not entirely agreed on the route to unity, the timing and conditions. However, even more pressing was the restoration of confidence within the GDR itself. This was to be achieved through monetary, economic and social union with the Federal Republic. Political union could then be negotiated in a calmer atmosphere. On 18 May 1990 Dr Theo Waigel, Finance Minister of the Federal Republic, and Dr Walter Romberg, his GDR counterpart, signed the treaty establishing a monetary, economic and social union of the two states. The signing ceremony took place in Bonn and this symbolised the fact that this was not a coming together of equal partners. The GDR government was virtually handing over the running of its financial and economic system to West Germany. In clause after clause it agreed to adjust its institutions and regulations to those of the Federal Republic and the European Community. As paragraph one of the 'Protocol on Guidelines' stated, 'The law of the German Democratic Republic will be modelled on the principles of a free, democratic federal and social order governed by the rule of law and be guided by the legal regime of the European Community.'[5] The first clause of the section on economic union laid down that, 'Economic activity should primarily occur in the private sector and on the basis of competition.' The GDR currency was to disappear and be replaced by the Deutsche Mark, issued and controlled solely and exclusively by the Bundesbank, the Federal Bank, in Frankfurt am Main. The Bundesbank was in effect taking over the State Bank of the GDR.

> The Deutsche Bundesbank shall exercise the powers accorded it by this treaty and by the Deutsche Bundesbank Act in the entire currency area. It shall establish for this purpose a provisional office in Berlin with up to 15 branches in the German Democratic Republic, which shall be located in the premises of the State Bank of the German Democratic Republic.

The treaty opened the door to private banking in the GDR, including West German banks. The legal system was also to be brought in line with that of the Federal Republic. This was a very complex problem even when GDR lawyers were enthusiastic about the change, and by no means all supported the move. Unemployment insurance, health, insurance, public health, accident insurance, pensions – all these had to be brought in line with existing practice in the Federal Republic. The same was true of labour unions and employers' organisations.

False dawn for the Western SPD

In the West Lafontaine and Horst Ehmke, Deputy Chair of the SPD Bundestag group, attacked the treaty. Lafontaine, SPD Minister-President of the Saar, had greatly strengthened his position on 28 January by increasing his party's vote from 49.2 per cent in 1985 to 54.4 per cent in 1990. He saw the way forward as constant attacks on the costs of rapid unification. But following the East German elections, some Social Democrats expected heavy losses in Western regional elections. However the CDU failed to make headway in two more Western *Länder* on 13 May. In Northrhine-Westphalia it made slight gains, increasing its vote from 36.5 per cent (in 1985) to 36.7 per cent. The SPD, which had held sway in this *Land* for 24 years, saw its vote decline from 52.1 per cent to 50 per cent. The Greens increased their vote from 4.6 to 5 per cent. The threatened surge of the far right Republicans did not materialise and they only scored 1.8 per cent. The FDP vote declined slightly from 6 to 5.8 per cent. In Lower Saxony, where the CDU had been in government since the mid-1970s, the SPD took the lead, increasing its vote from 42.1 per cent in 1986 to 44.2 per cent. The CDU vote dropped from 44.3 to 42 per cent. The FDP vote remained on 6 per cent and the Green vote fell from 7.1 to 5.5. Once again the Republicans failed to make headway, achieving only 1.8 per cent. There an SPD–Green administration was formed. The SPD felt confident about its chances against Kohl in the federal elections set for December 1990 and Kohl was worried. To a degree the SPD had benefited from another factor no one had expected or welcomed. On 25 April Lafontaine was attacked during an election meeting by a woman with a knife. He sustained life-threatening injuries, but made a speedy recovery. The woman was later found to be mentally ill. Moreover, the party's critical line on unification, pursued despite some opposition from Social Democrats in the West, was less popular that it as assumed. The impression was given that the SPD was mean towards its 'brothers and sisters' in the GDR. This hurt it in the December 1990 first all-German federal elections.

Goodbye Marx and Engels

On 1 July 1990 the two German states were formally joined in a monetary, economic and social union. The (West) German mark or Deutsche Mark was introduced into the GDR as sole legal tender. Older East Germans remembered earlier currency changes which had taken place in 1957, 1964 and 1971. The familiar bank notes with the heads of Thomas Müntzer (5 marks), Clara Zetkin (10 marks), Goethe (20 marks), Engels (50 marks) and Marx (100 marks) disappeared. Gone too were the sad little coins which were lighter in weight than West European coins. They were similar to those circulated by the German occupation authorities when they were plundering Europe. Their very lack of weight undermined their credibility and the serious intent of those who had issued them. Few missed them. Under the treaty, 'Wages, salaries, grants, pensions, rents and leases as well as other recurring payments shall be converted at a rate of one to one. All other claims and liabilities denominated in mark of the German Democratic Republic shall be converted to Deutsche Mark at the rate of two to one.'[6] Money in bank accounts was converted into Deutsche Mark at the rate of 1:1 for the first 4,000 GDR marks of account holders between 14 and 60 years old. The over-sixties were allowed to convert 6,000 at this rate, and those under 14 2,000 GDR marks. Higher balances were converted at 2:1. This was a generous rate for, as we have seen, the GDR mark was being exchanged for 10:1 in December 1989 and traditionally had been exchanged for 5:1. East Germans went on a new shopping spree for every conceivable type of consumer good, for food and for cars. East German produce was left on the shelves. Industries in the GDR now faced full competition from West German products and goods imported into West Germany. Most East Germans preferred West German products even when there was little difference other than the higher price of the Western product. They lost orders at home and with their customers in the East. About a quarter to a third of all GDR foreign trade was with the Soviet Union alone. Nearly 500,000 jobs, directly or indirectly, depended on trade with the Soviets. As East European states freed their trade, they switched from GDR products to American, West European and Asian products. Unemployment rose rapidly in the GDR. The one for one exchange rate was criticised in many quarters. The influential former president of the powerful Bundesbank, Otto Pöhl, argued that it would increase inflation and discourage inward investment from abroad. Kohl, however, realised that it would be politically disastrous if East Germans saw their savings disappear, especially older people, who would have no chance of rebuilding them.

On 29 June Detlev Karsten Rohwedder, Chairman of the West German engineering group Hoesch, was appointed Chairman of the *Treuhandanstalt*, the trust body established by Modrow on 1 March 1990 to oversee the 'safeguarding' and/or restructuring of the 8,500-plus state-owned enterprises of the GDR. The Volkskammer agreed a new law, symbolically, on 17 June. This put the emphasis on the privatisation of state-owned enterprises.

141

Rohwedder was assassinated by RAF terrorists on 1 April 1991 before his mission was completed. Among the highlights of the trust's activities, in 1991, were the closing down of the GDR national airways Interflug, the end of the production of the Trabant car on 30 April, and at the end of July, the handing over of the GDR lottery to Berlin and the five *Länder*. The West German company with the same name bought 51 per cent of the shares in Carl-Zeiss Jena, the world famous optics firm. The rest were held by the Carl-Zeiss Foundation, administered by the government of Thuringia. In 1992 the famous DEFA studios were sold to a firm controlled by the French CGE. By March 1992, 20 per cent of the firms privatised had been sold in management buyouts, but these were mainly the smaller businesses. The GDR shipbuilding industry presented a particular problem in that 80 per cent of its orders were from Soviet customers who could not pay for the vessels ordered. Eventually the yards were sold to a Norwegian firm, Kvaerner, and the Bremen firm Vulkan. Heavy subsidies were involved. What became later one of the most controversial decisions was the sale of Leuna/Minol to a consortium of the German Thyssen and the French state oil enterprise Elf.

The trust faced criticism from abroad for allegedly favouring West German firms. Of course German firms had many natural advantages over foreign competitors of language, geography and local knowledge. Nearer home it was attacked for incompetence, cronyism and corruption. Certainly there were a number cases where property speculators managed to get their hands on properties at knockdown prices. It was only in August 1991 that the executive of the trust passed rules governing insider trading by those working for the *Treuhand*. Another problem was analysing just how much GDR businesses were worth. Outside assessors were needed who had knowledge of particular industrial sectors and they were likely to be drawn from competitors and potential buyers. Some West German trade union leaders were also appointed to the board of the trust. By January 1992, the number of employees working for firms controlled by the trust had fallen from 4,080,000 in 1990 to 1,650,000. What had happened to the rest? Unemployment was the fate of 336,000, 455,000 had retired or were on government-financed work creation programmes (ABM), and about 640,000 had changed their jobs or professions.[7] Ownership disputes, poor infrastructure, environmental problems, poor image and lack of Western life-style facilities hampered efforts to attract outside, especially non-German, investors. East Germans found themselves competing against low-paid but skilled Czechs and Poles, and highly paid but highly productive West Germans.

On 15 June 1990, agreement was reached on the ownership of GDR property, including land, which had been confiscated, since the setting up of the GDR in 1949, from GDR citizens who had gone West illegally.

Basically, this was to be restored to them. This was a difficult and emotional problem. In the main, those affected were people with a family home or smallholding which they had forfeited by 'deserting' the GDR. In many cases their property had been handed over to loyal SED members who had lived in the properties for as long as thirty or forty years. In some cases they were faced with West Germans knocking on their doors demanding to be let in. Property seized before the setting up of the GDR did not come within the scope of the settlement.

As the economic situation deteriorated, protests and strikes followed. On 5–6 July there were strikes in the metal and engineering industries. These were settled on 13 July with pay increases of 20 per cent, a 40-hour week and a 12-month job-security guarantee. Strikes by chemical workers got them a 35 per cent pay increase and a promise of payment for a '13th month' in the year. Rail workers also took strike action, which led to pay increases. In August it was the turn of public service employees, including public transport, to take part in warning strikes.[8] Controversy continued long after about the increases in pay. Some, both trade unionists and employers, believed they speeded up the rise in unemployment. Farmers were among the hardest hit by the new economic situation of outside competition. Their industry had been heavily subsidised, productivity was low and there was chronic overmanning. In the new situation they could not compete with agricultural products from West Germany and other EC countries. On 15 August 250,000 farmers took part in demonstrations and erected blockades in the streets. Although they got DM 1,650 million in emergency aid, their situation remained precarious.[9] Many of them failed over the following years.

In May 1990 a special fund was announced by Kohl's government, the 'Fund for German Unity'. The Federal government and the *Länder* were prepared to guarantee 115 bn marks over five years as a down payment towards the rehabilitation of the German economy. So much needed to be done to bring the roads, railways, airports, streets and housing up to modern standards. The devastation wrought by the Soviet armed forces to large tracts of land over the previous forty years was not yet clear.

Two Plus Four

The Treaty on Monetary, Economic and Social Union committed the two German states to national unity in accordance with article 23 of the Basic Law of the Federal Republic of Germany 'as a contribution to European unification, taking into account that the external aspects of establishing unity are the subject of negotiations with the Governments of the French Republic, the Union of Soviet Socialist Republics, the United Kingdom of

Great Britain and Northern Ireland and the United States of America'. The Germans recognised that unity could only be achieved by agreement between Moscow, Bonn and the three Western Powers. A number of consultations on the basis of 'Two Plus Four', meaning the foreign ministers of the four victor powers of 1945 and the foreign ministers of the two German states, were already underway by the time the Treaty on Monetary, Economic and Social Union was signed.

For Kohl and his Foreign Minister Genscher, a breakthrough came on their visit to Moscow on 10–11 February 1990. By then they had good relations with Gorbachev. Undoubtedly Gorbachev's visit to West Germany in June 1989 had made a great impression on the Soviet leader. *Der Spiegel* (5 June 1989) reported poll findings which revealed that 73 per cent of West Germans had a positive attitude to the Soviet Union. This compared with only 13 per cent in 1983. It also published a poll showing that Gorbachev was much more popular in West Germany than Bush, Mitterrand or Thatcher. Scenes of almost hysterical enthusiasm confronted the Soviet leader, the kind of reception he did not experience at home. He needed German help and the Germans were ready to oblige. He was clear that the SED regime was dead. In February 1990 Gorbachev agreed on the principle of German unity, leaving it to the Germans themselves to decide the timing and method. The Germans assured him on the question of frontiers, economic aid and other matters but insisted on Germany remaining in NATO. Gorbachev later summed up the situation at that time as follows, 'We had managed to clear up the misunderstandings, which was most important at that particular stage. However, there was still a long and dangerous road before us.'[10]

On 14 February the foreign ministers of the four allies and the two German states agreed to begin formal talks on the process to achieve German unity. Later that month, 24–5 February, Kohl and Bush met at Camp David and agreed on German unity. Germany was to remain in NATO, and the USA would continue to act as guarantor of stability in Europe. Kohl was the first German Chancellor to be honoured by a visit to Camp David. The leaders of both superpowers were courting Kohl! Such treatment could only help his political friends in the East German elections.

The first meeting of the Two Plus Four talks was held in Bonn, involving East and West German officials and representatives of the four powers on 14 March four days before the GDR elections. This was followed by a meeting of the foreign ministers in Bonn on 5 May at which the security implications of German unity were discussed. James Baker, US Secretary of State, took the opportunity to underline that the USA regarded the existing frontiers as unassailable and that a united Germany would comprise the Federal Republic, the GDR and Berlin, 'not more and not less'.[11] Baker put the emphasis in his contribution on the ending of all the residual rights of the four wartime allies. The united Germany would be fully sovereign. The following month, on 7 June, the Warsaw Pact meeting in Moscow announced that it was giving up its old, ideological, hostile view of the West and that in future the terms 'East' and 'West' should be, once again, merely geographical terms.[12] On Germany, the Pact members stressed that German unity in its external aspects should be on the basis of satisfying the legitimate security interests of Germany's neighbours and the recognition of the inviolability of frontiers in Europe. The next day NATO welcomed the Warsaw Pact's declaration and also went on record that German unity would be a considerable contribution to stability in Europe. The documents seem to reveal that everything was going ahead smoothly, but there were still doubters in many quarters and it needed little to bring them out.

The Oder–Neisse Line

After the visit to Camp David, on 25 February, Kohl caused a furore by appearing to hesitate on the frontier issue. At a press conference, he pulled back from stating clearly that the Oder–Neisse frontier was the final frontier between the two countries, Germany and Poland. He argued that this was a matter for a freely elected government and freely elected parliament of a united Germany. He also said that nobody would link the question of the unity of the nation with a change in existing frontiers.[13] On the same occasion Bush emphasised that the United States recognised the inviolability of the existing frontiers in Europe and formally recognised the existing German–Polish frontier. Another interesting aspect of the press conference was the emphasis the two leaders put on the European Community as an anchor of European stability. They therefore wanted European integration to be speeded up. Their aim, they said, was political union via the single market and currency union. It was Kohl's remarks about the frontier, however, which caused a storm. Margaret Thatcher, the British Prime Minister, made it clear that she would only support German unification if Germany recognised the Oder–Neisse Line. Kohl's European Community colleagues took the same position. As we saw in Chapter 8, Margaret Thatcher did little to hide her unease at the prospect of German re-unification. She dwelt on the past. In an interview with *The Sunday Times* (25 February 1990) she commented, 'You cannot just ignore the history of this century as if it did not happen, and say, "We are going to unify and everything else will have to be worked out afterwards." That is not the way.'

The result of such apparent equivocation by Kohl was that by February 1990 well over half the population of Poland feared the consequences of the restoration of German unity. The Polish Prime Minister, Tadeusz

Mazowiecki, stated that all such ambiguous statements on the issue had convinced the Poles that they were correct in demanding that the border be confirmed before Germany's re-unification.[14] A remarkable event which worried some Poles was the success of ethnic Germans living in Upper Silesia in recent local elections. For the first time, they had been allowed to stand. The greatest success was in Turawa, where Germans won all 21 council seats.[15] Most people outside Poland had no idea that there was still a significant German minority living there. In Britain, Thatcher and her government agreed with the Poles on the frontier issue. Indeed, Kohl's prevarication on the Oder–Neisse issue was greeted with anger and incomprehension in Britain, France and elsewhere. Why had Kohl wavered on the frontier issue taking up such a legalistic position? Firstly, because of course what he said was the exact legal position. He could not *presume* that the GDR electors would vote for parties which would opt for joining the Federal Republic. Nor could he speak for the GDR. Undoubtedly, he was hoping to strengthen the CDU's support in the coming March elections in the GDR, and his party's support in the regional elections in Lower Saxony and Northrhine-Westphalia in May, mentioned above. In both parts of Germany there were millions who had lost their homes, or whose parents had lost their homes, in the territories beyond the Oder–Neisse Line. Most did not believe they would ever get them back, but they wanted an occasional recognition that they too had suffered. Kohl's wavering was a hint that he understood, that his heart was in the right place. Kohl also had in his mind the relative success of the far right Republicans in earlier recent elections, although he must have known that the achievement of German unity would seriously undermine their credibility.

Kohl's remarks about the German–Polish frontier caused headaches for Bush, who had to carry on much behind-the-scenes diplomacy. At home he had to contend with the worries of Polish-Americans and Jewish-Americans. Arthur Miller, one of America's best-known writers and of Jewish origin, contributed to the debate with an article in the *New York Times Sunday Magazine* on 6 May 1990. He had good things to say about West German progress since 1945, but worried because the Germans had not fought for democracy themselves. It was a system imposed by the Allies.

> Does the Federal Republic of Germany arouse lofty democratic feelings in its citizens' minds, or is it simply a matter of historical convenience invented by foreigners? To be sure, this system has helped the nation to prosper as never before, but the issue is how deep the commitment is to its democratic precepts, how sacred are they, and if they will hold in hard times.

Earlier in the year, Yitzhak Shamir, the Israeli Prime Minister, had expressed his views on Germany. In a statement he said that even forty years of democracy were not yet a guarantee against a repetition of the past.[16] To demonstrate their goodwill, the speakers of the Bundestag and the Volkskammer, Professor Rita Süssmuth and Dr Sabine Bergmann-Pohl, paid a joint visit to Israel. The women gave Israelis a totally different image of Germany from the usual stereotype and undoubtedly helped to create a better climate of opinion in Israel towards the new Germany, which was by then only weeks away. It was the only such joint initiative.[17]

'The terrible suffering inflicted on the Polish people'

On 21 June 1990 the Bundestag and the Volkskammer in identical resolutions overwhelmingly voted to approve the Oder–Neisse Line as the final frontier between Germany and Poland. In the 400-strong Volkskammer only 6 members opposed the resolution and 18 abstained. In the 519-strong Bundestag 487 members voted in favour and 15 against,[18] including Dr Herbert Czaja, chairman of the organisation representing the expellees and refugees. The resolution of the two parliaments stated that the Bundestag (and Volkskammer) was

> anxious to make a contribution through German unity to the development of a peaceful order in Europe in which frontiers no longer divide, which enables all European nations to live together in mutual trust and engage in comprehensive co-operation for the common benefit, and which ensures lasting peace, freedom and stability.

The Bundestag expressed consciousness 'of the terrible suffering inflicted on the Polish people through crimes perpetuated by Germans and in the name of Germany'. But it also expressed consciousness of 'the great injustice done to millions of Germans who have been expelled from their native regions'. The Oder–Neisse Line had been originally accepted by the GDR in 1950, but not by West Germany. The resolution 'expressed its will' that the course of the frontier between the united Germany and Poland 'be definitely confirmed by a treaty under international law'. It accepted it as that defined in the treaty of 6 July 1950 between the GDR and Poland, the treaty between the two states of 22 May 1989, and the treaty between the Federal Republic and Poland 'concerning the basis for Normalising their Mutual Relations' of 7 December 1970. Brandt's SPD–FDP government had been responsible for the 1970 treaty. The resolutions also underlined that the 'the two sides [Germany and Poland] have no territorial claims whatsoever against each other and that they will not assert such claims in the future'.[19] The resolutions of the two parliaments changed nothing but helped to assuage Polish and other people's fears about where Germany was heading.

147

On the following day, 22 June, a second round of the Two Plus Four talks at ministerial level was held in East Berlin. On the agenda were the defence aspects of a united Germany. Eduard Schevardnadze, Soviet Foreign Minister, started by reminding his colleagues that their meeting was taking place on the 49th anniversary of the 'treacherous attack by fascist troops' on the Soviet Union. He believed that, as in the past, the situation in Germany was but a mirror image of the broader situation in Europe. He was optimistic about the progress being made. The frontier question would be resolved by reference to the Görlitz treaty of 1950 between the GDR and Poland and the 1970 Warsaw Treaty between the Federal Republic and Poland. He expected a united Germany to relinquish, like the majority of states, the right to manufacture, own, maintain or station nuclear weapons on its territory. He proposed a transitionary period during which the four powers would reduce their forces in the GDR and the Federal Republic by 50 per cent and later withdraw them from Germany altogether. He also proposed that within six months of a government of a united Germany being established the four powers should withdraw their forces from Greater Berlin. For a period of five years, the Soviet Foreign Minister continued, treaties entered into by the GDR and the Federal Republic would continue to be valid. This would mean that neither NATO nor the Warsaw Pact forces would move forward from their existing areas of operations in Germany.[20]

Meanwhile, time was running out for the GDR's old diplomatic élite. There was an air of uncertainty, defeat and despondency in GDR embassies around the globe. Most of those deployed knew that they had little chance of remaining in the service after unification. In many cases the issue was simply, 'Will I get a pension?' One of the last engagements of the GDR's Ambassador to the United Kingdom, Joachim Mitdank, was to open an exhibition at Nottingham University on the GDR's first, and last, free elections of March 1990. This was his first, and last, visit to the East Midlands university. He was, in effect, opening an exhibition revealing how his political friends were defeated. A loyal SED member, Mitdank had been in the GDR's diplomatic service since 1956 and had had two tours of duty in Finland. Between 1968 and 1978 he was head of the department responsible for relations with West Berlin, ensuring that the GDR got the best deal when it allowed West Berliners visas to visit their relations in the East. Mitdank was replaced a few weeks before unification by a young woman pastor.

'This rushed take-over by the Germans'

In July 1990 a memorandum was leaked to the British paper *The Independent on Sunday* and to *Der Spiegel* which claimed to be the results of the deliberations of six historians, two American and four British, on Germany. They had been asked by Mrs Thatcher to let her have their thoughts on the Germans at a seminar at Chequers in March. Although what was allegedly said was by no means all negative, nor was it very flattering to the Germans. The leaked memo did nothing to improve the international atmosphere as the date set for German unity approached. A modest counterblast was fired by the Director of the influential American Institute for Contemporary German Affairs, in Washington, DC, and the Director of the Institute of German, Austrian and Swiss Affairs of Nottingham University. They felt convinced that the majority of British and American social scientists, historians and other specialists on German affairs did not share the views expressed in the leaked memorandum.[21] However, worse was to come. Nicholas Ridley, Trade and Industry Minister in Thatcher's government and a close associate of the Prime Minister, was prepared to articulate fears she could not. In an infamous interview with the weekly *Spectator* (14 July 1990) he claimed that European Monetary Union was a German racket designed to take over the whole of Europe. 'This rushed take-over by the Germans on the worst possible basis, with the French behaving like poodles to the Germans, is absolutely intolerable. . . .' Although papers like the *Sun* and *The Daily Express* claimed their readers overwhelmingly supported Ridley in his anti-German outburst, the surprising thing for some was that many Conservative MPs, and very many ordinary voters, disagreed with him. According to *The Independent* (13 July 1990), polls revealed that 64 per cent of British people approved of German unification and 71 per cent were in favour of attempts to unify Western Europe. Sixty per cent also had either a lot of trust or some trust in West Germans. Only 29 per cent thought a united Germany posed a threat to European peace, and most of them were the older generation who had memories of the war. Thatcher was forced to remove Ridley from her government. The Ridley incident and the leaked memo looked, in retrospect, as sad rearguard actions by British opponents of German unity.

For Kohl the final triumph came in July 1990 when he visited Gorbachev in the Caucasus. Gorbachev and Kohl had a number of one-to-one meetings, as well as talks with their foreign ministers. At these meetings the two leaders agreed that a united Germany could belong to NATO. Kohl and Gorbachev also agreed on the strength of the German armed forces with a maximum strength of 370,000 men for the united Germany. This represented a cut. They also agreed that the Soviet forces in Germany would be withdrawn over a four-year period. Germany, it was agreed, would enjoy full and unrestricted sovereignty but would renounce forever the possession of nuclear, chemical and bacteriological weapons. Kohl gave the Soviet leader various undertakings to cover the costs of the Soviet withdrawal from Germany as the Soviet state was in no position to house its returning troops. Gorbachev records that he told Kohl, 'We cannot forget the past. Every family in our country suffered in those years. But we have to look towards Europe and take the road of co-operation with the great German nation.'[22]

The grand coalition collapses

De Maizière's coalition fell apart in the summer of 1990 because of differences over the electoral system and ministerial portfolios. The CDU, and the West German Christian Democrats, the DSU and the PDS favoured retention of the existing electoral law for the elections due in December 1990. The Social Democrats and FDP in both parts of Germany wanted the existing West German electoral system used throughout Germany. In protest the FDP withdrew from the coalition on 24 July. De Maizière requested the two FDP members of the coalition to continue at their posts. Negotiations on unification also led to disagreements between the CDU and the SPD. The SPD parliamentary group in the Volkskammer voted on 7 August to remain in the government, but reversed this decision on 19–20 August after the Minister-President had made changes in the government against the SPD's wishes. Walter Romberg lost his post for allegedly mismanaging state funds since the introduction of monetary union and failing to give leadership in his ministry. Also dismissed was the SPD-backed independent Peter Pollack. Gerhard Pohl and Kurt Wünsche resigned. Against the advice of Richard Schröder, its Chairman, the SPD Volkskammer group voted, on 19 August, by 60 votes to 5, to leave the coalition. The following day the remaining SPD ministers resigned from the coalition. De Maizière decided to take over the Foreign Ministry himself and gave Jürgen Kleditzsch the additional responsibility for Labour and Social Affairs. Hans-Joachim Meyer added Research and Technology to his responsibilities. Lothar Engel was put in charge of Trade and Tourism and Gottfried Haschke took on Food, Agriculture and Forestry. Richard Schröder was probably right that withdrawing from the coalition at this stage was not the best policy for the SPD.[23] It meant that the Christian Democrats alone would lead the GDR into unity with West Germany. Fears that the break-up could delay unification were also voiced, as the Unity Treaty would require a two-thirds majority, which de Maizière did not have.

Separately from the other resignations, Axel Viehweger resigned because of accusations that he worked for the Stasi, which he denied.[24] In fact, a list 68 members of the Volkskammer who were suspected of Stasi activities was presented on 15–16 September 1990 by the parliamentary committee responsible. The Volkskammer appointed Pastor Joachim Gauck, himself a Stasi target, as commissioner responsible for the Stasi files. A member of

Bündnis 90, Gauck had chaired the Volkskammer committee entrusted with dissolving the Ministry for State Security and its successor, the Office for National Security. The files found by the committee covered 4 million East Germans, 2 million West Germans and an unknown number of foreigners.

The GDR leaves the Warsaw Pact

Rainer Eppelmann's most important formal engagement as Minister for Disarmament and Defence was to sign the documents taking the GDR out of the Warsaw Pact. This happened in September 1990. It was an incredible story which neither he nor anyone else could have imagined even a year before. This hardly known, humble clergyman from Berlin, who had been the object of so much Stasi attention, who had been imprisoned for eight months for refusing to serve in the NVA, here he was, the successor to Admiral Theodor Hoffmann.

Eppelmann's job had not been easy, even though by the time he took over everyone expected re-unification to take place. There was the problem of keeping the higher echelons of the NVA happy so that they did not attempt to take matters into their own hands. After all, for them collectively, they were to surrender the machine they had built up. Individually, they did not seem to have a future. It looked like the disbanding of the NVA was not far off – or was it? Admiral Hoffmann, no longer a minister, was, however, still the highest serving officer. This was surprising given his membership of the SED and total loyalty to it. On the other hand, he had not advanced up the party ladder and the navy appeared to be the least politicised branch of the NVA. Eppelmann had to get the best professional advice available to keep the NVA out of politics and maintain discipline within the ranks. He had to confront the possibility that the ordinary servicemen, conscripts and professionals alike, would simply stop obeying orders. There had been a mutiny of conscripts in January 1990 at the Beelitz base, south-west of Berlin. In March 1990, in Berlin, soldiers of the élite guards regiment Friedrich Engels demonstrated in protest about their poor living conditions and against having to take part in goose-stepping ceremonial duties on the Unter den Linden.[25] Discipline was weakening as many young men could not see the point of military training in an army which was discredited, doomed and without *raison d'être*. Conscripts were deserting or simply not returning from leave.

Eppelmann did his best to keep matters under control. Various talks took place, starting with a meeting between Eppelmann and his opposite number in Bonn, Dr Gerhard Stoltenberg, on 27 April.[26] It is significant that the meeting took place in the Holiday Inn Hotel at Cologne–Bonn Airport rather than at the Federal Ministry of Defence. After talks with

151

Eppelmann and Hoffmann at Strausberg, headquarters of the GDR defence ministry, on 28 May, the West German side was worried that there had been no 'house-cleaning' in the NVA of hard-line senior SED officers. Hoffmann and Eppelmann seemed to believe that the Warsaw Pact would continue to exist and that the NVA would have a bridging function between East and West. The officer corps of the NVA believed that it had a secure future.[27] Indeed, earlier, on 2 May, Eppelmann told the first conference of NVA commanding officers to be held under his command that although German unity was the aim, after it was achieved there would still be a second German army in the former GDR. This would be an army which was not part of any alliance but would have as its function the security of the former GDR.[28] The continued existence of the NVA (or something similar) seemed to be emphasised on 20 July 1990, the anniversary of the 1944 officers' bomb plot against Hitler, when NVA troops were required to take a new oath of allegiance to the now democratic GDR. Eppelmann thanked the officers of the NVA for preventing a 'Chinese situation'. Five days earlier Gorbachev and Kohl had agreed on the size of the German armed forces and the Soviet withdrawal from Germany. On 10 August the two ministers, Eppelmann and Stoltenberg, met again and agreed to send a civilian and military liaison group from Bonn to Strausberg, to gather information for planning the armed forces of the united Germany. In secret, on 14 August, Stoltenberg appointed General Jörg Schönbohm of the Bundeswehr as commander-designate of Bundeswehr-Kommando Ost, as the former GDR territory was to be known in Bonn's defence ministry. He would take over the units of the former NVA immediately on unification of the two states. His task was mainly one of disbanding the NVA, securing all stores and building up Bundeswehr forces there. Apparently, the GDR officials and officers responsible were still not clear that the NVA would cease to exist.

As unity drew closer, Eppelmann came under increasing pressure. He embarked on a partial demobilisation of the NVA. It was reduced from 175,000 to 103,000. The military intelligence service, the military prosecutors and the propaganda units were disbanded. A few days before the 3 October unity deadline, he instructed his permanent secretary, Werner Ablass, to retire the generals and admirals and all officers over 55 and all members of the Political Main Administration, the SED's political officers within the NVA.[29] Admiral Hoffmann was retired on 15 September from a force he had joined in 1952 when it was still officially a police unit. Schönbohm arrived at Strausberg on 2 October to find that the troops there were still wearing their old uniforms. At midnight, at a small reception, he took over. The guards he had met earlier were now kitted out in Bundeswehr uniforms. The NVA had ceased to exist. It had cost the people of the GDR an awful lot, which could have contributed to their living standards. Perhaps there was a minority that took pride in its ceremonial events. But many more, especially foreign visitors, were put off a state that put so much emphasis on archaic military rituals, which reminded them of an earlier even uglier time. Unlike the Bundeswehr, it was a force built on 'unconditional obedience' ('unbedingte Gehorsamkeit'), as its training manuals emphasised, and hatred of Bundeswehr troops 'who would be ready to commit any crime, like their US models'. The NVA had only been on active service once and that was to take part in the invasion of a friendly neighbour. In the end 6,000 officers and 11,000 NCOs of the NVA were taken into the Bundeswehr on a trial basis for two years. Of these, about 3,000 officers and 7,600 NCOs were given the opportunity for longer service.[30] Of the navy's 8,500 personnel, 7,000 were dismissed. Most of their ships were sold abroad or scrapped. It is not surprising that when General Schönbohm visited the fleet on 11 October he found a 'depressed atmosphere among the men'.[31] Schönbohm's task did not end on 3 October; his job of disbanding the NVA, disposing of its equipment and integrating elements of it into the Bundeswehr went on throughout 1991.

The Volkskammer and the Bundestag vote for unity

On 12 September 1990, the representatives of the two German states and the four Allies signed the Treaty on the Final Settlement with Respect to Germany. The signing of the ten-article treaty took place in Moscow. In the case of the GDR, de Maizière acted as Foreign Minister. Under article 6, Germany had the right 'to belong to alliances, with all the rights and responsibilities arising therefrom'. The four powers agreed in article 7 to 'terminate their rights and responsibilities relating to Berlin and to Germany as a whole'. Germany 'shall have accordingly full sovereignty over its internal and external affairs'. Article 4 laid down that Soviet troops would withdraw from Germany by the end of 1994. Until this time no NATO troops, including those of the Bundeswehr assigned to NATO, would be stationed in the former GDR. Article 1 was of particular importance for Poland and the Czech Republic. 'The united Germany and the Republic of Poland shall confirm the existing border between them in a treaty that is binding under international law.' Germany renounced all territorial claims 'now and in the future'. The Germans also undertook to amend articles 23 and 146 of the Basic Law accordingly. Article 23 covered the area of jurisdiction of the Basic Law, which, after naming the Western *Länder*, laid down, 'It is to be put in operation in other parts of Germany after their admission' ('In anderen Teilen Deutschlands ist es nachderem Beitritt in Kraft zu setzen'). The GDR had chosen this route. Remote though this was, there was the nagging fear that a former German part of Poland or even the Kaliningrad (Königsberg) area of the Soviet Union might apply. Article 146 of the Basic Law laid down that it would lose its validity on the day that a constitution was inaugurated which had been agreed by the free decision of the German people. One other important aspect of the Treaty was that, in article 2, the Germans re-affirmed their renunciation of the manufacture and possession of and control over nuclear, biological and chemical weapons.

The Volkskammer voted on 23 August, with nearly three-quarters of the members in favour, for the entry of the GDR to the area of jurisdiction of the Basic Law (the West German constitution) according to its article 23. The Unity Treaty between the two states was signed on 21 August. The Treaty was then ratified by the two parliaments on 20 September with the PDS, *Bündnis 90* and the Greens voting against. In the Bundestag, the vote was 442 in favour and 47 against with 3 abstentions. The anti-votes were the Greens and 13 Christian Democrats.[32] The Bundesrat, the *Länder* chamber of the German parliament, agreed the treaty on the following day. Richard von Weizsäcker, the Federal President, signed the treaty on 29 September, thus completing the legislation on unity. On that day thousands marched from West to East Berlin to protest against the terms of the treaty. The votes in the two parliaments, however, had revealed that these demonstrators were not representative of German opinion.

'The war is finally over'

The GDR CDU merged with the West German CDU on 1 October 1990 at a congress in Hamburg. Kohl was elected Chair by 98.5 per cent of the vote and de Maizière Deputy Chair by 97.4 per cent. Volker Rühe was returned as General Secretary. The enlarged ten-member presidium included three members from the GDR. The Social Democrats of East and West had merged already on 27–8 September. They re-elected Hans-Jochen Vogel as their Chair, Lafontaine as their Chancellor candidate and the East German Wolfgang Thierse as Deputy Chair.

On 2 October the Allied Kommandatura met for the last time in Dahlem, West Berlin, where it had been quartered since 1945. On the same day the city councils of the two parts of Berlin declared the end of the division of the city.

On the night of 2–3 October official celebrations took place in front of the Reichstag and, a few yards away, at the Brandenburg Gate. The music of Beethoven, Brahms and Mendelssohn filled the air. There was the inevitable firework display and the singing of the national anthem. *The Guardian* correspondent David Gow wrote that 'Germany, an economic and political colossus in the heart of Europe, was reborn today on the stroke of midnight. . . . More than a million people witnessed the historic end of two separate German states' (3 October 1990). There were much smaller counter-demonstrations against unification in a few places. In Berlin, several thousand protested their opposition. These were from several far left groups, including the anarchist fringe from West Berlin. On that night, President Bush said in a televised address, 'The last remnants of the wall remain, there at the heart of a free Berlin – a ragged monument in brick and barbed wire – proof that no wall is ever strong enough to strangle the human spirit, that no wall can ever crush a nation's soul.'[33] De Maizière recalled Germany's murderous past, including the Holocaust, and urged all Germans to regard it as a permanent spur to serve reconciliation and contribute to understanding among the peoples of the earth. He called the end of the GDR 'a farewell without tears'.[34] Czech President Václav Havel commented, 'The war is finally over.'

The Bundestag had been enlarged from 519 to 663 members to include 144 representatives of the former GDR nominated by the Volkskammer. They included 63 CDU, 8 DSU, 9 FDP, 33 SPD, 7 *Bündnis 90*/Greens and 24 PDS. The first session of the enlarged parliament was held in the old Reichstag building in Berlin on 4 October. Five members of the outgoing GDR government were sworn in as members without portfolios. They were de Maizière, Bergmann-Pohl, Günther Krause, all CDU, and Hansjoachim Walther (DSU) and Rainer Ortleb (FDP). This was a transitional solution until the federal elections of December 1990. One of the first acts of the new Bundestag was to ratify the Treaty on the Final Settlement on 5 October. The Bundesrat ratified it on 8 October.

Further victories for Kohl

In the elections for the parliaments of the five restored *Länder* – New Brandenburg, Mecklenburg-West Pomerania, Saxony, Saxony-Anhalt and Thuringia – on an average turnout of 68.77 per cent, the CDU won enough votes to form governments in all but New Brandenburg, where Manfred Stolpe formed a coalition with the FDP. In Saxony, Professor Kurt Biedenkopf, General Secretary of the West German CDU, 1973–77, formed a CDU-only government (see Table 11.2).

As the federal elections approached, Lafontaine saw the lead he had held at the beginning of the year disappear totally. The SPD was fighting to limit the damage as far as possible. The smaller opposition parties were struggling to get enough votes to gain re-entry into the Bundestag. Kohl's victory proved to be greater than expected. Turnout was down, only 78.6 per cent in the West, compared with 84.3 per cent in 1987, and 74.7 per cent in the former GDR, compared with an astonishing 93.4 per cent in March 1990.

155

Table 11.2   Länder elections, 14 October 1990 (percentages)

	New Brandenburg	Mecklenburg-West Pomerania	Saxony	Saxony-Anhalt	Thuringia
CDU	29.4	38.3	53.8	38.99	45.4
SPD	38.3	27.0	19.09	26.0	22.8
PDS	13.4	15.7	10.22	11.98	9.7
FDP	6.63	5.5	5.26	13.51	9.3
Bündnis 90	6.4	2.2	5.6*	5.29*	6.5*
Greens	2.84	4.2			
DSU	1.15†	1.9†	3.58	1.7	3.3
Others	1.88	3.1	2.45	2.52	3.0

* Includes the Greens
† Republicans in Brandenburg, CSU in Meckenburg-West Pomerania
Source: Adapted from Keesing's Record of World Events, News Digest for October 1990, 37762.

Perhaps this was due to a degree of apathy in face of Kohl's seemingly inevitable victory. The election law, which had been much debated, allowed parties to stand in just one part of Germany, that is, 'election region West' or 'election region East'. This was designed to give smaller, but significant parties in the former GDR a better chance of getting representation. Had the earlier West German law been transferred to the whole of Germany, parties would have had to get either 5 per cent throughout the united Germany or win three seats directly. The West German Greens and Bündnis 90/Greens of the former GDR had miscalculated badly by not getting together before the election. As the figures in Table 11.3 show, they got 5 per cent together. The West German Greens lost their representation in the Bundestag with their 3.8. Their colleagues in the East gained 6 per cent in 'election region East'. The PDS attracted only 2.4 per cent in the whole of Germany but 11.1 per cent in the East. The far-right Republicans gained 2.3 per cent in the West and 1.3 per cent in the East.

The SPD saw its vote slump in the West compared with the last two federal elections, its 35.7 per cent compared with 37 (1987) and 38.2 (1983). The only consolation for the party was that it had increased its vote compared with March in all five Länder of the former GDR. In the West, the SPD took losses everywhere except in the Saar. Lafontaine could be relieved that on his home territory his party's vote had increased from 43.5 (in 1987) to 51.2 per cent. The CDU, on the other hand, saw its vote rise slightly in the West from 34.5 in 1987 to 35.7 per cent. In the former GDR it gained 41.8, which compared with 40.8 in the March elections. The FDP percentage rose in both parts of Germany: in the West from 9.1 in 1987 to 10.6, in the East 12.9 compared with 5.3 for the BFD in March. Bündnis

Table 11.3   Results of federal election, December 1990

	Percentage vote	*Seats gained*
CDU	36.7	319*
SPD	33.5	239
FDP	11	79
CSU	7.1	
Greens (West)	3.8	0
PDS	2.4	17
B90/G**	1.2	8
Rep	2.1	0

* CDU/CSU
** *Bündnis 90*/Die Grünen in former GDR only

Source: *Küschners Volkshandbuch: Deutscher Bundestag 12. Wahlperiode 1990.*

90/the Greens with 6 per cent did better than *Bündnis 90* and the Greens had done fighting separately in March, when their combined total was 4.9. Kohl was riding high after his December victory, and although the SPD, the *Bündnis 90*/the Greens and the PDS improved their respective positions, he won again in 1994.

Switzerland and Sweden as models?

Some abroad still feared Germany 45 years after the end of hostilities. It is therefore worth mentioning that Kohl's Christian Democrats (CDU/CSU/DSU) received a higher percentage vote in 1990 than the Nazis had gained in the last two democratic Weimar elections of 1932 and the not so free election of January 1933. Kohl never sought the 'charisma' that many claimed for Hitler. Hitler would have thought his *Volk*, as they were in the early 1990s, were not worthy of him. Any of Germany's neighbours who read it would have been relieved to see the results of a survey for the daily *Süddeutsche Zeitung* (4 January 1991). This revealed that 40 per cent of Germans saw Switzerland as a future model for Germany. Sweden came second, attracting 29 per cent. Japan and Italy were joint third with 10 per cent each. The three Western victor states – France, the USA and Britain – attracted 8, 6 and 2 per cent respectively.

United Germany in 2000

In 2000, eleven years after German unity has been restored, the Federal Republic looks in remarkably good shape as the leading state in the European

Union of 15 states, 12 of them being even more closely united in the single currency, the euro. Berlin was a huge building site, and it has once again became the home of the German parliament and government. Many towns in the former GDR have been transformed. Unemployment, however, remains a problem. At the end of 1999, of the 3,900,000 'looking for work' in Germany, 1,300,000 of them were in the former GDR.[35] In spite of this unemployment, most East Germans are better off in material terms, not to mention personal freedom, than they were under Honecker's SED. This is especially true of the elderly whose pensions had risen from 55.6 per cent of the West German level in 1990 to 110 per cent in July 1998.[36] The PDS has survived and prospered mainly in the former GDR helped by the persisting unemployment, some inevitable GDR nostalgia, and its attempts to present itself as a left, democratic, anti-establishment party. Kohl, who did so much for German unity, and his CDU, meanwhile, have been struck a savage blow by allegations of corruption. After years in the wilderness, the Social Democrats, led by Gerhard Schröder, joined by the Greens, gained a remarkable federal election victory in 1998.

The SPD-led coalition was part of a wave which swept Labour into office in Britain, a left-of-centre government in France, and similar forces in other EU states. Austria was an exception, where the influx of foreigners seeking asylum and/or work had been an important factor in the decline of the Social Democrats. The problem of asylum seekers and migrants was one facing the whole of the EU and one which has helped the far right to consolidate in a number of states. In the united Germany these forces remain on the margin. Will they remain there?[37] Other problems facing Germany and its EU partners are the ageing of their populations, the threat of 'globalisation', the rise of the Asian economies and the poverty in many other mainly 'Third World' areas. There were also threats to European security, which were as real as any posed by the Warsaw Pact before 1990 and had been almost overlooked in the euphoria of the opening of the Wall and its aftermath. It remains to be seen whether the German Social Democrats and their colleagues in the Socialist International can meet these challenges.

Notes

1. Details from *Die Volkskammer der Deutschen Demokratischen Republik 10. Wahlperiode: Die Abgeordneten der Volkskammer nach den Wahlen vom 18. März 1990*, Staatsverlag der DDR, 1990.
2. Karl Kaiser, *Deutschlands Vereinigung: Die internationalen Aspekte*, Bergisch Gladbach, 1991, pp. 205–7.
3. *Die Welt*, 25 May 1990.
4. *Frankfurter Allgemeine Zeitung*, 25 September 1990.

5. Cornelia Heins, *The Wall Falls: An Oral History of the Reunification of the Two Germanies*, London, 1994, p. 271.
6. *The Unification of Germany in 1990: A Documentation*, Press and Information Office of the Federal Government, Bonn, April 1991.
7. Birgit Breuel (ed.), *Treuhand intern Tagebuch*, Frankfurt am Main, 1993, pp. 408–20.
8. *Keesing's Record of World Events*, News Digest for 1990, 37660.
9. *Ibid.*
10. Mikhail Gorbachev, *Memoirs*, London, 1997, p. 685.
11. Quoted in Kaiser, *Deutschlands Vereinigung*, p. 211.
12. *Ibid.*, p. 224.
13. *Ibid.*, p. 202.
14. *Keesing's Record of World Events*, 37660.
15. *Die Welt*, 2 June 1990.
16. Renata Fritsch-Bournazel, *Europe and German Unification*, New York/Oxford, 1992, p. 182.
17. *Ibid.*
18. *Keesing's Record of World Events*, 37536.
19. Kaiser, *Deutschlands Vereinigung*, p. 232.
20. *Ibid.*, p. 239.
21. *Politics and Society in Germany, Austria and Switzerland*, Vol. 3, No. 1, 1990.
22. Gorbachev, *Memoirs*, pp. 685–8.
23. Schröder was interviewed by the author.
24. *Keesing's Record of World Events*, 37718.
25. *Berliner Morgenpost*, 15 March 1990. For Beelitz, see Jörg Schönbohm, *Two Armies and One Fatherland*, Providence, RI, 1996, p. 36.
26. *Ibid.*, p. 17.
27. *Ibid.*, p. 19.
28. *Ibid.*, p. 18.
29. *Ibid.*, p. 26.
30. *Ibid.*, p. 206.
31. *Ibid.*, p. 69.
32. Stefan Brauburger, 'Deutsche Einheit' in Werner, Weidenfeld and Karl-Rudolf Korte (eds), *Handwörterbuch zur deutschen Einheit*, Bonn, 1991, p. 125.
33. All quotations are from *The Unification of Germany* (see above).
34. *The Guardian*, 3 October 1990.
35. Press release, Embassy of the Federal Republic of Germany, London, 11 February 2000.
36. Klaus-Peter Schwitzer, 'Ältere und alte Menschen in den neuer Bundesländern in Zweiten Jahr nach der Wende', in *Aus Politik und Zeitgeschichte Beilage zur Wochenzeitung Das Parlament*, 22 October 1999, 33.
37. The author attempted to deal with the German far right in his 'in Klaus Larres and Panikos Panayi (eds), *The Federal Republic of Germany Since 1949*,' Harlow/New York, 1996. See also the contribution by Panayi in the same volume.

Chronology

1945   US President Roosevelt dies, Truman replaces him. End of the Second World War after atomic bombs dropped on Japan. British Labour victory. Orwell's *Animal Farm* published. Forty-six nations meet in San Francisco to set up United Nations. The KPD, SPD, CDU and LDP are licensed in the Soviet Zone of Germany. They form the 'Unity Front of Anti-Fascist Democratic Parties'. July/August: Potsdam conference of Churchill (Attlee), Stalin and Truman on Germany.

1946   Forced merger of SPD with Communists in Soviet Zone of Germany to form SED. FDJ founded with Erich Honecker as Chairman. 'Equal wage for the same work irrespective of gender' introduced.

1947   Prussian state officially abolished by Four Allies. Marshall Aid announced. II congress of SED. Women's organisation, DFD, founded in Soviet Zone.

1948   June: West Berlin blockaded by Soviets. Czech Communist coup. Stalin–Tito split. NATO established. State of Israel proclaimed. NDPD, DBD and JP (Young Pioneers) founded in Soviet Zone. Denazification officially ended in Soviet Zone. KVP, para-military People's Police, founded.

1949   Two German states set up. Adenauer West German Chancellor. Pieck GDR President. Mao takes over in China. Soviets become nuclear power. Orwell's *Nineteen Eighty-Four* published. May: End of Berlin blockade.

1950   Korean War. Ministry for State Security (MfS) established in GDR. Poland and GDR recognise Oder–Neisse Line as their common frontier. III congress of SED.

1951   World Festival of Youth and Students held in East Berlin.

1952   SED proclaims 'building of socialism'. Slansky show trial in Prague. *Länder* replaced by *Bezirke* as administrative units. GST established. Stalin note on united, neutral Germany published.

1953   6 March: Stalin dies. Chemnitz renamed Karl-Marx-Stadt. 17 June: Revolt in GDR crushed by Soviets.

1954   Ministry of Culture established in GDR. Elvis Presley makes his first recordings. French defeated in Vietnam. IV congress of SED.

1955   Adenauer and Khrushchev agree on diplomatic relations between Bonn and Moscow. Austria, freed from four-power occupation, declared neutral. May: First *Kampfgruppen* parade in Berlin.

1956   1 May: GDR armed forces (NVA) proclaimed, having developed from KVP. Khrushchev denounces Stalin. Hungarian revolution. Anglo-French Suez operation. KPD banned in West Germany.

1957   Rome Treaties. Adenauer's greatest victory in West German election. Ghana, first black African colony to gain independence. Soviets launch first artificial earth satellite. 'Youth culture' recognised in US. July: 'Harich group' condemned in GDR. November: Mielke takes over as Minister for State Security.

1958   EEC is born. Ulbricht defeats Wollweber and his other rivals in SED Politburo. V congress of SED. Algerian revolt by French Right. De Gaulle takes over as President of Fifth Republic.

1959   Khrushchev threatens West Berlin. Castro takes power in Cuba.

1960   Pieck dies and is replaced by Ulbricht as GDR head of state.

1961   12 April: Soviet cosmonaut Yuri Gagarin first human successfully launched into space. August: Berlin Wall built. Sino-Soviet split. Solzhenitsyn's *One Day in the Life of Ivan Denisovich* published in Soviet Union. Bay of Pigs invasion of Cuba fails.

1962   Compulsory military service in GDR introduced. US–Soviet missile crisis over Cuba.

1963   Gigantic march on Washington, DC, for Black civil rights addressed by Martin Luther King. President Kennedy assassinated. VI Congress of SED.

1964   Khrushchev ousted. Major US military involvement in Vietnam.

1966   SPD joins CDU/CSU in grand coalition in West Germany. Cultural Revolution in China.

1967   Arab–Israeli 'Six Day' War. Greek military coup. Che Guevara killed in Bolivia. VII congress of SED.

1968   8 April: New GDR constitution. GDR sends independent team to Olympic Games in Mexico. Student revolt in Paris and elsewhere. Warsaw Pact forces invade Czechoslovakia and destroy 'socialism with a human face'. Swedish Social Democrats win absolute majority of votes.

1969   Brandt elected West German Chancellor. American moon landing. Cambodia, followed by Iraq, recognises the GDR. These are the first states outside the Soviet bloc to do so.

1970   Meetings of Brandt and Stoph at Erfurt (19 March) and Kassel (21 May).

1971   31 January: Telephone traffic between East and West Berlin restored. 3 May: Honecker replaces Ulbricht as SED leader. Chile and GDR take up diplomatic relations. Twenty-eight states have recognised GDR.

1972   SPD achieved best electoral result since FRG established. Basic Treaty signed between GDR and Federal Republic (West Germany). The Volkskammer legalises abortion. Exceptionally, 14 members vote against and 8 abstain. Munich Olympic Games: GDR ahead of West Germany in medals table, on third place.

1973   Britain recognises GDR, followed by Franco Spain, Japan and 12 other states. GDR and West Germany admitted to UNO. Yom Kippur War, followed by oil crisis. Solzhenitsyn's *Gulag Archipelago* published in Paris. Allende coalition overthrown by Pinnochet in Chile. Death of Ulbricht.

1974   US recognises GDR. Schmidt replaces Brandt as West German Chancellor. Fall of dictatorship in Portugal and Greece.

1975   End of Vietnam War. First personal computer introduced in US. Friendship Treaty between USSR and GDR signed in Moscow. GDR newspapers no longer published on Sundays because of costs.

1976   23 April: Palast der Republik opened on Marx-Engels-Platz. 18–22 May: IX congress of SED. End of dictatorship in Spain. Swedish Social Democrats defeated. Mao dies. Carrillo completes his *'Eurocommunism' and the State*. Wolf Biermann banned from returning to GDR. Robert Havemann placed under house arrest.

1977   Rudolf Bahro arrested. Honecker visits Vietnam, Philippines and North Korea.

1978   Chancellor Kreisky of Austria visits GDR. Military instruction introduced into GDR schools. GDR cosmonaut Sigmund Jähn goes into space with Soviet *Sojus 31*.

1979   Honecker and Stoph visit India. Honecker visits Libya, Angola, Zambia and Mozambique. Soviet invasion of Afghanistan. Revolution in Iran. Second oil crisis.

1979 Reagan inaugurated US President (in office to 1988). Polish unrest. GDR takes second place at Moscow Olympics after US boycotts Games. Honecker and Stoph visit India.

1980 Chancellor Helmut Schmidt visits Honecker in GDR. Honecker pays official visits to Cuba and Austria.

1981 Mitterrand elected French President. April: X congress of SED. 13 December: Martial Law proclaimed in Poland.

1982 Schmidt falls and is replaced by Kohl (CDU). Falklands War. Honecker visits Syria, Cyprus and Kuwait. Pastor Eppelmann and Robert Havemann publish Berlin Appeal of the unofficial peace movement of GDR.

1983 Kohl wins West German election. Apple introduces the 'mouse' to personal computers. Fidel Castro visits GDR. Five hundredth anniversary of birth of Martin Luther celebrated in GDR.

1984 Canadian Prime Minister Pierre Trudeau pays official visit to East Berlin. Honecker makes official visits to Finland and Algeria. Austrian Chancellor, Fred Sinowatz, visits GDR.

1985 Gorbachev elected CPSU leader. Honecker pays first official visit to a NATO country, Italy, and is received by the Pope. Honecker and Strauß meet in Leipzig.

1986 Chernobyl nuclear explosion. XI congress of the SED in Berlin. Honecker pays official visit to Sweden.

1987 17 June: Death penalty abolished in GDR. September: Honecker pays official visit to West Germany. October: Honecker makes official visit to Belgium.

1988 January: Honecker makes a state visit to France. May: Chancellor Kohl makes a private visit to the GDR. June: Austrian Chancellor Vranitzky makes official visit to GDR. August: European Community and GDR take up official relations. October: Honecker makes official visit to Spain. December: Yugoslav President visits GDR.

1989 January: Swedish Prime Minister, Ingvar Carlsson, visits GDR.

6 February: 20-year-old Chris Gueffroy shot dead attempting to cross Berlin Wall. He is the last victim.

7 May: SED accused of falsifying local election results.

2 June: Tiananmen Square massacre in Beijing.

10/11 September: Hungary opens frontier to West allowing GDR citizens to pass to Austria. Thousands take this route.

7 October: 40th anniversary of founding of GDR.

7 October: SDP founded.

10 October: 'Miracle of Leipzig'.

18 October: Krenz replaces Honecker as SED/GDR leader.

10/11 November: GDR frontier posts opened.

13 November: Modrow elected Minister President of GDR.

7 December: First meeting of 'Round Table' of government and opposition.

8/9, 15/16 December: Extraordinary SED congress.

15/16 December: Special congress of the CDU that freed the Christian Democrats from their dependence on the SED.

December: Helmut Kohl visits Dresden on 19 December and is warmly received amid calls for re-unification.

1990   18 March: First democratic elections in GDR.

1 July: German mark becomes official currency of GDR.

GDR votes for German re-unification from 3 October.

Kohl wins first election of re-united Germany. Mandela released from prison in South Africa.

1991   Gorbachev overthrown. End of Soviet Union.

Brief biographies

Berghofer, Wolfgang (1943–), worked for FDJ, playing a decisive part in the organisation of the World Festival in Berlin in 1973. SED/PDS Mayor of Dresden, 1986–90.

Bergmann-Pohl, Dr Sabine (1946–), specialist for lung diseases, joined CDU in 1981. Elected as CDU member of Volkskammer, March 1990. Elected Volkskammer President and was *de facto* head of state of GDR to unification.

Bohley, Bärbel (1945–), painter, civil rights activist, imprisoned; founder Women for Peace, 1982; co-founder of New Forum; member of the Berlin *Land* parliament.

Böhme, Ibrahim (1944–99), co-founder of the East German SDP, later member of SPD executive. He was exposed as a Stasi informer.

Brandt, Willy (1913–92), Chancellor of Federal Republic, 1969–74; Governing Mayor of West Berlin, 1957–66; Chairman of SPD, 1964–87, then honorary chair.

Brie, André (1950–), son of a diplomat, attended school in China and North Korea. Studied international relations in Potsdam, where he later lectured. Embraced Gorbachev's ideas and helped to found PDS in 1989–90, becoming deputy Chair in June 1990. Resigned from his position after it was revealed he had been a Stasi informer for twenty years until 1989.

Bush, George (1924–), US President (Republican), 1989–1993, Vice-President, 1981–1989.

De Maizière, Lothar (1940–), professional musician then lawyer. Joined CDU in 1956; Chairman of the GDR CDU, 1989–90; Prime Minister of GDR, April 1989–October 1990; Deputy Chair of united CDU to 1991. Resigned from all offices after accusations of Stasi activity.

Dickel, Friedrich (1913–93), Minister of Interior of GDR, 1963–89; deputy Minister of Defence, 1956–57, 1959–63. Served in International Brigades in Spain and as Soviet agent.

Eppelmann, Rainer (1943–), pastor, civil rights activist, co-founder of DA; CDU since 1990; Minister for Disarmament and Defence, 1990. Member of the Bundestag, 1990– .

Fischer, Oskar (1923–). Ex-Wehrmacht soldier who climbed FDJ ladder. GDR Foreign Minister, 1975–90; Deputy, 1973–75.

Friedrich, Professor Walter (1929–), born in Silesia; joined SED 1948; studied psychology at Leipzig; 1966–90 founder and director of Central Institute for Youth Research in Leipzig; 1984 awarded Fatherland Gold Service Medal.

Genscher, Hans-Dietrich (1927–), Chairman of FDP, 1974–85; Foreign Minister of Federal Republic, Deputy Chancellor, 1974–92. Studied law in Halle and Leipzig, left GDR 1952. LDPD member, 1946–52, then FDP. Minister of Interior, 1969–74.

Gerlach, Manfred (1928–), Chairman of LDPD, 1967–90; head of state of GDR, 1989–90. Founder of illegal youth group, Leipzig, 1943; arrested by Gestapo, 1944. Cofounder FDJ; member Volkskammer, 1950–90; Deputy Chair of Council of State, 1960–89. Accused of denouncing colleagues to Soviets, withdrew from FDP in 1993.

Gorbachev, Mikhail (1931–), General Secretary of the CPSU, 1985–91.

Götting, Gerald (1923–), Chairman of the GDR CDU, 1966–89; General Secretary, 1949–66; member of Volkskammer, 1950–90; President of Volkskammer, 1969–76; Deputy Chair of Council of State, 1960–89. Expelled from CDU in 1991.

Gysi, Gregor (1948–), son of Klaus Gysi, Minister of Culture; studied law in Berlin; joined SED 1967; Chair, SED–PDS/PDS, December 1989–December 1992; Chair of PDS in Bundestag, 1990– . Accused of Stasi activity.

Hager, Professor Kurt (1912–98), ZK Secretary responsible for science, education and culture; member of Politburo, 1963–89; member of Council of State, 1976–89. He was expelled from the PDS–SED in 1990.

Heym, Stefan (1913–), born Chemnitz, the son of a Jewish salesman. Refugee US, served US Army as Lieutenant in psycho-warfare. Left US because of McCarthyism threat, returned to GDR 1952. Journalist and novel writer, *Hostages* (1952), *The Crusaders* (1948), *5 Days in June* (1976), etc. Served as loyal dissident but was criticised by Honecker and expelled from Writers' Union 1979; elected to Bundestag on PDS ticket in 1994.

Hoffmann, Admiral Theodor (1935–), volunteered for GDR 'Sea Police', 1952; joined SED, 1956; Commander of GDR navy and Deputy Minister of Defence, 1987–89; Minister of Defence, 1989–90, head of NVA, April–September 1990.

Honecker, Erich (1912–94), born Saar, West Germany, son of a miner. Chairman, FDJ, 1946–55; First/General Secretary of SED, 1971–89; GDR head of state, 1976–89; expelled from SED 1989, arrested January 1990 but released because of poor health.

Honecker, Margot (1927–), born Halle, daughter of a shoemaker. Worked as telephonist and secretary, joining KPD/SED in 1945. Chair of Young Pioneers, 1949–53. Married Erich Honecker, 1953. Deputy Minister of People's Education, 1958–63; Minister, 1963–89. Resigned from SED/PDS in February 1990 and lived in Chile from 1993.

Jaruzelski, General Wojciech (1923–), served in the Polish forces mobilised by the Soviets in Second World War. Later became youngest general in Polish forces and Minister of Defence in 1968. In 1971 elected to the Politburo, becoming First Secretary of the Polish United Workers' Party in 1981. President of Poland, 1989–90. Helped to avoid a Soviet invasion of Poland in 1981.

Keßler, Heinz (1920–), born in Silesia, worked as a metal turner, deserted from Wehrmacht (1941) to Red Army. Founder member NKFD; joined KPD and FDJ in 1945; served as commander of 'Air Police,' 1950–52; member Volkskammer, 1950–89; Deputy Minister of Defence, 1957–85; commander of Air Force, 1957–67, and then other defence responsibilities; GDR Minister of Defence, 1985–90; Politburo member 1986–89; expelled from SED 1989, briefly arrested then released. In 1993 sentenced to seven and half years' jail for deaths on Wall.

Kohl, Dr Helmut (1930–), studied law and history in Frankfurt am Main and Heidelberg, joined CDU in 1947. Minister-President of Rhineland-Palatinate, 1969–76; Chancellor of Federal Republic, 1982–98; in 2000 forced to resign as honorary Chair of CDU because of accusations of illegal funding activities.

Krenz, Egon (1937–), head of FDJ, 1976–83, candidate member, 1974–83, full member of Politburo, 1983–89; General Secretary of SED, October–December, 1989; member of the Council of State, 1981–84, Deputy Chair, 1984–89, Chair, 1989; Chairman of National Defence Council, 1989. Expelled from SED in January 1990.

Lafontaine, Oskar (1943–), studied physics in Bonn and Saarbrücken; SPD Minister-President of the Saar, 1985–98; Chancellor-candidate of SPD in 1990 election. Finance Minister in Schröder's SED–Green government, 1998–99.

Luft, Christa (1938–), joined SED, 1958; appointed Professor of Economics, 1971, at University for Economics (HfÖ), then its Rector, 1988–89; Minister for Economic Affairs and Deputy Chair of Council of Ministers, 1989–90; PDS member of the Bundestag, 1994– .

Maleuda, Günther (1931–), joined DBD in 1950; Chair, 1987–90; member of Volkskammer, 1981 and President of Volkskammer, November 1989–March 1990; Deputy Chair of Council of State, 1987–89. PDS member of Bundestag, 1994–98.

Masur, Professor Kurt (1927–), born in Silesia, studied music in Leipzig. Chief conductor of the Dresden Philharmonic Orchestra, 1967–72; Chief Conductor of the Gewandhaus Orchestra in Leipzig, 1970–90; Chief Conductor and Musical Director of the New York Philharmonic Orchestra, 1990.

Mazowiecki, Tadeusz (1927–), Catholic journalist, helped to forge links between the Catholic intelligentsia and workers' movement Solidarity. Became adviser to Lech Wałeşa in 1981. Was appointed the first non-Communist head of government in the Warsaw Pact states in August 1989.

Meckel, Johannes Markus (1952–), son of a pastor, expelled from school for political reasons. After studies at church seminaries, caretaker then vicar/pastor, 1980–88. Involved with various peace, human rights and ecumenical groups. Co-founder SDP, 1989; Deputy Chair then Chair, 1990; member of Volkskammer, 1990. As Foreign Minister of GDR, 1989 (April–20 August), took part in negotiations in Warsaw, Moscow, Washington, Bonn, Geneva and Strasbourg. Member of Bundestag, 1990– .

Mielke, Erich (1907–), Minister for State Security, 1957–89; Deputy, 1955–57; expelled from SED in 1989.

Mittag, Günter (1926–94), Member of the Politburo, 1966–89; ZK Secretary for the Economy, 1962–73, 1976–89. Expelled from SED in 1989.

Mitterrand, Francois (1916–96), studied law in Paris and was active in right-wing politics. After supporting the Vichy regime he joined the resistance to the Nazis. He served in numerous post-war governments and from 1971 was leader of French Socialists. French President, 1981–95. Established a close relationship with Chancellor Kohl.

Modrow, Hans (1928–), FDJ functionary in Brandenburg, Mecklenburg and Berlin, 1949–61; First Secretary SED Dresden, 1973–89; member of the Volkskammer, 1957–90; head of GDR government, November 1989–March 1990; PDS member of the Bundestag, 1990–94.

Pieck, Wilhelm (1876–1960), GDR President, 1949–60; leader of exile KPD in Moscow.

Poppe, Gerd (1941–), studied physics at Rostock University. From 1968 civil rights activist in various opposition groups. Member of the Bundestag, 1990–98.

Schabowski, Günter (1929–), joined FDJ in 1950 and SED in 1952; studied journalism at Leipzig University; member of Politburo, 1984–89; expelled from SED–PDS in 1990.

Schalck-Golodkowski, Alexander (1932–), joined SED in 1955 and entered Ministry of Foreign Trade. Recruited to Stasi in 1967. Served as Deputy Minister for Foreign Trade, 1967–75. From 1974 worked directly for Günter Mittag; from 1975 as State Secretary in the Ministry of Foreign Trade. ZK member 1986–89. Charged with various offences but never convicted.

Schäuble, Wolfgang (1942–), studied law and economics at Freiburg and Hamburg. Joined CDU in 1965; Minister for Special Tasks, 1984–98; Head of the Chancellor's Office, 1989–91; Minister of Interior, 1991–98; Chair of CDU/CSU Bundestag joint group, 1991– ; Chair of CDU 1998– .

Schmidt, Helmut (1918–), son of a schoolteacher, wartime officer who studied economics at Hamburg. Elected to the Bundestag in 1953. Served as Deputy Chair of SPD, 1968–83; Minister of Defence, 1969–72; Chancellor of Federal Republic, 1974–82. Carried on the policy of 'small steps' towards the GDR as inaugurated by Brandt.

Schürer, Gerhard (1921–), Chairman of State Plan Commission, 1965–90; candidate member of Politburo, 1973–89; expelled from SED–PDS in 1990.

Schwanitz, Wolfgang (1930–), joined SED and Stasi in 1951. Candidate member of ZK, 1986–89; Head of Office for National Security, 1989–90.

Seiters, Rudolf (1937–), studied law and politics in Münster. Joined CDU in 1958; Bundestag member since 1969. As Federal Minister for Special Tasks and Head of Federal Chancellor's Office, April 1989–November 1991, played a key role in negotiations with GDR. Minister of Interior, 1991–93. Vice-chair of CDU/CSU Bundestag group, 1993–98.

Shevardnadze, Eduard (1928–), son of a Georgian schoolteacher, made his career in the Communist youth movement and CPSU. As Georgian Minister of the Interior exposed corruption and ousted party secretary to take over himself in 1972. Served as Soviet Foreign Minister, 1985–90, taking a leading part in the negotiations leading to German unity. President of Georgia, 1992– .

Stoph, Willi (1914–99), Chairman of Council of Ministers of GDR, 1964–73, 1976–89; Minister of Interior, 1952–55; Minister of Defence, 1956–60; head of state, 1973–76. Expelled from SED in 1989 and arrested; released on health grounds.

Thatcher, Margaret (1925–), first British woman Prime Minister, 1979–90. Leader of the Conservative Party, 1975–90.

Tisch, Harry (1927–95), Chairman of FDGB, 1975–89; candidate member of Politburo, 1971–75; member, 1975–89; expelled from FDGB and SED in December 1989.

Ulbricht, Walter (1893–1973), born in Leipzig, served apprenticeship as carpenter. Served in First World War before helping to found KPD. Member KPD Politburo, 1929–46. *Émigré* in Paris, Prague and Moscow, 1933–45. First Secretary of SED, 1953–71; GDR head of state, 1960–73.

Ullmann, Wolfgang (1929–), studied theology in West Berlin and Göttingen, pastor, civil rights activist, co-founder DJ, deputy chairman of Volkskammer, 1990. Member of the Bundestag, 1990–94, then European Parliament for *Bündnis '90*/the Greens.

Waigel, Theodor (1939–), studied law and politics in Munich and Würzburg. Chair of CSU, 1988–99. As Federal Minister of Finance, April 1989–October 1998, played a key role in negotiations with the GDR on financial aspects of unification and subsequent development of former GDR.

Bibliography

Journals/newspapers

Deutschland Archiv, The Economist, German Comments, German History, German Politics, German Studies Review, Keesing's Record of World Events, Neues Deutschland, Das Parlament, Politics and Society in Germany, Austria and Switzerland, Der Spiegel, Stern, woche im bundestag.

Books:

(London is omitted where that is the place of publication.)

Biographies

Axen, Hermann, *Ich war ein Diener der Partei*, Berlin, 1996.

Bahr, Egon, *Zu meiner Zeit*, Munich, 1996.

Bernstein, Carl and Marco Politi, *His Holiness John Paul II and the Hidden History of Our Time*, 1997.

Brentzel, Marianne, *Die Machtfrau Hilde Benjamin 1902–1989*, Berlin, 1999.

Cole, Alistair, *François Mitterrand*, 1997.

De Bruyn, Günter, *Vierzig Jahre: Ein Lebensbericht*, Frankfurt am Main, 1996.

Doder, Dusko and Louise Brancoe, *Gorbachev: Heretic in the Kremlin*, 1990.

Falin, Walentin, *Politische Erinnerungen*, Munich, 1993.

Filmer, Werner and Heribert Schwan, *Oskar Lafontaine*, 1990.

Genscher, Hans-Dietrich, *Erinnerungen*, Berlin, 1995.

Goldstein, Kurt, *Wir sind die letzten – fragt uns*, Marburg, 1999.

Gorbachev, Mikhail, *Memoirs*, 1997.

Gorbachev, Mikhail, *Wie es war: Die deutsche Wiedervereinigung*, Berlin, 1999.

Hager, Kurt, *Erinnerungen*, Berlin, 1996.

Hoffmann, Admiral Theodor, *Das letzte Kommando: Ein Minister erinnert sich*, Herford, 1993.

Honecker, Erich, *Moabiter Notizen*, Berlin, 1994.

Jäckel, Hartmut (ed.), *Ein Marxist in der DDR: Für Robert Havemann*, Munich, 1980.

Jürgens, Urda, *Raisa*, 1990.

Kalinka, Wener, *Schicksal DDR: Zwanzig Porträts von Opfern und Tätern*, Berlin, 1997.

Keßler, Heinz, *Zur Sache und zur Person*, Berlin, 1996.

Kohl, Helmut, *Ich wollte Deutschlands Einheit*, Berlin, 1996.

Kotschemassow, Wjatscheslaw, *Meine letzte Mission*, Berlin, 1994.

Krenz, Egon, *Herbst, '89*, Berlin, 1999.

Kwizinskij, Julj A., *Vor dem Sturm: Erinnerungen eines Diplomaten*, Berlin, 1993.

Leonhard, Wolfgang, *Child of the Revolution*, Chicago, 1967.

Lippmann, Heinz, *Honecker and the New Politics of Europe*, New York, 1972.

Loeser, Franz, *Die unglaubwürdige Gesellschaft*, Cologne, 1984.

Loeser, Franz, *Sag nie du gehst den letzten weg: Ein deutsches Leben*, Cologne, 1986.

Luft, Christa, *Zwischen Wende und Ende Eindrücke: Erlebnisse, Erfahrungen eines Mitglieds der Modrow-Regierung*, Berlin, 1992 and 1999.

Mittag, Günter, *Um jedem Preis*, Berlin/Weimar, 1991.

Modrow, Hans, *Ich wollte nur die Perestroika*, Berlin, 1999.

Reichenbach, Alexander, *Chef der Spione: Die Markus-Wolf-Story*, Stuttgart, 1992.

Schäuble, Wolfgang, *Der Vertrag: Wie ich über die deutsche Einheit verhandelte*, Stuttgart, 1991.

Shub, David, *Lenin*, Harmondsworth, 1966.

Strauß, Franz Josef, *Die Erinnerungen*, Berlin, 1989.

Teltschik, Horst, *329 Tage: Innenansichten der Einigung*, Berlin, 1991.

Thatcher, Margaret, *The Downing Street Years*, 1993.

Wolf, Markus, *Die Troika*, Berlin, 1989.

Wolf, Markus, *Spionagechef im geheimen Krieg*, Munich, 1997.

Wolf, Markus with Anne McElvoy, *Man Without a Face*, New York, 1997.

Peet, John, *The Long Engagement: Memoirs of a Cold War Legend*, 1989.

Prokop, Siegfried (ed.), *Ein Streiter für Deutschland: Auseinandersetzung mit Wolfgang Harich*, Berlin, 1996.

The end of the GDR

Bahrmann, Hannes and Christoph Links, *Chronik der Wende: Die Ereignissse in der DDR zwischen 7. Oktober 1989 und 18. März 1990*, Berlin, 1999.

Behrend, Hanna (ed.), *German Unification: The Destruction of an Economy*, 1995.

Bortfeldt, Heinrich, *Von der SED zur PDS: Wandlung zur Demokratie?*, Berlin, 1991.

Bortfeldt, Heinrich, *Washington–Bonn–Berlin: Die USA und die deutsche Einheit*, Bonn, 1993.

Breuel, Birgit (ed.), *Treuhand intern Tagebuch*, Frankfurt am Main, 1993.

Czichon, Eberhard and Heinz Marohn, *Das Geschenk: Die DDR im Perestroika-Ausverkauf*, Cologne, 1999.

Darnton, Robert, *Berlin Journal, 1989–1990*, New York, 1993.

Dennis, Mike, *Social and Economic Modernization in Eastern Germany from Honecker to Kohl*, New York, 1993.

Fischer, Alexander and Günther Heydemann (eds), *Die politische 'Wende' 1989/90 in Sachsen Rückblick und Zwischenbilanz*, Weimar, 1995.

Flug, Martin, *Treuhand-Poker: Die Mechanismen des Ausverkaufs*, Berlin, 1992.

Förster, Peter and Walter Friedrich, *Jugend im Osten: Politische Mentalität im Wandel*, Leipzig, 1996.

Gedmin, Jeffrey, *The Hidden Hand: Gorbachev and the Collapse of East Germany*, 1992.

Gerlach, Manfred, *Mitverantwortlich als Liberaler im SED-Staat*, Berlin, 1991.

Glaser, Hermann, *Die Mauer fiel, die Mauer steht: Ein deutsches Lesebuch 1989–1999*, Munich, 1999.

Greenwald, G. Jonathan, *Berlin Witness: An American Diplomat's Chronicle of East Germany's Revolution*, Pennsylvania, 1993.

Heins, Cornelia, *The Wall Falls: An Oral History of the Reunification of the Two Germanies*, 1994.

Herles, Helmut and Ewald Rose (eds), *Vom Runden Tisch zum Parlament*, Bonn, 1990.

Hertle, Hans-Hermann, *Der Fall der Mauer*, Opladen, 1996.

Hertle, Hans-Hermann and Stephan Gerd-Rüdiger (eds), *Das Ende der SED: Die letzten Tage des Zentralkomitees*, Berlin, 1997.

Heydemann, Günther, Günther Mai and Werner Müller (eds), *Revolution und Transformation in der DDR 1989/90*, Berlin, 1999.

James, Harold and Marla Stone (eds), *When the Wall Came Down: Reactions to German Unification*, New York, 1992.

Joppke, Christian, *East German Dissidents and the Revolution of 1989: Social Movement in a Leninist Regime*, New York, 1995.

Keithly, David M., *The Collapse of East German Communism: The Year the Wall Came Down, 1989*, Westport, CT, 1992.

Krenz, Egon, *Wenn Mauern fallen: Die friedliche Revolution: Vorgesichte – Ablauf – Auswirkungen*, Vienna, 1990.

Kuhn, Ekkehard, *'Wir Sind Das Volk!': Die friedliche Revolution in Leipzig, 9. Oktober 1989*, Berlin/Frankfurt am Main, 1999.

Lapp, Peter Joachim, *Ausverkauf: Das Ende der Blockparteien*, Berlin, 1998.

Lewis Derek and John R. P. McKenzie (eds), *The New German: Social, Political and Cultural Challenges of Unification*, Exeter, 1995.

Maier, Charles S., *Dissolution: The Crisis of Communism and the End of East Germany*, Princeton, 1997.

Markovits, Inga, *Die Abwicklung: Ein Tagebuch zum Ende der DDR-Justiz*, Munich, 1992.

Mitter, Armin and Stefan Wolle (eds), *Ich liebe euch doch alle!*, Berlin, 1990.

Modrow, Hans, *Aufbruch und Ende*, Hamburg, 1991.

Neugebauer, Gero and Richard Stöss, *Die PDS: Geschichte, Organisation, Wähler, Konkurrenten*, Opladen, 1996.

Opp, Karl-Dieter, Peter Voss and Christiane Gern, *Origins of a Spontaneous Revolution: East Germany, 1989*, Michigan, 1995.

Philipsen, Dirk, *We Were the People: Voices from East Germany's Revolutionary Autumn*, Duke, 1993.

Przybylski, Peter, *Tatort Politbüro, Bd 2: Honecker, Mittag und Schalck-Golodkowski*, Berlin, 1992.

Rein, Gerhard (ed.), *Die Opposition in der DDR*, Berlin, 1989.

Reißig, Rolf and Gert-Joachim Glaeßner (eds), *Das Ende eines Experiments: Umbruch in der DDR und deutsche Einheit*, Berlin, 1991.

Reuth, Ralf Georg and Andreas Bönte, *Das Komplott: Wie es wirklich zur deutschen Einheit kam*, Munich, 1995.

Rheinischer Merkur (ed.), *Zurück zu Deutschland: Umsturz und demokratischer Aufbruch in der DDR*, Bonn, 1990.

Richter, Michael, *Die Staatssicherheit im letzten Jahr der DDR*, Weimar, 1996.

Schüddekopf, Charles (ed.), *'Wir sind das Volk!': Flugschristen, Aufrufe und Texte einer deutschen Revolution*, Reinbek bei Hamburg, 1990.

Smith, Patricia (ed.), *After the Wall: Eastern Germany Since 1989*, Boulder, CO, 1998.

Statistisches Bundesamt, *DDR 1990: Zahlen und Fakten*, Wiesbaden, 1990.

Tieding, Wilfried (ed.), *Ein Volk im Aufbruch: Die DDR im Herbst '89*, Dresden, 1990.

Weidenfeld, Werner and Karl-Rudolf Korte (eds), *Handwörterbuch zur deutschen Einheit*, Bonn, 1991.

Weilemann, Peter R. *et al. Parteien im Aufbruch: Nichtkommunistische Parteien und politische Vereinigungen in der DDR*, St Augustin, 1990.

Zwahr, Hartmut, *Ende einer Selbstzerstörung: Leipzig und die Revolution in der DDR*, Göttingen, 1993.

GDR: history, politics, economy

Auerbach, Thomas, 'Vorbereitung auf den Tag X. Die geplanten Isolierungslager des MfS' (BstU), Berlin, 1995.

Barth, Bernd-Rainer, Links, Christoph, Müller-Enbergs, Wielgons, Jan, *Wer war Wer in der DDR*, Frankfurt am Main, 1995.

Berg, Hermann von, *Marxismus-Leninismus: Das Elend der halb deutschen halb russischen Ideologie*, Cologne, 1986.

Bundesministerium für gesamtdeutsche Fragen, *A bis Z ein Taschen- und Nachschlagebuch über den anderen Teil Deutschlands*, Bonn, 1969.

Bundestag, Der Deutsche (ed.), *Materialien der Enquete-Kommission 'Aufarbeitung von Geschichte und Folgen der SED-Diktatur in Deutschland'*, Baden-Baden/Frankfurt am Main, 1995.

Behnke, Klaus and Jürgen Wolf (eds), *Stasi auf dem Schulhof*, Berlin, 1998.

Busch, Bertold *et al., DDR: Schritte aus der Krise*, two volumes, Königswinter, 1990.

Childs, David, *The GDR: Moscow's German Ally*, 1988.

Childs, David and Richard Popplewell, *The Stasi: The East German Intelligence and Security System*, 1996.

Doernberg, Stefan, *Kurze Geschichte der DDR*, Berlin 1964.

Dokumentationszentrum Alltagkultur der DDR (ed.), *Fortschritt, Norm und Eigensinn: Erkundungen im Alltag der DDR*, Berlin, 1999.

Eberle, Henrik and Denise Wesenburg (eds), *E. H. Einverstanden*, Halle, 1999.

Engler, Wolfgang, *Die Ostdeutschen*, Berlin, 1999.

Förster, Peter, Walter Friedrich and Kurt Starke, *Das Zentralinstitut für Jugendforschung Leipzig 1966–1990: Geschichte, Methoden, Erkenntnisse*, Berlin, 1999.

Frenzel, Paul, *Die rote Mark: Perestroika für die DDR*, Herford, 1989.

Friedrich-Ebert-Stiftung, *Zur Kulturpolitik in der DDR*, Bonn-Bad Godesberg, 1989.

Fricke, Karl Wilhelm, *Die DDR-Staatssicherheit*, Cologne, 1989.

Fulbrook, Mary, *Anatomy of a Dictatorship: Inside the DDR, 1949–1989*, 1995.

Gelb, Norman, *The Berlin Wall*, 1986.

Glaeßner, Gert-Joachim (ed.), *Die DDR in der Ära Honecker*, Opladen, 1989.

Henkel, Rüdiger, *Im Dienste der Staatspartei: Über Parteien und Organisationen der DDR*, Baden-Baden, 1994.

Janson, Carl-Heinz, *Totengräber der DDR: Wie Günter Mittag den SED-Staat ruinierte*, Düsseldorf/Vienna/New York, 1991.

Jeffries, Ian and Manfred Melzer (eds), *The East German Economy*, 1987.

Karau, Gisela, *Grenzerprotokolle: Gespräche mit ehemaligen DDR-Offizieren*, Frankfurt am Main, 1992.

Knechtel, Rüdiger and Jürgen Fiedler, *Stalins DDR: Berichte politisch Verfolger*, Leipzig, 1992.

Koehler, John O., *Stasi: The Untold Story of the East German Secret Police*, Boulder, CO, 1999.

Kopstein, Jeffrey, *The Politics of Economic Decline in East Germany 1945–89*, Chapel Hill, NC, 1997.

Krisch, Henry, *The German Democratic Republic: The Search for Identity*, Boulder, CO, 1985.

Leonhard, Wolfgang, *Das kurze Leben der DDR: Berichte und Kommentare aus vier Jahrzehnten*, Stuttgart, 1990.

Leptin Gert, *Die deutsche Wirtschaft nach 1945: Ein Ost–West-Vergleicht*, Opladen, 1970.

Ludz, Peter Christian, *DDR Handbuch*, Bonn, 1979.

McAdams, A. James, *Germany Divided: From the Wall to Reunification*, Princeton NJ, 1993.

McCauley, Martin, *The German Democratic Republic Since 1945*, New York, 1983.

Macrakis, Kristie and Dieter Hofmann (eds), *Science under Socialism: East Germany in Comparative Perspective*, Cambridge, MA, 1999.

Maier, Harry, *Innovation oder Stagnation: Bedingungen der Wirtschaftsreform in sozialistischen Laendern?*, Cologne, 1987.

Modrow, Hans (ed.), *Das Große Haus*, Berlin, 1994.

Naumann, Gerhard and Eckhard Trumpler, *Der Flop mit der DDR-Nation*, Berlin, 1991.

Neubert, Ehrhart, *Geschichte der Opposition in der DDR 1949–1989*, Berlin, 1999.

Pfister, Elisabeth, *Unternehmnen Romeo: Die Liebskommandos der Stasi*, Berlin, 1999.

Philips, Ann L., *Seeds of Change in the German Democratic Republic: The SED–SPD Dialogue*, Washington, DC, December 1989.

Pike, David, *The Politics of Culture in Soviet-Occupied Germany 1945–1949*, Stanford, CA, 1992.

Poppe Ulrike (ed.), *Zwischen Selbstbehauptung und Anpassung: Formen des Widerstandes und der Opposition in der DDR*, Berlin, 1999.

Reif-Spirek, Peter and Bodo Ritscher (eds), *Speziallager in der SBZ Gedenkstätten mit 'doppelter Vergangenheit'*, Berlin, 1999.

Richter, Michael und Martin Rißmann (eds), *Die Ost-CDU*, Weimar, 1995.

Richter, Peter and Klaus Rösler, *Wolfs Westspione*, Berlin, 1992.

Schabowski, Günter, *Das Politbüro*, Reinbek bei Hamburg, 1990.

Schabowski, Günter, *Der Absturz*, Berlin, 1991.

Schäfer, Bernd, *Sozialismus und katholische Kirche in der DDR*, Berlin, 1999.

Schneider, Gernot, *Wirtschaftswunder DDR: Anspruch und Realität*, Cologne, 1990.

Schultke, Dietmar, *'Keiner Kommt Durch'*, Berlin, 1999.

Schwan, Heribert, *Erich Mielke: Der Mann, der die Stasi war*, Munich, 1997.

Seiffert, Wolfgang and Norbert Treutwein, *Die Schalck-Papiere DDR: Mafia zwischen Ost und West*, Rastatt/Munich, 1991.

Siebenmorgan, Peter, *'Staatssicherheit' der DDR*, Bonn, 1993.

Spittmann, Ilse, *Die DDR unter Honecker*, Cologne, 1990.

Staritz, Dietrich, *Geschichte der DDR*, Frankfurt am Main, 1996.

Suckut, Siegfried and Walter Süß (eds), *Staatspartei und Staatssicherheit: Zum Verhältnis von SED und MfS*, Berlin, 1997.

Thalheim, Karl C., *Die Wirtschaft der Sowjetzone in Krise und Umbau*, Berlin, 1964.

Thalheim, Karl C., *Die Wirtschaftspolitik der DDR im Schatten Moscows*, Hanover, 1979.

Torpey, John C., *Intellectuals, Socialism and Dissent: The East German Opposition and Its Legacy*, Minneapolis, 1995.

Torsten, Dietrich, Hans Ehlert and Rüdiger Wenzke (eds), *Im Dienste der Partei: Handbuch der bewaffneten Organe*, Berlin, 1999.

Veen, Hans-Joachim and Peter R. Weilemann (eds), *Die Westpolitik der DDR*, St Augstin, 1989.

Walther, Joachim, *Sicherheitsbereich: Literatur, Schriftsteller und Staatssicherheit in der Deutschen Demokratischen Republik*, Berlin, 1996.

Wallace, Ian (ed.), *East Germany* (World Bibliographical Series, Vol. 77), Oxford, 1987.

Weber, Hermann, *DDR: Grundriß der Geschichte 1954–1990*, Hanover, 1991.

Weitz, Eric D., *Creating German Communism, 1890–1990*, Princeton, NJ, 1997.

Wekentin, Falco, *Politische Strafjustiz in der Ära Ulbricht*, Berlin, 1999.

Wendel, Eberhard, *Ulbricht als Richter und Henker: Stalinistische Justiz im Parteiauftrag*, Berlin, 1996.

Wilkening, Christina, *Staat im Staate*, Berlin, 1990.

Wolle, Stefan, *Die heile Welt der Diktatur: Alltag und Herrschaft in der DDR 1971–1989*, Berlin, 1998.

Woods, Roger, *Opposition in the GDR under Honecker 1971–85*, 1986.

Zank, Wolfgang, *Wirtschaft und Arbeit in Ostdeutschland 1945–1949*, Munich, 1987.

Zauberman, Alfried, *Industrial Progress in Poland, Czechoslovakia and Eastern Germany 1937–1962*, 1964.

Zimmermann, Hartmut (ed.), *DDR-Hanbuch*, 2 volumes, Cologne, 1985.

Other books on Soviet bloc/Eastern Europe

Aldcroft, Derek H. and Steven Morewood, *Economic Change in Eastern Europe Since 1918*, 1995.

Andrew, Christopher and Oleg Gordievsky, *KGB: The Inside Story*, New York, 1990.

Crampton, J. R., *Eastern Europe in the Twentieth Century and After*, 1997.

Frankland, Mark, *The Patriots' Revolution*, Chicago, 1992.

Furtak, Robert, *The Political Systems of the Socialist States*, Brighton, 1986.

Lawrence, Alan, *China under Communism*, 1998.

Lomax, Bill, *Hungary 1956*, 1976.

Naimark, Norman and Leonard Gibianski, *The Establishment of Communist Regimes in Eastern Europe, 1944–1949*, Oxford, 1998.

Pittman, Avril, *From Ostpolitik to Reunification: West German–Soviet Political Relations Since 1974*, Cambridge, 1992.

Sodaro, Michael, *Moscow, Germany and the West: From Khrushchev to Gorbachev*, Ithaca, NY, 1991.

Solzhenitsyn, Alexander, *The Gulag Archipelago*, 1974.

Westmood, J. N., *Endurance and Endeavour: Russian History 1812–1992*, 1993.

Winberg, Chai (ed.), *Essential Works of Chinese Communism*, New York, 1968.

Other books on Germany

Ash, Timothy Garton, *In Europe's Name: Germany and the Divided Continent*, New York, 1993.

Barzel, Rainer, *Es ist noch nicht zu spät*, Munich, 1976.

Childs, David, *Germany in the 20th Century*, 1991.

Fritsch-Bournazel, Renata, *Europe and German Unification*, New York/Oxford, 1992.

Geiss, Imanuel, *The Question of German Unification, 1806–1996*, 1997.

Hacke, Christian, *Weltmacht wider Willen: Die Aussenpolitik der Bundesrepublik Deutschland*, Frankfurt am Main, 1993.

Heydemann, Günther and Lothar Kettenacker, *Kirchen in der Diktatur*, Göttingen, 1993.

Jain, Rajendra K., *Germany, the Soviet Union and Eastern Europe 1949–1991*, 1993.

Kaiser, Karl, *Deutschlands Vereinigung: Die internationalen Aspekte*, Bergisch Gladbach, 1991.

Kennan, George, *The German Problem: A Personal View*, Washington, DC, 1989.

Larres, Klaus and Panikos Panayi (eds), *The Federal Republic of Germany Since 1949*, Harlow/New York, 1996.

Marsh, David, *The Germans: Rich, Bothered and Divided*, 1989.

Morse, James S. (ed.), *Beyond the Cold War: American Foreign Policy and the German Question*, Owning Mills, MD, 1993.

Nawrocki, Joachim, *Relations between the Two States in Germany*, Bonn, 1985.

Pittman, Avril, *From Ostpolitik to Reunification: West German–Soviet Political Relations Since 1974*, Cambridge, 1992.

Richie, Alexandra, *Faust's Metropolis: A History of Berlin*, 1998.

Schuh, Petra and Bianca von der Weiden, *Die deutsche Sozialdemokratie 1989/90*, Munich, 1996.

Steininger, Rolf, *Deutsche Geschichte seit 1945*, 2 volumes, Frankfurt am Main, 1996.

Steury, Donald P. (ed.), *On the Front Lines of the Cold War: Documents on the Intelligence War in Berlin, 1946 to 1961*, Washington, DC, 1999.

Watson, Alan, *The Germans: Who Are They Now?*, 1992.

Weisenfeld, Ernst, *Welches Deutschland soll es sein? Frankreich und die deutsche Einheit seit 1945*, Munich, 1986.

Zelikow, Philip and Condoleezza Rice, *Germany Unified and Europe Transformed: A Study in Statecraft*, Cambridge, MA, 1995.

Articles

Childs, David, 'The Revolution in the GDR', *Politics and Society in Germany, Austria and Switzerland*, Vol. 2, Nos 1–2, 1990.

Hendriks, Gisela, 'The Oder–Neisse Line Revisited', *Politics and Society in Germany, Austria and Switzerland*, Vol. 4, No. 3, 1992.

Keminsky, Annette, ' "Mehr produzieren, gerechter verteilen, besser leben": Konsumpolitik in der DDR', *Aus Politik und Zeitgeschichte: Beilage zur Wochenzeitung Das Parlament*, 9 July 1999.

Ludwig, Michael, 'The Foreign Policy of the New Polish Government and the German Question', *Politics and Society in Germany, Austria and Switzerland*, Vol. 3, No. 2, 1991.

Noelle-Neumann, Elisabeth, 'The German Revolution: The Historic Experiment of the Division and Unification of a Nation as Reflected in Survey Research Findings', *International Journal of Public Opinion Research*, Vol. 3, No. 3, 1991.

Padgett, Stephen, 'British Perspectives on the German Question', *Politics and Society in Germany, Austria and Switzerland*, Vol. 3, No. 1, 1990.

Reich, Jens, 'Zehn Jahre deutsche Einheit', *Aus Politik und Zeitgeschichte: Beilage zur Wochenzeitung Das Parlament*, 7 January 2000.

Roesler, Jörg, 'Jugendbrigaden im Fabrikalltag der DDR 1948–1989', *Aus Politik und Zeitgeschichte: Beilage zur Wochenzeitung Das Parlament*, 9 July 1999.

Süssmuth, Rita, 'Zehn Jahre deutsche Einheit: Die innere Befindlichkeit der Gesellschaft', *Aus Politik und Zeitgeschichte: Beilage zur Wochenzeitung Das Parlament*, 7 January 2000.

Thompson, Peter, 'The GDR Election: An Eyewitness Account from Berlin', *Politics and Society in Germany, Austria and Switzerland*, Vol. 2, No. 3, Summer 1990.

Videos

Ch. Links Verlag, *Chronik der Wende*, 1999.

Spiegel TV, Hamburg, *Fünf Wochen im Herbst: Protokoll einer deutschen Revolution*, 1989.

Map

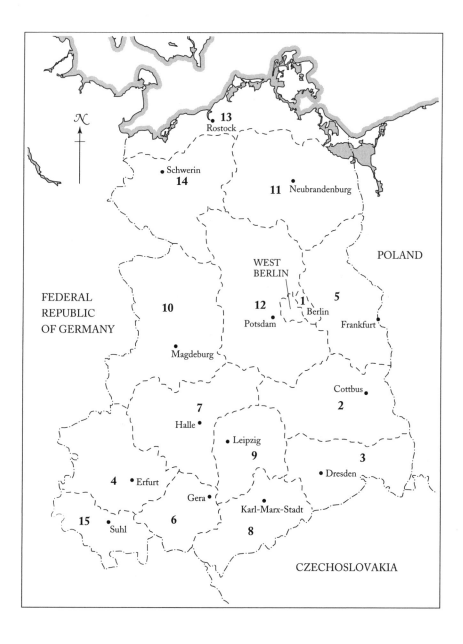

FEDERAL
REPUBLIC
OF GERMANY

POLAND

CZECHOSLOVAKIA

WEST
BERLIN

13 Rostock

Schwerin
14

11 Neubrandenburg

12 Potsdam
1 Berlin
5
Frankfurt

10

Magdeburg

Cottbus
2

7 Halle

Leipzig
9

3 Dresden

4 Erfurt

Gera
6
Karl-Marx-Stadt
8

15 Suhl

Index of names

183

General index